WHEN HATE GROUPS COME TO TOWN

A Handbook of Effective Community Responses

Second Edition
Revised and Updated

Published by the

CENTER FOR DEMOCRATIC RENEWAL

P.O. 50469, Atlanta, GA 30302-0469 • 404-221-0025

23699

Published in association with
The Black Belt Press
Montgomery, Alabama.

Printed in the United States of America by
Wells Printing Co.
Montgomery, Alabama.

ISBN 1-881320-05-7

The opinions and ideas expressed in this publication are solely the responsibility of the Center for Democratic Renewal and Education, Inc. Any support or assistance received in connection with the publication of this manual cannot be taken as an endorsement of the content of this manual, in whole or in part.

This publication is not meant to provide legal advice. Individuals and organizations interested in the legal issues discussed in this manual should consult with their own attorney.

CENTER FOR DEMOCRATIC RENEWAL

P.O. Box 50469
Atlanta, GA 30302-0469
404/221-0025

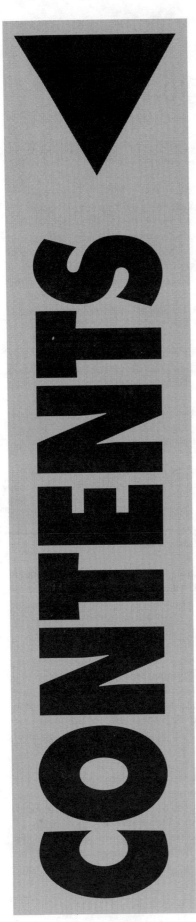

CONTENTS

CONTRIBUTING WRITERS AND EDITORS

Charles Fulwood is the president of Geneva Communications, an Englewood, New Jersey-based media consulting firm. Mr. Fulwood has worked closely with the CDR since its earliest days as the National Anti-Klan Network. Mr. Fulwood has worked extensively with a wide range of non-profit organizations such as Amnesty International, the Natural Resources Defense Council and others.

Zoltan Grossman is a cartographer and activist in Madison, Wisconsin. He has been active in Native American support work since 1978 and is one of the founding members of the Midwest Treaty Network.

Daniel Levitas is the executive director of the Center for Democratic Renewal. Prior to coming to CDR in 1989, he served as research director for the Des Moines, Iowa-based rural advocacy group, PrairieFire Rural Action, where he developed and implemented programs to monitor and counteract far right, anti-Semitic hate groups throughout rural America.

George Littleton is a writer and editor with the Black Belt Communications Group in Montgomery, Alabama. He is also publisher of the Eclectic *Observer*, a small weekly newspaper in Elmore County, Alabama.

Georgia Lord practices law in Atlanta, Georgia. An honor graduate of Emory University College of Law, Ms. Lord specializes in civil rights litigation. She has held many leadership positions with the National Lawyers Guild, including a term on its National Executive Committee.

Jonathan Mozzochi is the research associate with the Coalition for Human Dignity based in Portland, Oregon, where he specializes in tracking far right individuals and organizations.

Suzanne Pharr is a founding member of the Women's Project, based in Little Rock, Arkansas. The author of *Homophobia: A Weapon of Sexism*, Ms. Pharr is a nationally-known writer, lecturer, organizer and activist.

Loretta Ross is the national program director for the Center for Democratic Renewal in Atlanta. Prior to her tenure at CDR she was the program director for the National Black Women's Health Project and also served as director of women of color programs for the National Organization for Women in Washington, D.C.

Rabbi A. James Rudin is the Director of Interreligious Affairs for the American Jewish Committee. An internationally recognized expert in the field of Jewish-Christian and interfaith relations, Rabbi Rudin is the author of many books and articles on Judaism, Christianity, and Islam. He is also an expert on the activities and effects of destructive cults.

Mab Segrest is a Durham, North Carolina-based writer and activist. She is the author of *My Mama's Dead Squirrel and Other Stories: Lesbian Essays on Southern Culture*, and (with Leonard Zeskind) *Quarantines and Death: The Far Right's Homophobic Agenda*. Ms. Segrest is a founder and was the first director of North Carolinians Against Racist and Religious Violence. She is currently coordinator for the U.S. Urban-Rural Mission of the World Council of Churches and serves as a member of the CDR board of directors.

Carol Smith was director of the Farm Crisis Project of the Jewish Community Relations Bureau of Kansas City and Women's American ORT from 1986 to 1988. A Kansas native and folk music artist, she is vice president of the board of the Missouri Rural Crisis Center. She has served on the Kansas Interfaith Rural Life Committee and the Missouri Interfaith Coalition on Rural Issues.

Nelson Thayer, Jr. is a third year law student at the University of Pennsylvania specializing in constitutional and civil rights law. In 1992, Mr. Thayer served as a legal intern in the Criminal Section of the U.S. Justice Department. In 1990 and 1991, Mr. Thayer interned with the Center for Democratic Renewal.

H. Randall Williams is executive editor of the Black Belt Communications Group and the Black Belt Press in Montgomery, Alabama. He is a former member of the CDR board of directors and was the founding director of the Southern Poverty Law Center's KLANWATCH project.

Lynora Williams served as executive director of the Center for Democratic Renewal from 1986-1989. She is a writer, editor and human rights activist. She is currently communications associate with the AIDS Action Council in Washington, D.C. From 1991-1992 she served as African Governance Program Coordinator at the Carter Center of Emory University.

Leonard Zeskind is the research director for the Center for Democratic Renewal. From his offices in Kansas City, Zeskind has monitored the activities of far right, racist and neo-Nazi groups and individuals for more than 15 years. The author of numerous background reports, articles and CDR publications, Zeskind is considered one of the foremost experts on hate group activity nationally and internationally.

ACKNOWLEDGMENTS

This project would not have been possible without the generous support of the General Board of Global Ministries of the United Methodist Church. In particular we wish to thank Eli Rivera and the members of the Racial/Ethnic Ministries Working Group of the United Methodist Church.

We are deeply appreciative of the talent, indefatigable effort and patience of our editors, H. Randall Williams and George Littleton, and the entire staff of the Black Belt Communications Group in Montgomery, Alabama.

We are especially grateful to all the writers who contributed to the manual, and to those persons who served on the editorial committee: Charles Fulwood, Daniel Levitas, Mab Segrest, Loretta Ross and Leonard Zeskind. Thanks also to: Margaret Quigley and Jean Hardisty of Political Research Associates for their editorial comments; Kevin Berrill and the National Gay and Lesbian Task Force for providing up-to-date information on hate crime legislation; CDR board members Anne Braden and Lu Walker for their input concerning the organizational history of CDR; former CDR Northwest Coordinator Deni Yamauchi for providing material and input about anti-Asian violence; and to former CDR Executive Director Lynora Williams, CDR intern Carrie Flieder and Nelson Thayer and all other CDR staff and interns who labored with us and contributed their effort and insight during this two-year project.

The information presented in this manual was drawn from the experiences of hundreds of communities and thousands of individuals with whom CDR has worked over the years. We are deeply indebted to all of them for placing their trust in us so that we could share some of those experiences with you.

*The publication of this manual was made possible
by the generous support of:*

The General Board of Global Ministries
of the United Methodist Church
New York, New York

Shefa Fund
Philadelphia, Pennsylvania

Unitarian Universalist Social Concerns Grants Panel,
Minneapolis, Minnesota

Max and Anna Levinson Foundation
Santa Fe, New Mexico

Father Gary Jarvis Peace and Justice Memorial Lecture Endowment
Kansas City, Missouri

HOW TO USE THIS MANUAL

The purpose of this manual is to help individuals and communities respond appropriately to hate group activity and bigoted violence. Such violence and activity comes in many stripes — anti-Semitism, gaybashing, violence against Asians and other minorities, and terrorism against African Americans, to name just a few. Because there is such wide variety of hate violence today, this manual is organized to provide an overview of the problem and the different hate groups involved, and to allow the reader to easily locate those sections covering particular problems.

PART 1, "Understanding Racism and Bigotry," seeks to define the nature and problem of racism and prejudice as well as the victims in today's world. In simplest terms, Part I provides the reader of this manual with a statement of the problem of hate violence.

PART 2, "The White Supremacist Movement Today," identifies the major players in the variegated field of today's far right. After a brief overview of the history of racism in America, the different groups and their leaders are identified. These groups include the "traditional" hatemongers such as the Ku Klux Klan and the American neo-Nazis, but there are also growing problems with young people being recruited into racist and neo-Nazi organizations, the so-called theological justifications for hate promoted by the Identity church, and the progression of bigotry into the mainstream of American politics under such far right leaders as David Duke and Lyndon LaRouche.

PART 3, "Responses to Hate-Motivated Activity," contains guidelines for responding to particular brands of hate violence. It is the largest and most important part of the manual. This section is arranged so users can easily identify the type of hate activity they are encountering and provides insight into forming an appropriate response.

This section includes information about: passing hate crime laws at all levels of government and examines the legal rights of hate groups and their victims; recruitment of and responses to racist and skinhead youth on campus and in the larger youth culture; responses to anti-government, anti-Semitic racists who sow seeds of hate among financially troubled farmers; different types of religious hatred, false theologies, and how churches and synagogues can counter such activity; the Native American experience and some model responses to anti-Indian activity; responses to far right and racist violence in the workplace and the political arena; and ways in which police, human relations experts, and elected officials might respond to hate violence.

PART 4 of this manual includes resources to use when countering hate activity. These resources include lists of organizations that can provide assistance in particular areas; resolutions by various organizations opposing hate violence; an annotated bibliography, and other material that focuses on the problem of hate activity and proper responses to it.

Portions of this manual can be freely photocopied and distributed to help communities which are trying to respond appropriately to hate activity. Many of the sidebars and pullouts are particularly useful in giving background information on particular individuals and movements, and in explaining various methods hate groups use to gain media attention and to recruit new members.

WHAT IS THE CENTER FOR DEMOCRATIC RENEWAL?

The Center for Democratic Renewal (CDR) emerged from the response to the violent resurgence of the Ku Klux Klan a decade after the civil rights movement. The focus and purpose of CDR, and the organization's attempt to promote constructive, non-violent responses to hate groups and bigoted violence, has been shaped by the relationship between the white supremacist movement and the larger society.

The grassroots movement that arose among African Americans for civil rights in the 1950s and 1960s shook the nation to its core. Many white people joined this effort. The freedom movement also brought to center stage long-standing struggles of other people of color, women and gays and lesbians among others. For a brief moment it set the agenda for the country and won passage of the landmark 1964 Civil Rights Act and 1965 Voting Rights Act.

By the end of the 1960s, Klan membership had dwindled to a mere few thousand nationwide. Seven years later, however, in 1975, a militantly violent and racist backlash emerged. By the spring of 1976, according to award-winning journalist Patsy Sims,

"the Klan began popping up like crabgrass: throwing its hood into the vice-presidential race; infiltrating the Marine Corps; protesting busing in Boston and Louisville; joining the textbook fight in Charleston, West Virginia; creating a scandal in the New York State prison system; prompting the Illinois legislature to conduct a major investigation; burning crosses from California to Maryland; going to court to sue and be sued, and appearing on national talk shows."

The current KKK surge began in the mid-70s

By 1979, there were an estimated 11,500 members of various Klan factions throughout the United States. In May of that year, members of the Invisible Empire Knights of the Ku Klux Klan attacked civil rights marchers led by the Southern Christian Leadership Conference in Decatur, Alabama, shooting into the crowd. Seven months later, on November 3, 1979, a gang of Klansmen, Nazis, and other white supremacists murdered five anti- Klan protestors in cold blood in front of TV cameras on the streets of Greensboro, North Carolina. On April 20, 1980 — in celebration of Hitler's birthday — a carload of Klansmen drove through the African American community in Chattanooga, Tennessee, firing a shotgun, injuring five women. Remarkably, nobody was killed.

NAKN was born in response to these developments. With minimal staff and little funding, NAKN was established in 1979 as a loose-knit network of organizations and civil rights activists dedicated to responding to the resurgence of racist violence and Klan activity across the South. NAKN was organized by the joint work and institutional support of the Interreligious Foundation for Community Organization (IFCO), the Center for Constitutional Rights (CCR), the Southern Christian Leadership Conference (SCLC), and the Southern Organizing Committee for Economic and Social Justice (SOC). Its

NAKN organized in response to hate groups

early leadership came from people like the Rev. C.T. Vivian, a former key aide to Dr. Martin Luther King, Jr., and a longtime civil rights activist who had organized his first non-violent direct action to protest segregation in 1945 with a series of sit-ins in Peoria, Illinois; Marilyn Clement, then executive director of CCR; the Rev. Lucius Walker of IFCO, and Anne Braden of SOC.

From the beginning, NAKN's individual supporters were black and white, Catholic and Protestant, Jewish and gentile, and these people were determined to make it representative of the broadest possible constituencies. Through intentional and intense efforts in its early years, it worked closely with a wide range of civil rights groups, religious denominations, labor organizations, civic leaders, and grassroots activists.

NAKN organized rallies and demonstrations — recruiting more than 10,000 participants to Greensboro in the wake of the 1979 shootings; worked with other civil rights groups such as CCR to win landmark legal cases against Klan members responsible for racist violence; initiated an educational campaign with the National Education Association that produced a widely-used Anti-Klan Curriculum; monitored hundreds of Klan meetings and marches; organized national conferences and

Thousands marched in Greensboro in reaction to the murders of five people by Klansmen and Nazis.

local workshops; and held press conferences and published reports which exposed the inner workings of Klan organizations and their relationship to institutional racism. Public hearings involving members of Congress were held in Washington with victims of racist violence from across the country coming to testify. A 1983 lawsuit filed by NAKN against the Justice Department, along with a mass petition campaign, highlighted the failure of government lawyers to aggressively prosecute the perpetrators of hate violence.

The case studies and information presented in CDR's first edition of *When Hate Groups Come to Town* drew primarily on these early experiences, and focused largely on Klan-related activity and racist violence throughout the South. The first manual was an attempt to answer, in a way that would be most useful to the broadest audience, the key questions people were likely to confront when hate groups came to their communities.

In the mid-1980s, the nature of the KKK and Nazi threat changed again

By the mid-1980s, the situation had changed dramatically, once again. Political campaigns using racist imagery exacerbated racial tensions and mainstream politicians helped to legitimize white supremacist concepts like opposition to civil rights and "reverse discrimination." With Klan membership declining, other white supremacist groups were making headway by more carefully disguising their message of hate. Across the farm belt, activists with the far right group, the Posse Comitatus, sought to recruit financially troubled farmers

with promises of low-interest loans and theories about an "international Jewish banking conspiracy."

Promoters of "Christian Identity" masked their religion of racism and anti-Semitism in theological language, seeking converts and "soldiers" in the upcoming "war of Armageddon." NAKN expanded its activities in response, working with farm organizations, churches and Jewish groups to combat the rural radical right and its theology of hate.

White supremacists sought out seclusion and new recruits in the Pacific Northwest, at the same time as the region served as a base of operations for a new wave of criminal activities by organized racists. Followers of several different neo-Nazi groups including the Aryan Nations in Idaho engaged in counterfeiting, murder, bank robbery, bombings, and paramilitary training. They plotted to overthrow the government, abolish democracy, and establish a "white, Christian republic."

In 1985, NAKN formally announced it had expanded its mission and changed its name to the Center for Democratic Renewal, becoming a national clearinghouse for information on constructive responses to hate group activity and bigoted violence. Through its programs of research, public education, leadership training, crisis intervention, community organizing and technical assistance, CDR expanded its work to hundreds of communities across the United States helping people combat racism, anti-Semitism, religious intolerance, and homophobia.

By disseminating reliable information about the complex social, political and criminal aspects of hate groups, the CDR provides a much-needed analytical perspective on far right organizations and individuals.

By examining racial and ethnic trends in American society, the CDR also assesses the extent to which racist, anti-Semitic and homophobic appeals by demagogues and others are receiving widening public support. Bringing this complex message to the general public, and using it to build an effective "fire wall" of community-based resistance to racism and bigotry, is the focus of CDR's programs.

Today the activities of CDR are national and international in scope. Its research and reports are used by a diverse array of journalists, academics, organizers, law enforcement agencies, public policy makers, religious leaders and human relations professionals. The organization's agenda has broadened to encompass the concerns and interests of Asian Americans, Native Americans, Latinos and immigrants. The CDR was the first national non-gay civil rights organization to launch a nationwide campaign against anti-gay violence, working with groups such as the National Gay and Lesbian Task Force and others. In the Northwest, the organization provided research, training and technical assistance to dozens of grassroots groups, municipal agencies, and Indian tribes, helping to stem the tide of hate group activity throughout the region. In 1991, CDR established a statewide Georgia Anti-Racist Project to expand its work with dozens of rural communities and grassroots groups in the state. The project combines resistance to hate group activity with the affirmative work of advancing voting rights, ending discrimination in public services, and building long-term community organizations.

With the passage of the Federal Hate Crimes Statistics Act in 1990 and dozens of new state hate crime laws on the books, a good portion of the debate over hate group activity and bigoted violence moved to the public policy arena. New organizations emerged at the local, state and even national level, and already existing groups are seriously examining what they can do to respond.

At the same time as these positive developments are occurring, there is a resurgence of racism in the political and cultural mainstream of American life. The backlash against civil rights that started in the late 1960s had by the mid-1980s won control of our government at many levels. The idea that victims of racism are to blame for their own problems, and the idea that whites in America are now the main victims of discrimination, have become government policy.

The success of white supremacists like David Duke in the electoral arena are a harbinger of what is to come as political candidates become more adept at manipulating bigotry to achieve votes and more inclined to resort to the politics of fear. Other trends include: the increasing youthfulness of those involved in hate groups and bigoted violence — both on campuses and in communities; a rising tide of anti-Asian violence; a sharp escalation in the frequency and savagery of anti-gay hate crimes; more sophisticated attacks on Native American treaty rights; and mounting fears of foreigners (xenophobia), immigrants, and even Spanish-speaking American citizens.

White supremacy threatens the culture of pluralism and the practice of democracy in America. Many hate groups promote a Hitler-like fascism and violate the human rights of people of color, religious minorities, and gays and lesbians. Efforts to undermine racial and social justice and to establish white supremacy are not vestiges of a former era. They are the beginnings of a phenomena which, if permitted to expand unchecked, will envelope ever larger segments of the United States population.

This manual was written with all these factors in mind, because as the nature of the problem changes, so must the responses. The information presented here should contain something useful for everyone: community leaders, grassroots activists, students and teachers, public policymakers, law enforcement professionals, clergy and human relations experts and concerned citizens.

This manual is based on the notion that racist skinheads, Klan members and other neo-Nazis are not simply "fringe groups" whose only goal is to generate publicity for themselves. And it will hopefully offer constructive alternatives to those who believe "the less said, the better," when hate groups come to town.

The mission statement of the Center for Democratic Renewal

"Founded in 1979 as the National Anti-Klan Network, the Center for Democratic Renewal is a multi-racial organization that advances the vision of a democratic, diverse and just society free of racism and bigotry. It helps communities combat groups, movements and government practices that promote hatred and bigotry and is committed to public policies based on equity and justice."

It is never easy to judge what is the most appropriate or effective response to organized hate group activity and acts of bigoted violence, but one unfortunate fact remains clear: most situations evoke no response.

In contrast, CDR's goal is to reach the broadest possible audience with the message that positive actions can be taken to respond to hate groups. From Portland, Oregon to Blakely, Georgia, this manual will show how the actions of people and groups have made a remarkable difference. Elsewhere, the combined efforts of city governments, state legislators and religious leaders have had an equally important effect.

The people of this country really do have the capacity, working together, to create the society CDR calls for in its mission statement — "a democratic, diverse, and just society free of racism and bigotry." The key is what each of us does at the local level, where we live. Hopefully this manual will be useful to people throughout our land who are working where they are to make the vision a reality.

Efforts to eliminate violent bigotry must be coupled with strategies to uphold democracy, expand pluralism, empower the disenfranchised and defend democratic traditions and the vision of an inclusive society. The CDR seeks to promote *democracy without bigotry*, thus the need for *democratic renewal*. It is not sufficient to be against hate groups; building a society free of injustice requires the promotion of a vision which, in the words of CDR Board Chairman Rev. C.T. Vivian, "raises great ideas up to the level of conscience where men will deal with them. We want to raise issues, not guns or knives...we want to live in a society where we can come to men and women and say to them, these are the things for which we struggle, not with brutality, but with the truth of the human spirit, with the heart filled with understanding." ☐

UNDERSTANDING 1

Racism and Bigotry: How Hate Crimes Begin

Understanding Racism
and Bigotry:
How Hate Crimes Begin

Introduction

To develop an effective response to Klan and neo-Nazi groups, it is important to understand the ideas and social structures from which these groups emerge. While a complete analysis is beyond the scope of this handbook, this text does pinpoint the intersection between the ideas of white supremacists and the larger problem of bigotry.

The following pages discuss racism: its history as well as its current impact on African Americans and other distinct racial-ethnic groups. The section on anti-Semitism explains the role that hatred of Jews plays in the far right. The section on gender, sexuality and anti-gay bigotry explores homophobic violence and violence against women.

The problem of hate violence — violence directly attributable to prejudice — is serious. But many victims never come forward. Except for cases where injury or death is involved, hate-inspired incidents are too often treated as pranks or as breaches of the social etiquette. A burning cross, for example, that unmistakable symbol of the Ku Klux Klan, is frequently investigated by police as if it were just a juvenile prank, or a case of trespassing or arson. A swastika carved into a synagogue door may be regarded simply as vandalism.

The victims of hate violence include thousands who have been harassed, injured, and even murdered because of their race, religion, national origin or sexual orientation. African Americans, **Victims fall into many different categories** Latinos, Arab Americans and Asian Americans are harassed and attacked whether they are new immigrants or their families have been in North America for three centuries. Native Americans continue to be targets of racist violence, even after a policy of genocide decimated their populations. Lesbians and gay men are frequently persecuted by those who fear and hate their victims' sexual orientation, and the AIDS epidemic has only intensified this problem. Jews and Jewish institutions are frequently attacked because of the millennia-old virulence of anti-Semitism.

Hate violence is often committed by individuals acting on impulse. But it can also erupt from a mob made volatile by organized hate groups or demagogues and

Unless someone is seriously hurt, many hate crimes are disregarded by the authorities and the public.

Center for Democratic Renewal • P.O. Box 50469, Atlanta, GA 30302-0469 • 404/221-0025

Historically, violent Klansmen, such as those who attacked the Freedom Riders near Anniston, Ala., in 1961, used every means at their disposal to terrorize minorities...

opportunists. It is sometimes coldly calculating, well-planned, and thoroughly executed.

Violence coupled with bigotry, oppression, economic deprivation and the denial of basic rights are all tools of social control. After the Civil War, former Confederate soldiers launched a violent guerilla war to prevent the former slaves from voting and holding public office. After they succeeded, a wave of lynchings — which continued into modern times — forced African Americans to remain without rights. In the 1960s, violent attacks against African Americans, civil rights activists and others were intended to stop the civil rights movement. Racial violence today is often intended to prevent the racial integration of neighborhoods or to punish interracial couples for breaking with socially accepted mores.

Historically, some of the most frightening and brutal hate violence has been committed by organized racists, members of far right groups who plan their acts of violence and wear them as badges of honor. Such white supremacist groups develop and promote many theories to justify their terrorist actions. They tell their followers that crime and welfare abuse by African Americans, immigration by Mexicans and Asians or a fictional Jewish conspiracy has resulted in a decline in status for white people.

In every area of the country where hate organizations have been extremely active, there have been correspondingly high levels of bigoted violence. On the other hand, there are also regions which have experienced high levels of bigoted violence without correspondingly high numbers of organized white supremacists.

Even when they are not members of hate groups, violent freelance racists look to the Ku Klux Klan and to

Nazi-type organizations for inspiration. The symbols of the independent racist are often those of the KKK and the Nazis — the burning cross, the swastika, the anonymous phone call in the night. The United States Civil Rights Commission reported that a major role of organized white supremacist groups is to provide the rhetoric of justification for other violent racists.

It is often tempting to ignore Klan and neo-Nazi organizing and bigoted violence. It is sometimes easier to characterize the far right as misfits or simple "extremists" rather than face the larger problem of widespread racism, homophobia, and anti-Semitism. But the first step to confronting hate violence is understanding how racism has played a crucial role in the United States and how the struggle against it — from the time of Columbus until today — has shaped our ideals of democracy.

Decades ago, W.E.B. DuBois, a leading African American scholar, remarked that, "The problem of the twentieth century is the problem of the color line." As we near the end of that century, it seems sadly evident that DuBois was correct. From today's vantage point, it is painfully evident how far we still have to go to fulfill the proposition of the Declaration of Independence: "that

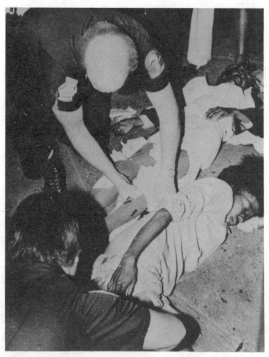

...The pattern continued twenty years later when innocent black women in Chattanooga, Tenn., were randomly shotgunned by drunken Klansmen...

Center for Democratic Renewal • P.O. Box 50469, Atlanta, GA 30302-0469 • 404/221-0025

...Even whites are targeted when they, like Viola Liuzzo—murdered by Klansmen near Selma, Ala., in 1965—are involved in civil rights or other activities opposed by violent white supremacists.

all men are created equal."

Today, one of the greatest barriers to the promise of democracy is the evil of racism. It is a difficult evil to combat, because people disagree about what it means, what causes it, and even whether it exists.

The movement against racism and bigotry is large and broad-based

Before launching efforts to respond to hate groups in any community, it is important for human rights advocates to know they are not alone. In fact, the movement to counter hate groups and bigoted violence consists of hundreds of national, regional, statewide, and local organizations, in addition to the thousands of individual volunteers who collect information, assist victims, and help organize community responses. A listing of some of these groups is contained in the resource section of this manual.

At the national level, each targeted community has its own civil rights organizations such as the National Association for the Advancement of Colored People (NAACP), the National Gay and Lesbian Task Force, the American Jew-

ish Committee, the American Arab Anti-Discrimination Committee, and the National Network Against Anti-Asian Violence among others. Many of these groups have local chapters or affiliates.

National organizations which monitor hate groups and document hate crimes include the Center for Democratic Renewal headquartered in Atlanta, Georgia, the Klanwatch Project of the Southern Poverty Law Center in Montgomery, Alabama, the National Institute Against Prejudice and Violence in Baltimore, Maryland, Political Research Associates in Boston, Massachusetts, and the Anti-Defamation League of B'nai B'rith.

Regional and statewide community-based monitoring agencies include the Northwest Coalition Against Malicious Harassment based in Seattle, Washington, North Carolinians Against Religious and Racist Violence, the Montana Human Rights Network, the Coalition for Human Dignity based in Portland, Oregon, and the Arkansas Women's Project. Efforts are underway as of this writing to establish other similar statewide monitoring and documentation projects.

State and municipal Human Relations (or Rights) Commissions provide support to local communities and, depending on size and scope, can offer considerable assistance to organizations and individuals working to oppose hate groups. More information on these commissions is contained in Part 3 of this manual.

In addition to those groups which work fairly exclusively on racism and the elimination of bigotry, many national organizations such as the YWCA, the United Auto Workers' Union and the National Education Association have anti-racist commitments expressed through the establishment of national departments, task forces and committees which provide resources through their member groups and affiliates.

Efforts to combat bigotry are particularly strong within the religious community. Denominations and

"Equality in America" workshop, Washington, Penn., May 1990

Center for Democratic Renewal • P.O. Box 50469, Atlanta, GA 30302-0469 • 404/221-0025

agencies such as the United Methodist Church, the American Jewish Committee, the Presbyterian Church (U.S.A.), the National Council of Churches' Racial Justice Working Group, and the United Church of Christ, among others, contribute generously to the efforts of organizations that work to oppose racism and bigotry nationally and locally.

There are many different opinions about the most effective strategies to counter the Klan and other white supremacists. Some want to ignore hate groups, while others want to launch potentially violent confrontations. Neither extreme is effective. It is best to use each crisis situation as an opportunity to build bridges and coalitions that will help heal the community through public education, non-violent actions, and strategic use of the media and government agencies. Each crisis is also an opportunity to curb the growth of hate groups through pro-active programs that target potential recruits and offer people critical information on a wide variety of subjects.

Some anti-bigotry organizations emphasize providing direct assistance to individuals and families victimized by hate crimes. Others provide support to victims while working to achieve changes in public policy and institutions (i.e., law enforcement) that will improve how hate crime victims are treated. Other strategies include prejudice reduction training geared at changing individual attitudes. Promoting multicultural education and cross-cultural understanding is part of the agenda of others. Organizations such as CDR research and document the activities of white supremacists and their sympathizers and assist communities to lessen their impact. While it is important to understand the distinctions between and limitations of these different approaches, all are legitimate strategies that may be combined to resist and overcome bigotry and violence.

The link between racism and white supremacists is fundamental

Many people now wrongly believe that racism is an insignificant part of American society. The cry of racism, they say, is an old complaint that has run out of steam. Racism, it is often argued, is a leftover phenomenon clung to by only a hard-headed minority. Racists who commit hate violence are an even smaller minority, many people say.

Because of the existing racial divisions in our society, there has not yet been an exact definition of racism that is widely accepted by all social groups. In fact, each social group experiences the reality of racism differently, and often draws differing conclusions about what it is.

This section of the handbook attempts to construct a description of racism which affirms this diversity of experience while providing the understanding necessary to combat racism.

Racism is a complex set of social, economic and political relationships, values and ideas in which one group of people asserts dominance over another based on perceived racial differences. Racism is distinct from prejudice, ethnocentrism, xenophobia and other forms of inter-group tensions — although it includes elements of each.

Ethnocentrism is a cultural preference which doesn't include the systematic ranking of social groups and clear

What is prejudice?

In his book *Prejudice*, sociologist Gordon W. Allport wrote, "Ethnic prejudice is an antipathy based upon a faulty and inflexible generalization. It may be felt or expressed. It may be directed toward a group as a whole, or toward an individual because he is a member of that group."

Allport outlined the following mechanisms for acting out prejudice: antilocution, or negative speech about the object of prejudice; avoidance; discrimination; physical attack; and extermination. His stages were not an argument that prejudice is necessarily expressed in an orderly progression but were simply a framework he used for studying the escalation of prejudice-induced action.

According to Allport:

"From the point of view of social consequences, much 'polite prejudice' is harmless enough — being confined to idle chatter.

"But unfortunately the fateful progression is, in this century, growing in frequency. The resulting disruption in the human family is menacing. And as the peoples of the earth grow ever more interdependent, they can tolerate less well the mounting friction . . . . It was Hitler's antilocution that led Germans to avoid their Jewish neighbors and erstwhile friends. This preparation made it easier to enact the Nuremberg laws of discrimination which, in turn, made the subsequent attacks upon Jews seem natural. The final step in the macabre progression was the ovens at Auschwitz."

hostility toward "out-groups." For example, each of us often prefers the music, food or religious practices of the group or community in which we grew up. Prejudice is something different. Sociologist Gordon W. Allport briefly defined prejudice as, "thinking ill of others without sufficient warrant." It is possible, however, to be prejudiced *in favor* of someone just as *against* them. For example, prejudice against black people in the United States has often taken the form of prejudice in favor of white people.

Allport describes prejudice as often the result of overcategorization; that is, making large generalizations from small amounts of fact. Unlike simple misconceptions, however, prejudices are "actively resistant to all evidence" against them. "Prejudgments become prejudices only if they are not reversible when exposed to new knowledge."

The National Council of Churches has described racism as prejudice plus power. While this shorthand definition is useful, it does not explain the complexity of racism.

Racism embraces a system of deeply entrenched legal and extralegal guidelines and codes for interaction between perceived racial groups. This system is often far more subtle than the Jim Crow codes which enforced legalized segregation or the South African apartheid system. It occurs on a spectrum which ranges from the vulgar to the sublime, from the very personal to the political, from the violent to the passive. It is a complex, deeply ingrained social behavior which has existed throughout American history. It is so entangled in our consciousness that there are few, if any, interracial social interactions free of the long shadow of racism.

As a set of ideas, racism attempts to explain cultural, social or behavioral differences as the natural result of biological differences. Racism argues that particular racial groups are inferior or superior to others based upon their biological make-up which cannot be altered.

Perceived racial differences, such as skin color or bone structure (phenotype), are supposed to explain social differences such as poverty, education level, political power, etc. In fact, race is not a biological concept, but a social concept.

In *Racial and Ethnic Competition*, Michael Banton noted: "Race relations are distinguished not by the biological significance of phenotypical features but by

Do different human races exist?

There has been a debate among anthropologists over whether or not distinct biological races exist among human beings; and if they do, what they mean. The idea of distinct races — rooted in biological differences — first emerged in the 16th century. At the time, supposed racial differences were based primarily on skin color and hair texture. Later, after Darwin's *Origin of the Species* was written, other racial indicators were used such as the cephalic index (measuring head size) and blood types. During the 19th century, some believed that there were even distinct European races — Alpine, Nordic, Celtic, Teutonic, etc.

But the evidence is clear that phenotypical differences (differences in skin color, hair texture, etc.) do not sharply define biological differences among groups of human beings. *Within* supposed racial groups the biological differences are often as great as *between* supposed racial groups. For example, a study of racial-biological differences among 15 population groups in central Africa by Jean Hiernaux concluded that the Tutsi of Rwanda were clearly distinct from at least 13 of the other groups. Yet no one to date has argued that a distinct Tutsi "race" exists.

Within the United States, Italians are considered part of the white racial population. Yet the skin tone and hair color of those native to southern Italy and Sicily more closely approximates that of those from northern Africa than it does the skin tone and hair color of those people from Sweden and Finland. Race is really a socio-historical concept. *Biology is not destiny.*

the social use of these features as signs which identify group membership and the roles people are expected to play."

For example, some white supremacists tell their followers that the high number of black men in prison is the result of a genetic predisposition to criminality among Africans. Other, more genteel racists, argue that crime in the African American community is the result of a "culture of poverty." Each of these propositions ignores the high level of unemployment, discrimination in the judicial system and other social and political factors which leads to high levels of incarceration for blacks as well as low-income whites.

The National Research Council's landmark 1989 study, *A Common Destiny: Blacks and American Society*, concluded that "The meaning of race is a matter of social interpretation...not a fact of biology or genetics." The National Research Council argued that race is a social and historical category which is not reducible to either class or ethnicity.

As a social structure, racism in the United States has meant the continuing dominance by white people over people of color. For example, the genocide practiced against Native Americans provided access to cheap land and upward mobility for some white people during the conquest of the West. Even when they were absolutely impoverished by the system of slavery which surrounded them, landless Southern whites still had more social standing than African slaves. Today, whites and people of color compete in different job markets, live in different housing markets and educate their children under different conditions. Many poor and working class white people lack access to political and real economic power. Yet white people as a whole are relatively privileged.

At its worst, racism causes some to define people of color as bestial, filthy, or mentally retarded. This is the most blatant form of racism which most people find unacceptable and easier to challenge and condemn. Yet many people perpetuate racism by trivializing even this most vulgar manifestation of it, categorizing it as outdated or shrugging it off.

More commonly, racism is shown when there is an equation between deprivation caused by poverty with racial inferiority. In this way, the consistent statistical indicators of the oppression of people of color — their poverty, unemployment, and low educational level — baffle and frighten white people.

Different cultural mores, values and traditions are often beyond the understanding of the dominant society, because these traditions have been distorted and romanticized.

Some people believe that while individual prejudices and racism may still exist, the basic institutional structures of racism were destroyed during the 1960s when legal segregation was struck down. In fact, some of the mechanisms of institutional racism have changed, but racism has not disappeared. It is a system which is capable of remaining essentially intact despite the banning of segregation and has adapted new methods for disempowering people.

For example, the image of the black rapist which motivated lynch mobs for over 200 years was re-employed to great effect during the 1988 presidential election. The now-infamous example of Willie Horton, a paroled repeat rapist, was widely seen as a broadside statement about the criminality of black men, even though the words "black rapist" were not uttered publicly. Laws, language and other practices have been altered mightily in the service of racism.

Racism's Early Roots

The road to successfully overcoming racism and combatting hate violence cannot be traveled without knowing where the journey began. Racism has much of its origins in the sixteenth century, when colonization of the New World began in earnest. It is from Europe's emergence from the Middle Ages onto a global stage that modern racism emerged. This racism was first practiced in the New World by the Spanish, Portuguese, British and French. Christopher Columbus's journals revealed a high degree of racist response to the people he encountered in the Caribbean Islands.

The sociologist Oliver Cox, in his book *Caste, Race and Class*, argued that racism was deeply bound up with

---

What whites think about non-whites: A survey on "Ethnic Images"

A December 1990 survey conducted by the National Opinion Research Center at the University of Chicago concluded that, "images about the work ethic of blacks are significantly related to...support for special treatment of blacks by the government ("affirmative action") and support for more governmental spending for blacks."

The survey gave a disheartening view of the actual level of racism in America:

- 62 percent of non-blacks thought blacks were more likely to be lazy than whites;
- 56 percent of non-blacks thought blacks are violence-prone;
- 53 percent of non-blacks said blacks are less intelligent than other groups;
- 78 percent of non-blacks said blacks are more likely than whites to "prefer to live off welfare" and less likely to "prefer to be self-supporting."

Hispanics were rated at similarly negative levels:

- 74 percent of non-Hispanics said Hispanics are more likely to prefer to live off welfare;
- 56 percent thought them more lazy;
- 50 percent thought them more violence-prone;
- 55 percent thought them less intelligent;
- 61 percent thought them less patriotic.

Asians as a whole fared better on the survey, though whites still held the following beliefs about Asians:

- 34 percent considered Asians more likely than whites to be lazy;
- 30 percent said they are more violence-prone;
- 36 percent said they are less intelligent;
- 46 percent said they prefer to live off welfare;
- 55 percent said they are less patriotic.

conquest and empire-building. In North America, these intertwined roots of racism were shown historically through the wholesale killing and dislocation of indigenous peoples throughout the Americas in order to take their land. Entire populations were simply wiped out — swept aside in order to make way for European settlers. As the United States expanded south and westward, racism against Mexican people was used to justify the takeover of parts of Mexico.

In order to develop the vast agricultural potential of the new territory, the brutal and devastating slave trade entered a boom period. The slave trade altered forever the continent of Africa, which even today suffers from severe economic instability brought on by the population exodus that occurred during the period and by other forms of exploitation that continued under colonial rule.

The dehumanization of Africans began in earnest as they were subjected to the Middle Passage, in which conditions brought them almost to the brink of genocide. These

Earning Power in the U.S.

- Black men 25 years and older with four or more years of college on average earned $31,380 in 1989.
- White men 25 years and older with four or more years of college on average earned $41,090 in 1989.
- Black women 25 years and older with four or more years of college on average earned $26,730 in 1989.
- White women 25 years and older with four or more years of college on average earned $27,440 in 1989.
- Black men 25 years and older with four years of high school but no college earned on average $20,280.
- White men 25 years and older with four years of high school but no college earned on average $26,510.
- Black women 25 years and older with four years of high school but no college earned on average $16,440.
- White women 25 years and older with four years of high school but no college earned on average $16,910.

—*Results from U.S. Census Bureau released September 1991 from a study conducted in 1989 and 1990.*

Economic Crisis Breeds Violence

Economic hard times often bring out the worst in people. There has been a backlash among some white working people blaming the very people who are still at the bottom of the economic system. In contrast to the artificial impression that African Americans are benefiting from white economic problems, recent census data reveals that African Americans make one-half the wages of whites and have one-tenth the wealth available to them.

A 1989 study by the National Research Council of the National Academy of Sciences showed that while African Americans had made significant gains relative to whites between the 1940s and the 1970s the economic slowdown since then has affected African Americans disproportionately. In 1986, an African American family's median income was $17,604 while a white family's was $30,809. The rate of poverty for African Americans has consistently been two to three times the rate of whites, according to an article in Knight-Ridder newspapers.

Economic strains will likely continue in the 1990s. A policy of deindustrialization led corporations to automate or to relocate major industries to countries with cheaper labor and fewer labor standards. Capital in the United States was invested in expensive corporate takeovers and mergers rather than in retooling basic industries. The deregulation of capital has caused a crisis in the savings and loan industry (its bailout equals $100 billion a year), and the banking and insurance industries are also in trouble.

By 1991, union representation has declined to 17 percent of the work force from a high of 33 percent in the 1940s, and current union strength is concentrated in the older, heavy industrial sectors.

Cities went bankrupt in the 1980s under the double pressure of increased responsibility for social services and a reduced tax base. Financial bail outs for cities were often tied to cutbacks in services. States are also facing bankruptcy under this pressure.

Poor people face these times with a slashed safety net, and middle income people in the coming decade are likely also to feel some economic free-fall. There will be many competing explanations for these happenings, and finding ways to explain complex economic events in understandable terms is part of the challenge of countering far-right activity.

Center for Democratic Renewal • P.O. Box 50469, Atlanta, GA 30302-0469 • 404/221-0025

conditions were meant to break the spirit of the Africans, but to preserve just enough of their collective physical well-being that they could be productive laborers in bondage. Estimates vary widely, but at least 30 million women, men and children died as they were brought to the shores of the New World, packed in the holds of ships and chained like cattle, during this Middle Passage practice.

Though not subjected to outright slavery, many Asians were brought to America to fulfill the interests of the railroad barons and plantation owners who needed additional cheap labor.

Racism has been used to justify much of the brutality of the early periods in United States history. By dehumanizing Africans, Asians, Native Americans and Latinos, deadly practices found acceptance among a mass audience which might otherwise have rebelled against measures which were morally repugnant. A system with such deep and penetrating roots will not be easily changed.

Racism Today

Racism today plays an essential role in shaping the lives of both people of color as well as whites in the United States. Some of the primary manifestations of racism are in the workplace and the marketplace. As the world economy contracts and expands, it is convenient for the economic system to be able to call upon a set or

---

'Reverse Discrimination' and Affirmative Action

Racists are quick to blame white male unemployment on African Americans and affirmative action. They insist that there are fewer jobs because African Americans are getting all the work. But black economic progress has not been at the expense of whites. Indeed, despite advances by blacks, whites remain in control of 99.7 percent of the nation's gross national product, according to the Louisiana Coalition Against Racism and Nazism. Affirmative action programs have had little effect on white employment. A recent study of state contracts in Louisiana found that although African Americans comprise 31 percent of the state population, the state awards less than five percent of its contracts to minorities. If affirmative action really compromised opportunities for white males, the bulk of the criticism would be directed towards white women, the greatest beneficiaries of affirmative action.

---

group of workers at will — to bring them into the work force when many jobs are available, and to push them out when times are tight. Thus, racism is still used as a justification for policies of economic exploitation.

The most overt form of this is through job discrimination, primarily in the denial of equal access to jobs of all types.

A 1991 study by the Urban Institute found that equally qualified white applicants are three times more likely to get a job than African Americans.

The Institute conducted a job audit similar to those used by agencies testing for housing discrimination. Equally qualified African-American and white job applicants were sent to the same employers in Washington, D.C., and Chicago. All of the applicants were articulate and poised, conventionally dressed with the same job experience.

According to the study, whites were able to advance in the hiring process, where African Americans were not, in 20 percent of the cases. African Americans were able to advance in the hiring process, where whites were not, in 7 percent of the cases.

According to the Urban Institute, "These results show that despite extensive legislative and regulatory protections and incentives to hire minorities, unfavorable treatment of young black men is widespread and pervasive across firms offering entry level jobs. Moreover, the audit results indicate that reverse discrimination—favoring a black applicant over an equally qualified white—is far less common."

People of color in the United States also face exceptionally high rates of unemployment which decline only in times of tremendous economic growth. With each recession, more and more people of color experience long-term unemployment. Rarely are they rehired at the same rate as white workers. It is frequently argued that affirmative action has already solved this problem. In reality, affirmative action practices have barely scraped the surface of economic racism and do not create reverse discrimination.

For the first time, the actual standard of living of the average American is in decline and young people will not necessarily improve on their parents' economic status. For example, the *New York Times* reports that in 1973, a 30-year-old could make a mortgage payment with 20 percent of his or her income. By 1986, mortgages took 40 percent of the paycheck. These worsening economic times can only spell disaster for communities of color and a rise in scapegoating.

Though economic injustice in the workplace is a central aspect of racism, many other forms of racism remain.

• *PSYCHOLOGICAL AND CULTURAL RACISM* maintains a sense of superiority among whites and a sense of inferiority among people of color. The majority culture

The Constitution had to be rewritten to bar slavery and to extend equality under the law to African Americans

Amendment XIII. Section 1. Neither slavery nor involuntary servitude, except as a punishment for crime whereof the party shall have been duly convicted, shall exist in the United States or any place subject to their jurisdiction.

Amendment XIV. Section 1. All persons born or naturalized in the United States, and subject to the jurisdiction thereof, are citizens of the United States and of the State wherein they reside. No State shall make or enforce any law which shall abridge the privileges or immunities of citizens of the United States; nor shall any State deprive any person of life, liberty, or property, without due process of law; nor deny to any person within its jurisdiction the equal protection of the laws.

imposes its definition of beauty — the aquiline nose, the straight blonde hair, the white skin, the light-colored eyes — and also defines a set of social behaviors as racially superior.

Another pervasive and devastating effect of racism is the distortion of the consciousness of children of color by establishing a set of values which permanently cripple and shape their will and self-image. A child subjected to racism in his or her formative years must carry forever the psychological burden of his or her alleged inferiority. The rage at being victimized by racism is often turned inward, and is manifested in self-destructive behavior, constant self-doubt and self-deprecation, profound sorrow which has few outlets, confusion, and alienation from one's own community for fear of guilt by association.

• *SCIENTIFIC RACISM* is the attempt to rationalize the subordinate status of people of color through the claim that their "inferiority" is scientifically based. Scientific racists find ways of "proving" the superiority of white people. In the past they have also attempted to prove that white elites have attained their status based on their biological superiority over other whites. "Scientific" rationales were employed by the Hitler regime to prove the inferiority of Jews, Gypsies and Slavic peoples. In the United States, it has resulted in the forced sterilization of people of color.

The most notorious is the so-called science of eugenics, or the pursuit of a pure race through genetic engineering. In the 1990s, eugenics found vocal expression in the actions of former Louisiana State Representative David Duke, who promoted linking birth control to social aid. He hoped to establish a program that would provide cash payments to welfare recipients who agreed to temporary sterilization. Others legislators have followed with similar measures in other states.

• *POLITICAL DISENFRANCHISEMENT* of communities of color means they are systematically blocked from access to political power and excluded from meaningful positions in the legislative, executive and judicial branches of government. This continues to impact the ability of African American, Asian American, Native American and Latino communities to shape public policies which could address the special needs of their people.

In Los Angeles, for example, which has a large Latino population, it was not until 1990 that a Latino person was seated on the city's ruling commission. This event was forced by a protracted court battle which demanded that the city be redistricted to allow for greater Latino representation. This pattern is repeated in nearly every town, city, county and state in the nation where there are people of color. Although the civil rights movement won a greater measure of political representation by ending *de jure* disenfranchisement of African Americans and other people of color, much remains to be done.

• *UNEQUAL ACCESS TO BASIC SERVICES* in the areas of education, health, and social welfare continues to exist. Few measurements of national well-being are more accurate than are the percentage of its newborn babies who die during their first year of life and the average life expectancies of its population. Poor health, as shown by high infant mortality and shortened life expectancy, is widely accepted as an indication that people are being excluded in some way from basic social services. In 1991, the Journal of the American Medical Association noted that South Africa and the United States were the two countries with the widest gap in health standards within their populaces. This situation is directly attributable to poor race relations. At the beginning of the 1990s, while overall life expectancy continued to increase, it was decreasing for the African American community. (Whites born in 1988 could be expected to live to 75.6 years, while African Americans could be expected to live until 69.2 years.)

• *FOREIGN POLICY:* It also must be noted that racism is unmistakably a component in the formulation of United States foreign policy. Just as the drive for international power and markets sometimes requires the existence of racism to justify disregard for local populations, conversely this same disregard can be the wellspring from which policy decisions flow. Repeatedly throughout history, foreign policy decisions justified by racism have had a spillover impact on people of color at home.

During World War II, only Americans of Japanese descent were imprisoned in concentration camps — although the United States was also at war with Germany and Italy. During the Vietnam War a special racist vocabulary was developed for Southeast Asians; there was a similar occurrence during the Persian Gulf War.

> The basic interests and humanity of all people, including whites, are greatly damaged by racism.

Though there are many shared experiences among communities of color when it comes to racism, each community has experienced racism in a different way and has responded to it differently.

The Two Minds of White People

White people, those descended from European immigrants, have always been of two minds about race and racism. On one hand, ordinary white people have practiced the everyday rituals of racial discrimination and domination. On the other hand, white people have also fought against racism and for democracy — sometimes paying with their lives.

Many times white people have expressed their opposition to racism through the ideals of fairness, equal justice and patriotism. The term "white people" originated in the 17th century with the distinction between African chattel slaves and the indentured servants (and others) who could eventually earn or buy their freedom. During the 19th century, there was widespread discrimination against first Irish immigrants and later those from eastern and southern Europe. Eventually, however, the United States proved to be a "melting pot" for Europeans, even while many of the most recent immigrants have maintained distinctive ethnic identities.

Each wave of European immigrants has gradually assimilated the prevailing racist attitudes towards people of color — even if their forbearers didn't directly participate in the slave system or the genocide of Native peoples. A 1991 survey by the National Opinion Research Center, for example, revealed that a majority of white Americans believe that African Americans and Latinos are lazy, unpatriotic, breed crime, and are prone to violence. [See box on page 18.]

On the other hand, surveys of racial attitudes conducted since the 1930s show a gradual decline in racial prejudice and stereotyping. During the 1960s, there was a significant shift in white racial attitudes — as the nationwide debate on racial discrimination changed peoples' minds.

The basic interests and humanity of all people, including whites, are greatly damaged by racism. The system of racism includes many mechanisms to check anti-racist action by whites. White people who cross the color line — either through their social interaction, or through conscious participation in the anti-racist movement — also have been the target of bigoted violence.

Nevertheless, white people have more of an economic and social infrastructure by which to establish and achieve some measure of social advancement; and they face fewer economic and political barriers than do people of color.

Most whites deny that racism still exists because, to them, racism simply means overt, conscious expressions of white supremacy. And, to the extent to which they witness blatant white supremacy, the tendency is to dismiss it, believing it is simply a fringe phenomenon or else a problem limited to only a handful of ignorant individuals. This outlook also causes many whites to either minimize or dismiss the problems of institutional racism in American society, or to ridicule people of color who insist on exposing and combatting it. Additionally, many whites don't understand the social power that distinguishes racism from prejudice. Without properly understanding this power dynamic and its effects on

The Arab Stereotype:
VILLAIN WITHOUT A HUMAN FACE

Portrayed as either billionaires, bombers, or belly dancers, bedouin bandits or bundles in black — Arabs are hardly ever seen as ordinary people practicing law, driving taxis or healing the sick.

Featured since the early 1900s in more than 500 feature films and scores of television programs, Arabs still lack a human face. The typical screen Arab can be summarized in a handful of cliches: He uses terrorism and/or oil as a weapon against civilized societies. He supposedly worships a different deity than Jews and Christians, and is opposed to both religions. He treats women of his race as chattel, but prefers to kidnap and rape white, Western women. He delights in the torture of innocents. Although often presented as a coward, at the same time he willingly dies for his cause, because, we are led to believe, he does not appreciate human life as "we" do.

Children with Arab roots grow up without ever having seen a human Arab on screen, someone to pattern their lives after. (When 293 secondary school teachers were asked to name any heroic or humane Arab characters they had seen in movies, 287 could think of none.) Instead, they will see animated heroes Heckle and Jeckle pull the rug from under "Ali Boo-Boo, the Desert Rat," and Laverne and Shirley stop "Sheik Ha-Mean-ie" from conquering "the U.S. and the world." More than 250 comic books like *The Fantastic Four* and *G.I. Combat* have sketched Arab characters as "low-lifes" and "human hyenas."

Nicholas Kadi, an actor with Iraqi roots, makes his living playing terrorists — the kind of Arab villains who say "America," then spit — in such films as the 1990 release *Navy Seals*. Kadi admits that he does "little talking and a lot of threatening —

threatening looks, threatening gestures." The actor explains: "There are other kinds of Arabs in the world. I'd like to think that someday there will be an Arab role out there for me that would be an honest portrayal." The ugly caricatures have had an enduring impact on Arab Americans. To many during the Persian Gulf War, all Arabs became "camel jockeys," "ragheads" and "sandsuckers." Whenever there is a problem in the Middle East, Arab Americans are subjected to vicious stereotyping and incidents of violence and discrimination. Even White House staffers — according to Reagan's first education secretary, Terrel Bell — dismissed Arabs as "sand niggers."

But trends are not uniformly bleak. On television, at least, the worst stereotyping has declined. A few recent shows — like *Counterstrike, Shannon's Deal* and *Father Dowling's Mysteries* — have actually featured sympathetic Arabs and Arab Americans. Perhaps one day it will be possible to retire the stereotypical Arab to a media Valhalla.

—JACK SHAHEEN

(Shaheen, author of The TV Arab, *is a professor of mass communications at Southern Illinois University. Reprinted from* EXTRA! *A publication of Fairness and Accuracy in Reporting (FAIR). Vol. 5, No. 5. July/August 1992.)*

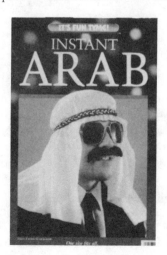

AMERICAN ARAB ANTI-DISCRIMINATION COMMITTEE

Anti-Arab products became common during the 1991 war in the Persian Gulf.

Center for Democratic Renewal • P.O. Box 50469, Atlanta, GA 30302-0469 • 404/221-0025

American society, whites who believe that racism is simply a matter of individual attitudes or ignorance also tend to conclude that simply changing individual behaviors will eliminate racism.

In fact, white racist attitudes are institutionally reinforced. For example, one of the most pervasive effects of racism towards African Americans is the irrational fear of African American men. The institutionalization of this fear is revealed in statistics shown in the box on page 19. African American men are half as likely to be employed as their equally qualified white counterparts, yet they receive prison sentences that are nearly twice as long when they commit the same crimes as whites. These conditions do not require conscious or deliberate reinforcement; a system of institutional racism perpetuates these conditions. It is exactly because institutionalized racism is so pervasive that it is especially difficult to dismantle.

African Americans

America's promise of democracy was fundamentally compromised from the outset by the enslavement of people of African origin and the systematic destruction of indigenous peoples throughout North America. Pivotal to democracy's survival today is the need to combat the persistent racism directed against African Americans who, with their relatively large numbers, are destined to play an increasingly major role in the nation's political and economic evolution.

Although direct knowledge of their African homelands was destroyed by the slave trade, African Americans have maintained many African traditions in the culture they built since their arrival here in the 17th century. Through distinctive contributions in religion, arts, science and politics, African Americans have also helped shape the national culture — often while being officially excluded from it.

African Americans were central to the early economic development of the United States. Slaves not only provided the cheap labor upon which agricultural development in the South rested, but they also provided the skilled labor which built the trading ships and industry of the South. The North and West also benefited from slave labor, since cotton was the chief export and cash crop of the new national economy. African slavery also facilitated the accumulation of capital during the 1800s helping the United States become a global industrial power in the 20th century.

This exploitation did not occur in a vacuum, however. African American protest was continuous and

> **United States 1990 African American Population:**
> 29,986,000, about 12 percent of the total U.S. population

intense. From the earliest pre-colonial era slave rebellions of the 16th century to the civil rights movement of the 1950s and 1960s, African Americans fought first for their freedom and basic human rights, and then to achieve a range of demands including educational equity, fair housing, and equal employment opportunity. Through these periods, Africans and African Americans met intense resistance from racists of all stripes, who assumed that terrorizing individual African Americans would halt the struggle for freedom. For example, it is estimated that at least 2,500 lynchings of African Americans occurred from 1882 to 1930 in ten Southern states. This violence reflected not only the extremes of racism, but also the intersection of race hate and sexual fears, as many of the lynchings were attributed to actual or suspected "miscegenation" or race-mixing between African American men and white women. Economic competition was also a factor; many lynching victims were African Americans who attempted to open stores, or start businesses such as newspapers that were perceived as competing with white-owned establishments.

White supremacy has been sustained by a complex, brutal system of laws and judicial decisions since the 17th century. Before the abolition of slavery, it was illegal to teach African Americans how to read or write. After slavery, the Supreme Court gave its approval to apartheid-like Jim Crow laws in its 1896 *Plessy v. Ferguson* decision, which legalized separate but equal facilities, which were indeed separate, but never equal. With the 1954 *Brown v. Board of Education* Supreme Court decision, the legal basis for Jim Crow segregation was defeated, yet the impact of judicially-sanctioned racism still exists within the legal system. The nation was stunned with disbelief in 1992 as it watched first the beating of Rodney King and then the shocking acquittal of four of the policemen involved. Feelings of rage and cynicism fueled the subsequent rebellion in south central Los Angeles where African Americans and Latinos viewed the acquittals as proof of institutionalized racism within the criminal justice system.

The 1992 Supreme Court decision in *R.A.V. v. City*

> At least 2,500 lynchings of African Americans occurred from 1882 to 1930 in 10 Southern states.

Center for Democratic Renewal • P.O. Box 50469, Atlanta, GA 30302-0469 • 404/221-0025

of St. Paul ruled that crossburnings, used by the Klan and their sympathizers to terrorize African Americans and drive them from their homes, are a protected form of free speech. In the contest between the First Amendment rights of white supremacists and the Thirteenth and Fourteenth Amendment rights of African Americans to live free of the incidences of slavery, the Supreme Court clearly favors the free speech rights of white supremacists.

Racism currently has a specific and immediate impact on all African Americans, regardless of social class, educational level, sexual orientation, or immigrant status. The most violent racism is frequently experienced when African Americans attempt to integrate neighborhoods and schools or to compete in the job market. Ongoing school desegregation efforts often result in violent clashes between white and African American students in high schools and on college campuses. Interracial dating and marriages are also key factors sparking hate violence against African Americans around the country. Struggles to achieve voting rights, equal access to public services and fair employment have also produced assaults, death threats, or racist harassment, as demonstrated by everything from the Klan's attacks on peaceful civil rights marchers in Forsyth County, Georgia, in 1987 to the rigorous campaign of anti-black and anti-Latino harassment waged against FBI agents by their white colleagues in the 1980s.

Hate violence against African Americans still reflects the stark brutality of earlier periods. For example, Michael Donald, a 21-year-old college student, was lynched in 1981 in Mobile, Alabama, by Klansmen. Other gangs of white youths were responsible for the deaths of Michael Griffith in New York City in 1986, Tony Montgomery in Reno, Nevada, in 1988, Timothy Moss in California's Simi Valley in 1992, and the lynchings of William Brooks and Carlos Stoner in North Carolina in 1992. These are just a few of the thousands of hate crimes experienced by African Americans in the past decade.

Racism can also take covert forms. Racist symbolism dominated presidential politics when Ronald Reagan campaigned against "welfare queens" and George Bush railed against repeat rapist Willie Horton; both deliberately exacerbated racial tensions without ever directly mentioning African Americans. The "reverse discrimination" propaganda of opponents of civil rights increases the resentment of white Americans against African Americans. Such myths and distortions deny the reality that power and control in American society are still a white monopoly, based upon centuries of "skin privilege."

Although it has become fashionable to appreciate such individual African Americans as Michael Jordan or Alice Walker, racism continues to deny the achievements of most other African Americans. A new, more sophisticated and academic form of racism has appeared, portraying African Americans as dysfunctional, hopeless, and inevitably linked to "a culture of poverty." This stereotype is reinforced by the constant barrage of statistics and images of drug-infested, crime-ridden African American communities.

The struggle to overcome racism against African Americans is intense and ongoing and takes many forms, whose descriptions are beyond the scope of this manual. However, civil rights organizations, religious groups, civic associations, student groups, women's organizations, and fraternities and sororities all employ a wide range of approaches to eliminate racism. Sometimes, African Americans are joined by whites and others who share their vision of creating a true democracy by purging racism from the mainstream and margins of American society. Other times, African Americans and their leaders have acted in virtual isolation, passing along their unfinished quest for justice to the next generation.

Native Americans

Prior to European colonization, the indigenous, aboriginal people of North America built stable communities and established civilizations.

Genocide — the extermination of an entire population — was practiced against Native Americans in order to push them from their lands to make way for white settlers. Disease also severely decimated the ranks of aboriginal peoples throughout the Western Hemisphere. From an estimated population ranging anywhere between 8.4 and 112.5 million throughout the Western Hemisphere prior to 1492, the American Indian population in the United States declined from about 600,000 in

---

Native American Population

861,500 Indians lived within or near Federal reservations as of January 1987

The largest Indian Reservations as of January 1989 were:
• Navajo (Ariz., N.M., Utah) 185,661
• Cherokee (Okla.) 87,059
• Creek (Okla.) 56,244
• Choctaw (Okla.) 26,884
• Pine Ridge (S.D.) 20,206
• Southern Pueblos (N.M.) 18,837
• Chickasaw (Okla.) 12,369

Center for Democratic Renewal • P.O. Box 50469, Atlanta, GA 30302-0469 • 404/221-0025

1800 to a mere 250,000 between 1890 and 1900. Meanwhile, the non-Indian population increased from approximately 5 million in 1800 to over 75 million in 1900 according to Russell Thornton's *American Indian Holocaust and Survival: A Population History Since 1492.* By 1980, the American Indian population had recovered to 1.37 million. The ignominious history of United States policy toward Native Americans involved countless methods of dehumanizing and robbing them.

In the late 1830s, the Cherokee Indians were forced from their lands, where they had established a mighty nation in what is now north Georgia and western North Carolina. They were relocated far from their home to Oklahoma, and forced to live in what can only be described as concentration camps. The long march to Oklahoma — the Trail of Tears — cost more than 8,000 lives, approximately one-third of the Cherokee population — and changed forever the Cherokee nation and the Indian experience. Other tribes experienced similar forced removals.

Though hundreds of thousands of Native Americans died in the 19th century as a result of such policies, a massacre which occurred in the northern Plains a century ago stands out as one of the most heinous incidents in United States history: the massacre at Wounded Knee in what is now South Dakota. In that massacre, an estimated 300 people, mostly women and children, were gunned down by the United States military.

Today, Native Americans live in grinding poverty on reservations and off, with the highest rates of unemployment and the greatest amount of disease of any population group in the country.

The conditions persist at the same time as many Americans maintain a simultaneous fascination and disrespect for Indian culture. While Indian jewelry and pottery are held in great esteem and many people adopt aspects of Indian spirituality, sports teams still are labeled the Braves, the Indians, the Redskins and similar names.

Indians always fought this domination with a variety of tactics, from outright warfare to courtroom battles. Much of today's struggle is in the courtroom, where many Native American groups are working to retrieve a measure of treaty rights and control over the resources on the land which has been left to them, as well as to regain control over Indian artifacts and burial grounds that are being taken over by museums and land developers. In a recent battle over Native American fishing rights in Wisconsin, racist whites adopted the slogan, "Save a Fish, Spear an Indian."

> **Many Americans maintain a simultaneous fascination and disrespect for Indian culture.**

Latinos

There are significant differences in the experiences of various Latino populations in this country. These differences are based on the historic relationship of Chicanos, Mexicans, Cubans, Puerto Ricans, Dominicans, and others to the United States government, white society, and each other. Of course, all suffer from language discrimination, in which institutions seek to impose English as the only acceptable language of discourse. A conservative social movement seeking to legislate "English Only" gained in strength in the 1980s as the Latino population in the United States sharply increased.

Puerto Ricans suffer not only from discrimination based on their skin color and language, but also from the colonization of their homeland. Puerto Rico became a colony of the United States in 1898 and has been occupied by the military ever since. Officially, a "commonwealth," the drive to become the 51st state has been stalled by the continuing strength of the pro-independence movement on the island and among Puerto Ricans on the mainland. Nevertheless, millions of Puerto Ricans have been forced to leave their homeland in search of jobs and economic opportunity.

Racism directed at Mexicans and Chicanos is based on skin color and language. It is also based on the conquest of Mexican lands during the 1845 war with Mexico. It can be traced to the arrival of the Spaniards to Mexico, three-and-one-half centuries earlier. When light-colored skin came into existence in that part of the continent, so did the preference for it, and the dark skin of the Indian was despised and belittled. White Spanish land owners were brutal taskmasters, and their finely-tuned racism was a large motivation for the revolution of 1810 which began to break the ties to Spain. Mexico has also been conquered by the British and French, in

---

United States 1992 Latino Population:

22,354,059, about 9 percent of total U.S. population

By Nationality:

• Mexican 13,495,938

• Puerto Rican 2,727,754

• Cuban 1,043,932

• Other 5,086,435

In recent years, Latinos in the U.S. have been the target of vicious anti-immigration campaigns. This photo was taken in 1992 in northwest Georgia, where Mexicans working in the poultry processing industry have been attacked by the KKK.

addition to losing half its national territory to the United States after more than thirty-six armed invasions of its sovereignty.

There has not been a self-defined term for Chicanos; they have been called Spanish, Hispanic, Mexican-American, Latin American — all terms imposed upon them by others, except the word Chicano, put into use by the movements of the 1970s. It simply means a person of Mexican descent born in the United States.

One of the most visible manifestations of racism against Chicanos in the United States has been the process of assimilation carried out in the public education system. Just as blacks were relegated to separate schools, so were Chicanos. As late as the 1960s, young children were punished and humiliated for speaking Spanish. Some who lived isolated within a white community would often change their birth names — Santiago to James, Olivares to Oliver — in a desperate effort to mask ethnic origin and avoid violence.

A focal point for anti-Latino action is through population control by the enforcement of unfair immigration practices. After each World War, Mexicans, many born and raised here, owning lands or businesses, were transported by railroad car out of the country and left destitute in Mexico. These actions were called the repatriation, Operation Wetback and other names. During the Depression, when the need for Mexican and Chicano labor was low, the United States suspended

welfare payments and people traveled to Mexico to avoid starvation. Whereas during the 1920s the United States absorbed a population of one million Mexicans, in the 1930s the country threw out about 500,000 people of Mexican origin, reported the President's Commission on Migratory Labor in 1951.

Most of the changes in immigration practices were part of an effort to control the size and make-up of the labor force, a practice which continues today. Armed force continues to be exercised by the United States Immigration Service which terrorizes exclusively Chicano neighborhoods, raiding factories, retail stores, and schools.

Economically and politically motivated immigration policies — sometimes in violation of international human rights standards — have similarly traumatic impact on many immigrants from Central and South America.

Asian Americans

Asian Pacific Americans are now the fastest growing minority in America and are frequently targeted for hate crimes. According to the 1990 Census, the Asian American population doubled from 1970 to 1980, and again from 1980 to 1990.

More than 30 sub-groups are included as Asian Pacific Americans, among them: Filipino, Korean, Thai, Mien, Hmong, Laotian, Indonesian, Pakistani, Samoan, and Micronesian.

Asian Pacific Americans are often called a model minority, but this stereotype ignores the long history of exclusion and discrimination which continues today. The first Asian immigrants came to America centuries before the Revolutionary War.

Asian immigration to America greatly increased in the late 1880s. They were scholars, farmers, laborers,

1990 U.S. Population of Americans of Asian and Pacific Island Descent

7,274,000, about 3 percent of total U.S. population

By country of origin:

- Chinese 1,643,924
- Filipino 1,403,882
- Japanese 843,784
- Asian Indian 814,688
- Korean 800,140
- Vietnamese 611,016
- Laotian 145,480.

Oriental rugs, *not* people

Asian groups should not be called Oriental. The term Oriental is considered offensive to most Asian Pacific Americans because: 1) it assumes the world's peoples should be divided into Oriental and Occidental and 2) to many, it painfully conjures up stereotypical Hollywood images of mysterious, opium-smoking caricatures in gambling dens. However, the term Oriental is appropriate to use for objects, such as Oriental rugs.

merchants and others. Despite the stereotype that these early Asian immigrants were poor and unskilled, United States customs figures show they came with a higher level of native literacy and more money than the average immigrant. However, with the post-Civil War depression and the rise of the white labor movement, Asian workers became economic scapegoats. Thousands were forcibly expelled from cities by angry mobs in the 1880s and early 1900s.

In 1882, the Exclusion Act successfully restricted immigration of Chinese laborers. This marked the first time that immigration laws would restrict one ethnic group. In all, over 600 pieces of legislation directed against Asian Pacific Americans were enacted by the early 1900s. These laws forbade them from citizenship, owning land, intermarriage, employment, and other forms of participation in American life. Subsequent immigration laws, in 1917 and 1924, virtually stopped immigration of new Asians to America for several more decades. The Exclusion Act was not repealed until 1943.

Even American citizens of Asian Pacific ancestry were viewed as unwelcome foreigners. This was dramatically illustrated during World War II when 120,000 Japanese Americans, the majority of whom were born and educated in the United States, were placed into internment camps, forced to abandon businesses, homes, and other property.

Anti-Asian bigotry continues today. In fact, there is evidence that it is increasing, due to deteriorating economic conditions and a rise in Asia bashing. Asians and Pacific Islanders, both overseas and in America, often have become economic scapegoats. Recent media headlines tout Asian investment as "America's New Invasion" or "Japan Wars," while ignoring investment by the British and Dutch, who are actually the largest foreign investors in America. Anti-Asian remarks are heard at the highest levels of government.

There is a false belief that Asian immigrants get ahead because they are given government money which other groups do not get. In truth, they get no such preferential treatment.

This country's experience in World War II, Korea and Vietnam have allowed forms of anti-Asian bigotry to continue. In these last three major conflicts, Asians were the enemy. This has continued to fuel anti-Asian hostility and hate crimes.

Asian Americans and Pacific Islanders are proportionately the most targeted racial group in such cities as Boston and Los Angeles. The frequency of attacks against Asians caused United States Justice Department official Martin A. Walsh to call hate crimes against Asians the fastest rising of any group.

Violence against members of the Asian community has had a devastating impact as many of the victims are new immigrants who are stunned by the vicious hatred of their attackers. These immigrants also have minimal historical interaction with social services, the criminal justice system and other means of support and redress.

Jews and Anti-Semitism

Anti-Semitism did not begin with the German Nazis and it did not end when Hitler committed suicide at the end of World War II. Conspiracy theories which blame Jews for economic, political and social problems have been a staple belief of far right racists. In the United States, as in other parts of the world, Jews are portrayed as the personification of evil — sometimes as Satan himself.

While "polite" anti-Semitism, which placed a ceiling on the achievement of individual Jews, has ebbed since

1986 Jewish Population

5,700,000, about 2 percent of total U.S. population

The total Jewish population in the world today is about 12,967,900; of those 3,562,500 live in Israel. Other countries with large Jewish populations are:

• Soviet Union 1,515,000

• Canada 310,000

• France 530,000

• Great Britain 326,000

Some of the countries with small Jewish populations are:

• Turkey 20,000

• Iran 22,000

• India 5,200

• Yemen 1,000

Scientific Racism and the term "anti-Semitism"

Jews were first described as "Semites" and anti-Jewish political movements described as "anti-Semitism" by the German writer William Marr in 1879. Marr wrote a book, *The Victory of Judaism Over Germandon, Regarded From the Nondenomination Point of Views*, and in 1879 founded the League of Anti-Semites. Marr was a follower of the new breed of "scientific racists" which attempted to describe all civilizations as having a racial origin. He wrote, "There must be no question here of parading religious prejudices when it is a question of race and when the difference lies in the *blood*."

One of the earliest "scientific racists," Count Gobineau, also believed that Jews were a threat to the racial purity of Europe because they were an admixture of white and black blood.

The term gained wider usage throughout Europe and the Americas after 1894 when Alfred Dreyfus, a Jewish French Army Captain, was falsely charged with treason. Dreyfus was exonerated after the author Emile Zola came to his defense, but not before a wave of anti-Jewish hatred engulfed France under the name "anti-Semitism."

The term "Semite" was derived from the description of a language grouping, which included both Hebrew and Arabic, but was transformed into a racial designation for Jews.

Although Jews are a distinct people, they are not a race. There are black Jews from Ethiopia and Yemen with African features. There are Jews from Syria, Iraq, Lebanon and other Arab countries who look much as their neighbors. And there are Jews of European and Arab descent — Ashkenazic and Sephardic — who resemble others from those areas. Israel, as a homeland for Jews from all parts of the world, is a multi-racial society.

Since it was first introduced, "anti-Semitism" has been the common usage for the complex of religious-based and supposed race-based hatred of Jews. Webster's dictionary defines anti-Semitism as "prejudice against Jews; dislike or fear of Jews and Jewish things."

Webster's dictionary defines Semite or Shemite as a "member of any of the peoples whose language is Semitic, including the Hebrews, Arabs, Assyrians, Phoenicians, Babylonians." Semitic is defined as a "major group of languages of southwestern Asia and northern Africa," which are then further divided into East Semitic, Northwest Semitic-which includes Hebrew, and Southwest Semitic-which includes Arabic, Ethiopic and Amharic."

Contrary to some current myths, the term Semite is not derived from the word "semi," to designate "half;" but from the word Shem, who was the eldest of the biblical Noah's three sons.

Despite the fact that the term "Semite" can be used to describe Arabs and Jews (and some North Africans) alike, anti-Semitism is used only to describe bigotry directed against Jews. Anti-Arab racism is derived from different sources and uses distinctive myths for its promotion. For example, Arabs are not mythologized as international bankers or grand manipulators of the media.

Some anti-Semites claim they are not anti-Semites by employing a verbal sleight of hand. First they claim that they are not anti-Arab; then they claim that since Arabs are Semites they are not anti-Semitic. At other times, they claim to be simply anti-Zionist, but nonetheless express many of the classic anti-Jewish myths.

Governments and powerful elites have often used anti-Semitism as a way to scapegoat Jews for political or economic problems. But anti-Semitism has also often been used by powerless people who seek relief from their own oppression. August Bebel, a German Social Democrat in the early 1900s, called anti-Semitism "the socialism of fools."

World War II, anti-Semitism practiced by people from all walks of life has remained a potent political force in the United States and around the world.

Denied the rights of citizenship accorded their Christian neighbors throughout Europe, Jews were forced to live in walled-off sections of cities called ghettos. Historians believe the first walled ghetto was probably established in Poland in 1266. The Breslau Church Council decreed at the time: "lest perchance the Christian people be...more easily infected with the superstition and depraved morals of the Jews dwelling among them...we command that the Jews shall be separated...by a hedge, a wall or a ditch."

Discrimination and segregation often boiled over into mass anti-Jewish riots known as pogroms, which resulted in thousands of deaths and the destruction of Jewish homes and synagogues. Increased religious fervor and nationalism often caused the riots and tens of

The Holocaust

The Nazi genocide of European Jewry was a major turning point in Jewish history. By 1945 one of every three Jews in the world had perished.

During their rise to power the Nazis blamed the Jews for Germany's troubles, often leading picket lines of Jewish shops and vandalizing synagogues. After the Nazis came to power they passed a set of laws which stripped Jews of their German citizenship and enforced discrimination. In 1938, a year before World War II started, dozens of Jews were killed, thousands sent to prison camps and shops and synagogues were destroyed in a large-scale anti-Jewish riot known as Kristallnacht.

As Germany conquered the rest of Europe, the Nazis extermination plans were assisted by like-minded political movements and governments in the occupied countries.

The destruction of European Jewry was so important to the Nazis that they diverted trains from moving troops and ammunition so they could be used to bring Jews to the concentration camps.

Despite repeated pleas by Jews and others all over the world, the Allies never bombed the railheads at Auschwitz — allowing the Nazi murder machine to continue operating throughout the war.

In fact, Jewish refugees from Nazi Europe were barred entry to the United States under the provisions of immigration law.

Although Jews played a central role in the Nazi demonology, they were not its only victims. Gypsies (Roma) were also singled out for extermination as a people. Gay men and lesbians, political dissidents and others were also sent to concentration camps and murdered.

The Protocols of the Elders of Zion

In 1903 an obscure Russian monk named Sergey Nilus published the *Protocols of the Elders of Zion*, claiming the book was the minutes of a secret meeting of Jewish leaders who were seeking to take over the world. The *Protocols* charged that Jews had a plan to control all political parties, the media, banking, indeed, whole economies. As described by the *Protocols*, Jews were both capitalists and communists, working under a master plan which hid their real objectives.

The *Protocols* quickly spread around the world, and special editions were printed in English, French, Spanish, German, Arabic and Japanese. Hitler's Nazis printed millions of copies, claiming "It is the duty of every German to study the terrifying avowal of the Elders of Zion."

In 1921 the London *Times* proved the *Protocols* was a forgery copied from a pamphlet written by Maurcie Joly in France which attacked Napoleon IV. Over 160 sections of the book were copied from Joly, only making changes to attack the Jews instead of Napoleon.

The *Protocols* were a fake designed to prove a conspiracy which didn't exist. But anti-Semites have concluded that even if it was a forgery, the international Jewish conspiracy exists nonetheless.

Henry Ford, the famed automaker, claimed, "...the *Protocols*...fit in with what is going on...they have fit the world situation up to this time. They fit it now."

Ford published his own series of anti-Semitic tracts in his newspaper, the Dearborn *Independent*. These articles were later collected as *The International Jew*.

Although Hitler is no longer publishing the *Protocols*, many others around the world still are. One English-language version by Angriff Press in California is distributed in the United States (Angriff Press is named after the newspaper of the SS in Nazi Germany.) It is sold by many Ku Klux Klan and neo-Nazi groups. But it is also circulated among people who do not regard themselves as racists, but claim to be "anti-Zionists."

thousands were murdered after 1096 when Crusaders marched through Europe on their way to the Holy Land.

In 1492 King Ferdinand and Queen Isabella ended the Moslem rule of Spain and began the infamous Inquisition, forcibly baptizing tens of thousands of Jews and burning the unrepentant at the stake. Many Jews publicly adopted Christianity, but privately practiced Judaism in secret.

During this entire period Jews were denied basic citizenship rights and were considered a separate nationality even if their families had lived in the area for centuries.

The emancipation of European Jewry began with the French revolution in 1789 which granted citizenship rights to individual Jews. It spread unevenly across Europe along with Napoleon's conquering armies. Full equality was not granted in Germany until 1871. The Russian Czars never granted Jews full equality, and in 1772 established a restricted area of residence in Eastern Europe, known as the Pale of Settlement. A series of government-directed pogroms swept across the Russian empire beginning in Odessa in 1871. They reached a fevered pitch in the 1890s and early 1900s. Between 1884-1903, 700,000 Jews fled Russia and Poland, over 500,000 settling in the United States.

At the same time that Jews were being granted individual citizenship rights, a new movement of scientific racists was burgeoning. Religious bigots had previously attacked Jews because they weren't Christians and were thought to be Satanic. But the new scientific racists declared that Jews were a race and that Jewish "characteristics" were genetic and hereditary.

Scholars have debated whether modern anti-Semitism has been based on religious bigotry, or is primarily racial-political in nature. What is certain is that modern anti-Semitism incorporates many of the powerful theologically-based myths, often expressed in racial terms. Anti-Semitism is neither simply religious bigotry or racism: it is a hybrid of both.

Jews were among the first European settlers in North America, many coming by way of small Jewish communities established earlier in Brazil and South America. As it was for other Europeans, the United States was largely a land of opportunity and free-

The Roma and World-wide Anti-'Gypsy' Bias

When was the last time you claimed that you had been "gypped" when you thought you had been cheated, or talked about a "gyp-joint" which sold shoddy goods at high prices? In the Funk and Wagnalls 1957 dictionary, the first definition listed for "gyp" is "swindler." In fact, the term is a pejorative, derived from the widely-held myths about Gypsies.

Actually, Gypsies is a misnomer for Romanies, or Roma. Roma are an ancient people of Dravidian origin whose ancestral homeland was India. After leaving there over a thousand years ago, probably in several separate migrations, Roma reached Europe in the mid- to late thirteenth century.

When Roma reached the Balkans, they were highly valued for their skilled craftsmanship, filling a necessary gap in a labor force depleted by the demand for men to fight in the Crusades. Measures to prevent Romani workers from leaving evolved into institutionalized slavery by 1360, affecting at least half of the entire Romani population. Slavery continued for over 500 years, until its abolition in 1864.

The other half of the Romani population dispersed through the continent reaching every country in Northern and Western Europe by about 1500. Because of this enforced movement, Roma are mistakenly known as a migratory people. Economic survival under oppressive conditions depended upon itinerant occupations, living by their wits (fortune telling is one example of this) and sometimes stealing in order not to starve. Although there is absolutely no evidence that Roma engage in criminal activities any more or less frequently than any other ethnic group, they have been greatly stigmatized as thieves.

Relentless persecution and violence reached a savage climax during the Nazi occupation of Europe.

After the collapse of Communism, nationalistic and xenophobic sentiments have exploded into violence, most often directed at Roma, Eastern Europe's unanimously despised ethnic minority.

Today there are approximately 12 million Roma in the world, with about one million residing in the United States. Roma frequently hide their ethnicity, fearing repercussions, prejudice or misunderstanding. The largest group of Roma in the U.S. are the Vlak (Wallachian or Roman), descendants of the Balkan slave population.

Source: Romani-Jewish Alliance.

dom for Jews. Nevertheless, anti-Semites in the United States have borrowed many of the myths and prejudices previously developed in Europe and elsewhere.

One of the goals of the Immigration Act of 1924 was to exclude Jews (as well as Catholics) from the United States. One of the popular arguments at the time was that Jews would bring down the intelligence levels in the United States because they had fared so poorly on IQ tests performed during World War I. Discrimination at the university level was used to prevent Jewish students from exceeding pre-determined numbers. The same kind of discrimination excluded Jews from using public facilities such as hotels or living where they wanted. Signs read "No Jews or Dogs Allowed."

Many of the remnants of institutional discrimination against Jews have relaxed over the past 30 years. Anti-Semitism, however, continues in American society and is a key element of the white supremacist movement.

Anti-Gay Bias and Homophobic Violence

Like race and religion, sexuality and gender have provoked violent hatred over the centuries. In cases such as the lynching epidemic in the American South, racism and sexual fears have worked together in brutal

Long-time Georgia white supremacist J. B. Stoner is an example of those who combine racism and anti-Semitism with anti-gay bias.

ways. Violence based on sexuality that targets gay men and lesbians is known as homophobic violence.

European explorers condemned the open acceptance of homosexuality among indigenous people in the Americas. Indians respected androgynous men, known as *berdache*, who dressed and acted as women. In fact, these men were often considered holy and had special ceremonial roles. Writes historian Peter Wood, "By the end of the era of Columbus, the fear of homosexuality had grown into a powerful force in Europe." One *conquistador* wrote home to the Spanish king about the "infamous people, Sodomites" and recommended "a war of fire and blood."

Homosexual acts in the British colonies of the Atlantic seaboard were punishable by death, along with capital sexual offenses that included not only rape and incest but also in some places even masturbation. Many of these sodomy laws still remain on the books although legal challenges have been brought in approximately half the states.

Many scholars of sexuality currently assert that homosexuality did not emerge as an identity in Europe and the United States until the late nineteenth century, when urbanization and industrialization brought large numbers of people into cities and out of more traditional kinship-based networks. It was then that the terms homosexual and heterosexual were coined. "Sexologists" such as Havelock Ellis, who were investigating questions of sexuality in the late 1800s, report an outpouring of stories from the newly labeled homosexual population. Comments historian Estelle Freedman, "[Medical writers] came to see homosexuality not as a discrete, punishable offense, but as a description of the person, encompassing emotions, dress, mannerism, behavior, and even physical traits… Abundant evidence survives from observers and participants that between the 1880s and the First World War, a sexual minority of sorts was in the making."

Just as the racism of the late nineteenth century was highly shaped by the scientific spirit of the time — with most objective measurements designed to support the superiority of Europeans or Aryans — modern homophobia was shaped in this atmosphere of social Darwinism, where survival of the fittest meant justification of exploitation. In an atmosphere where, many scientists believed, the propagation of the white race was the key to a nation's destiny, the homosexual's alleged inability to have children was seen as degenerate.

Many of the early sexologists, such as Ellis, argued for acceptance and humane treatment of these newly discovered homosexuals and supported repeal of laws criminalizing homosexual behavior. But the new discipline of psychiatry under Freud's influence attempted to cure homosexuals, through castration, hysterectomy, vasectomy, lobotomy, electroshock treatments, and drug

Center for Democratic Renewal • P.O. Box 50469, Atlanta, GA 30302-0469 • 404/221-0025

therapies such as the administration of hormones, LSD, sexual stimulants, and sexual depressants, according to Jonathan Katz in *Gay American History.*

Military purges of homosexuals during World War II helped to accelerate the self-identification of gay men and lesbians in the United States, and after the war there were increasingly large gay and lesbian subcultures in cities such as San Francisco. During the 1950s, the McCarthy era purged more gay people than Communists, a repression that also intensified gay and lesbian self-identification. It was in the late 1960s, spurred by the example of the African American freedom movement and by a feminist analysis of gender oppression, that large numbers of lesbians and gay men began to view themselves as an oppressed minority, rather than as criminal, sick or sinful. The Stonewall Riot in 1969, during which patrons of a gay bar fought back against police harassment, is one marker for the beginning of today's movement for gay and lesbian liberation.

One result of this movement — the increased visibility of gay men and lesbians and their institutions — has been the targeting of gay men and lesbians for hate violence, both by individuals and by organized hate groups. A 1987 report commissioned by the Justice Department found that homosexuals were the most frequent victims of hate crimes — a finding which the Justice Department then suppressed.

Widespread and institutionalized prejudice and discrimination compound the negative effects of violence against gay men and lesbians. The National Gay and Lesbian Task Force estimates that 75 percent of such attacks go unreported. In states with sodomy laws, police can and often do threaten to arrest hate crime victims for sodomy rather than the attacker. At the federal level, gay people are not protected by civil rights laws that are sometimes used to bring to justice attackers who conspire to deprive racial, ethnic, and religious minorities of their federally protected rights. The fact that homosexuals are subject to discrimination in employment, housing, and child custody as well as rejection by family members and friends deters reporting to the authorities and can further increase vulnerability to crime and violence.

In the 1970s and 1980s, Klan and neo-nazi groups were also quick to write newly visible lesbians and gay men into their ideology of hatred, and some articulated what they saw as a new opportunity to use homophobia to stir up other old animosities. The emergence of AIDS (Acquired Immune Deficiency Syndrome) in the 1980s as a major epidemic, which in this country initially affected gay men and increasingly affects communities of color, increased the level of anti-gay violence, now

> A 1987 Justice Department report found that homosexuals were the most frequent victims of hate crimes.

KLAN/NAZI VIEW OF WOMEN AND HOMOSEXUALS

In the August 1982 edition of National Vanguard, William Pierce, author of the neo-Nazi terror novel The Turner Diaries, wrote:

"the primary purpose of sexual activity is the upbreeding of the race. The strongest taboo, then, must be against any sexual activity which tends to degrade the race....

"Next in order of sinfulness is an act of symbolic degradation. The act of a man and woman intended to engender a healthy, white child should be viewed as a sacramental act. Even when a sex act is not specifically sacramental — i.e., not intended to produce children — it ought not to be of a nature which clashes with sacramental sex or which tends to undermine or distort the basic view of sexual activity.

"Thus bestiality and homosexuality are beyond the pale, just as interracial sex with a sterile partner (or involving contraception) is. Such acts cannot engender defective offspring directly, but they must inevitably poison the ethos of a people which permits them — and this will lead in turn to the abandonment of the primary taboo and then to racial decline.... Homosexuality is a disease, a perversion of the most pathological sort...."

considered a second epidemic by many gay and lesbian activists. If the Far Right targets gay men and lesbians because they are perceived as a threat to white reproduction, the New Right often scapegoats the gay and lesbian rights movement for changes in family structures in areas such as divorce, the need for increasing numbers of women to work outside the home, and the changes in sexual patterns and family structures brought on by new birth control technologies.

In February 1991, a study committee of the United Methodist Church recommended that the Methodist Church drop its statement that homosexuality is incompatible with Christian teaching and say only that the church has been unable to arrive at a common mind on the question. The same month, the Episcopal Church's Standing Commission on Human Affairs recommended that the church change its policy disapproving ordination of gay and lesbian clergy rather than leaving the issue to the discretion of local bishops. The Commission also recommended that the church consider blessing gay and lesbian couples' relationships. The Presbyterian Church's Special Committee to Study Human Sexuality voted to accept gay and lesbian people as full participants in the life of the church, to open ordination to the ministry to all regardless of sexual orientation, and to develop worship resources for the recognition of same-sex relationships. Of course, these findings are being debated vigorously within their denominations. But, in denominations with a membership of almost 15 million, they do show that in many cases the church is moving in a direction away from condemnation and toward inclusion of lesbian and gay peoples. Many rabbis of the Reconstructionist branch of Judaism perform same-sex union ceremonies.

Violence Against Women and Hate Violence

While violence against women is different in some ways from other forms of bias violence — for example, the majority of assaults and murders targeting women are carried out not by strangers, but by persons known to the victim — the bottom line is that there are more similarities than there are differences. Violence against women is motivated by misogyny and hatred just as gay bashing, and racist and anti-Semitic violence are the result of bigotry.

The fact that male violence against women exists at epidemic levels is reflected by the staggering statistics:

- The American Medical Association estimates that one in 12 women in the United States will be raped at some point in her lifetime. By some estimates, this comes to one woman every six minutes, yet only one in ten rapes are reported to law enforcement. Over 100,000 rapes were reported in 1990.
- The Federal Bureau of Investigation estimates that every 15 seconds a woman is battered somewhere in the United States, amounting to a total of three to four million women battered a year. Battering, in fact, is the single greatest cause of injury to women.
- Ninety percent of female homicide victims are murdered by men; 80 percent are murdered at home; 75 percent are murdered by husbands or boyfriends.
- One-fourth of the suicide attempts by women in the United States are preceded by assaultive relationships; the figure for women of color is one-half.
- More than 75 percent of battered women surveyed reported that their children are also physically or sexually abused by their batterers, initiating a cycle of violence often perpetuated in the next generation.
- Each year, domestic violence is the number one cause of women's homelessness; domestic battery accounts for more injuries to women than car accidents, rapes and muggings combined.

However, most state laws providing criminal and/or civil remedies for hate crimes frequently do not prohibit or address hate crimes motivated by gender. As of 1991, there were ten states that included gender in enhanced penalty laws. Debate about whether to include violence against women in the definition of hate violence has been growing since the passage of the 1990 Federal Hate Crimes Statistics Act (HCSA), which omitted gender as a protected class while including race, religion, ethnicity, and sexual orientation. This issue involves compelling arguments on both sides and is not yet fully resolved.

Rape: Study finds majority of victims are under 18 and know their attacker

▶ Continued from **A1**
partment Bureau of Justice Statistics's National Crime Survey for that year. The FBI's Uniform Crime Reports said 102,560 rapes were reported to police in 1990.

In the Atlanta area, according to authorities, about 2,000 rapes are reported every year.

Silence blurs count

"I really can't evaluate [the

Rape in America

A new National Women's Study shows that far more women were raped in 1990 than other government reports have said and that rape is a "tragedy of youth."

Conflicting totals for 1990   683,000

Age at time of rape
Younger than 11   Age 11 to 17
29.3%

The following positions, pro and con, represent a brief summary of the current debate.

PRO

There is no substantive difference between violence against women and hate violence against people of color, religious minorities, or lesbians and gay men. In all cases, the violence is used to intimidate and control a class of people. The violence enforces dominant/subordinate relationships and implicitly affirms the perceived superiority of one group over another: in the case of gender, men over

Violence against women is linked to the backlash against women's struggle for equality, just as the civil rights and gay rights movements led to hate violence against them.

women. Violence against women also resembles the most violent of hate crimes in that torture, terrorization and mutilation are often used. Many of the murders that do occur are extraordinarily violent.

Misogyny — the systematic hatred and objectification of women — is a powerful political force in our society, breeding and legitimizing violence against women by fathers, brothers, husbands, boyfriends and strangers. This violence is supported by public policies and laws that reinforce the domination of women by men.

In fact, misogyny and gender-motivated hate violence are so thoroughly integrated into the violent American mainstream that many experts predict that including statistics on the victimization of women will overwhelm the statistics on crimes committed because of sexual orientation, race and religion combined.

Regardless of the amount of aid, violence against women has reached epidemic levels with centers and shelters only able to handle a small percentage of the women and children who need their services. It is ironic to note that there are nearly three times as many animal shelters in the United States as there are shelters for battered women.

Violence against women should also be linked to the backlash against women's struggle for equality, just as the civil rights and gay rights movements have led to violent reactions by bigots and hate groups who have opposed them.

Organizations that fight hate groups should have a vital interest in adding the issue of violence against women to their agendas. The far right, white supremacist movement is fundamentally committed to establishing authoritarian control over individuals and institutions, in particular women and the family. Just as Hitler sought to make women in Nazi Germany automatons

and "breeders" for the "Aryan Race," so do today's hate groups.

It is time for an extended dialogue about legislative and social change strategies concerning the relationship between sexist violence and racist, religious and anti-gay/lesbian violence. The arguments against including sexist violence in hate crime legislation are similar to those given whenever another group (Asian Americans, lesbians and gay men, etc.) has worked to be included in civil rights strategies; that is, the reasons given appear to be stalling tactics to prevent the inclusion of women. Among the reasons given for not including gender are:

- The proposed legislation would be defeated.
- There are too many incidents to document.
- Other groups already document crimes against women.
- Violence against women is not a hate crime because in many cases the victim knows or is related to the perpetrator.
- The issues would become diffused and groups currently protected would suffer.

Some opponents also argue that gender-motivated violence does not fit the "classic" profile of a hate crime, in which the attacker does not know his victim. The truth is that by most accepted criteria, violence against women fits most definitions of hate crimes.

Male violence against women is characteristic of "patriarchal" cultures — cultures such as our own that are controlled by men and based on assumptions of male superiority and innate male rights over women. These assumptions perpetuate sex discrimination and violence, as reflected by the staggering statistics.

We are wasting precious time debating whether sexist violence is hate violence or even whether or not misogyny exists. It should be self-evident to all human rights advocates that gender should be included in the definition of hate violence. Not doing so both isolates female victims *and* creates barriers to potential alliances between women and a broad range of racial, ethnic, religious and sexual minorities. Our point of departure for discussion should be at the level of strategies.

Including gender in hate crime legislation will put the issue on the public agenda and keep it from being marginalized. It will send a message that violence against women cannot be minimized or placed in a separate, unrelated category of its own. Making the connection between all forms of bias violence will enable us to create a larger base of support. Instead of diverting attention from racist, religious or anti-gay/lesbian violence, including violence against women will focus more attention on the problem of all forms of hate violence because the movement will be inclusive of more people.

Women's organizations must put issues of race and sexual identity clearly on their agendas while civil rights organizations put issues of gender and sexual identity on theirs and gay and lesbian organizations address issues of race and gender. Until we manage this integration of issues and commit ourselves to addressing all of them, the movement against hate violence will be fragmented. □

CON

The issue of including gender in the language of federal and state hate crime laws is not a philosophical problem; it is a practical one with complicated implications for all parties concerned. Including gender should not be immediately embraced just because it seems philosophically or morally correct.

Ending violence against women can be more effectively accomplished through existing laws and programs and lobbying for different and more women-specific remedies instead of attempting to piggy-back the issue of gender onto the already overburdened and underfunded needs of other hate violence victims. For example, a bill to address violence against women estimates that the federal government should spend at least an additional $125 million per year to support centers and shelters, in addition to the money for law enforcement and the criminal justice system. This legislation, introduced by Senate Judiciary Committee Chair Joe Biden, would also stiffen penalties for sex offenders and expand the scope of federal civil rights protection for women. This bill should be strengthened

and supported by *all* civil rights advocates.

Although it is inadequate, the federal government currently allocates over $25 million annually for programs to end violence against women, and a much larger amount of support comes from local governments, foundations, and communities.

There are nearly 2,000 rape crisis centers and domestic violence shelters in the United States. In 1990 alone, according to the Justice Department, the Office of Victims of Crimes provided $125 million to support all victims programs, including more than 1,600 specialized programs for sexual assault and domestic violence. In contrast, the Hate Crimes Statistics Act (HCSA) contained *no* budget allocation for implementation, training or enforcement. No federal dollars have been allocated to combat hate violence other than the money spent by the government for a handful of prosecutions brought by the Justice Department against those involved in crossburning and racially-motivated murders. Likewise, the federal government has been gathering data on violence against women since 1973 — particularly statistics on victim-offender relationship through its National Crime Victimization Survey since 1979 — and has yet to produce its first report on hate violence motivated by race, religion, national origin andsexual orientation.

Currently, there is *no* government-sponsored center or shelter that responds to the needs of hate crime victims other than women. The only assistance comes from private and non-profit groups and primarily takes the form of telephone counseling, only a small step in the full range of services needed by hate crime victims. No federal dollars exist to assist victims of racist, anti-Semitic or homophobic violence, except for victim compensation funds, of which only a fraction of a percent goes to victims of these hate crimes.

Proponents of inclusion argue that adding gender to the HCSA will produce better data on violence against women and make it less of a marginalized issue. However, there is little indication this will occur. Whatever the weaknesses in current Justice Department procedures for tracking violence against women — and there are many — another mandate to collect data on violence against women will do little to remedy the problem.

> We are wasting precious time debating whether sexist violence is hate violence or even whether misogyny exists.

What is needed instead is pressure from women's rights groups and others to improve existing data collection methods at both state and federal levels.

Such pressure has already led to some significant improvements. For example, detailed information is now available on the relationship between offender and victim. What's more, there's nothing to prevent advocacy groups from legislatively mandating that the Justice Department's annual report on "Female Victims of Violent Crime" be renamed "Female Victims of Hate Violence."

Similarly, the fact that some data is not available at the state level can be addressed more effectively by lobbying state police agencies to make data available locally in a format similar to the aggregate federal statistics. This is because police already gather extensive data on female victims of crime (including assailant/victim relationship), yet they haven't even begun to gather other hate violence statistics.

If proponents of inclusion are hoping to enhance police treatment of women, adding gender to existing hate crime legislation is a step in the wrong direction. After all, only a handful of jurisdictions have programs to deal with hate violence motivated by race, religion or sexual orientation. If the goal is also to get police officers to define battering and other violence against women as hate violence, then that should be addressed through existing police training modules on "domestic violence" which practically all law enforcement officers receive.

If federal and state laws expand the definition of hate crimes to include gender, then the limited resources that the criminal justice system would have available to spend tracking and responding to nongender-related hate crimes would be severely depleted. This is a real issue that has significant implications for rape crisis centers and domestic violence shelters. For example, should these agencies be willing and/or required, in turn, to provide services to victims of all hate crimes?

If a woman needs help because female skinheads are terrorizing her, can she find shelter at the local battered women's center? Even more problematic, what if the victim is male? Should rape crisis hotlines and shelters be equipped to respond to all victims of hate violence? The likely answer to these questions is "no."

Advocates for inclusion argue that the solution is to provide more funding, and that adding gender to hate crime laws will build a larger base of support for victims of racist, religious or homophobic violence. The various bills to address violence against women that have come before Congress and state legislatures offer no such hope. Nothing in the language of any proposed legislation speaks to providing support for victims of racist, religious, or homophobic violence. In fact, the bills have been silent on the subject. Public policies that expand the definition of hate violence to include gender without directly addressing the issues of limited resources will not produce equitable treatment for other victims of hate violence.

It is ironic that this debate is occurring at a time when veteran organizers of the movement to combat violence against women are themselves questioning the effectiveness of strategies that have made that movement so dependent on police and the courts — two institutions that are widely regarded as bastions of sexism and racism.

The omission of gender as a protected class in hate crime laws does not stem primarily from sexism or ignorance on the part of other civil rights activists, but because of the very real and practical difficulties that arise when considering remedies for hate crimes. There are no easy answers to these dilemmas. More dialogue and debate is needed before proposals to change public policy are offered

It is possible that inclusion of gender might further cooperation between groups, and it may offer new opportunities for anti-racist groups to address sexism and for women's organizations to address racism and homophobia. However, the terrain of federally-controlled statistics is not the place to carry out this effort.

Instead of arguing whether the hate violence movement is sexist or the women's anti-violence movement is racist, the discussion should shift to the impact of proposed remedies and the strategies for building a strong, united movement that insists on the eradication of all bigotry. □

> If proponents of inclusion are hoping to enhance police treatment of women, adding gender to existing hate crime legislation is a step in the wrong direction.

HATE GROUPS 2

The White Supremacist Movement

Capsule history of a century of Ku Kluxery

There have been four periods of Klan growth since its formation after the Civil War. The first Ku Klux Klan was organized in 1866 by former Confederate Army officers to restore white supremacy in the defeated South. Klan and Klan-type guerilla groups murdered African American political leaders, terrorized the newly emancipated slaves and eventually helped topple the Reconstruction governments in the South. As a result of its success, the Klan disbanded. Many of its members became active in the 1870s in the resurgent Democratic Party.

In the 1920s the Klan re-emerged, this time as a nativist Protestant movement that had millions of members. Klansmen were elected to public office across the country, North and South. One of the Klan's major goals was halting Jewish and Catholic immigration from eastern and southern Europe. After Congress passed legislation in 1924 limiting immigration, the Klan collapsed in a series of public scandals and internal division. According to author Stetson Kennedy, who infiltrated the Klan between 1943 and 1951, the Klan's campaign against Presidential aspirant Al Smith in 1928 was the last significant anti-Catholic movement by Klan groups. By the 1970s, Klan leaders were recruiting members from Catholic backgrounds.

The third period of Klan growth occurred in the late 1950s and early 1960s when the Klan re-emerged to defend Jim Crow segregation by violently attacking the civil rights movement. The most prominent Klan group at that time was Robert Shelton's United Klans of America (UKA). Shelton was a racist and anti-Semite, but he avoided the symbolism and ideology of Nazism. The Mississippi White Knights, led by Sam Bowers, was the most secretive and murderous of the Klan groups of that period.

George Wallace's independent presidential campaign in 1968 attracted support from Klansmen and neo-Nazis, as well as the John Birch Society and White Citizen Councils. But by 1972 the Klan's failure to stop the civil rights movement resulted in a dramatic decline in membership.

What began as a white backlash against affirmative action, busing, and other civil rights gains quickly matured into a full-blown resurgence of the Klan in the late 1970s. The new leadership was younger and more media savvy. David Duke, who had been active earlier in neo-Nazi student groups, became a national leader of the Knights of the Ku Klux Klan. Unlike Shelton's old-style UKA, Duke added a gloss of sophistication and intelligence to the meanness and violence of the Klan's public image. He also added a naziesque ideology to the Klan's traditional racism. Neo-Nazism, with its emphasis on attacking Jews and supposed Jewish conspiracies, soon pervaded much of the Klan movement. The Klan became "revolutionary," organizing in conjunction with neo-Nazi groups to overthrow the United States government.

Even when Duke formally left the Knights of the Ku Klux Klan to form another white supremacist organization, the KKKK continued to make alliances with Hitler-worshipping organizations such as the Aryan Nations and the National Alliance. Klan members joined clandestine terrorist groups to fight what they termed the Zionist Occupation Government (ZOG).

THE CONTEMPORARY WHITE SUPREMACIST MOVEMENT

Introduction

Understanding the size and scope of the white supremacist movement is often the first step towards developing a response to it. This section contains an overview of major organizations and leaders, as well as the themes they use to recruit new followers. Readers should consult this section to understand the context in which the responses in the other parts of the handbook should be used. For example, different tactics are needed to counter Christian Patriot organizing in a middle-class suburb of Denver than are needed to stop skinhead violence in the San Francisco punk music scene. Both are different than the tactics needed to respond to a Klan march in the rural South.

The white supremacist movement is composed of dozens of organizations and groups, each working to create a society totally dominated by white Christians, in which the human rights of lesbians and gay men and other minorities are denied. Some groups seek to create an all-"Aryan" territory; others seek to re-institutionalize Jim Crow segregation. In each case, white supremacists believe that the United States government is controlled by non-whites or Jews or a combination of both. In their minds, the current system of institutionalized racism and discrimination simply does not exist. They seek to change the government either through terror and violence or by campaigning in the political mainstream or both.

Defining the White Supremacist Movement

Some groups consist of only a few individuals; others have tens of thousands of members and collect millions of dollars in contributions. Although individual leaders come and go, and specific organizations grow and decline rapidly, the white supremacist movement as a whole has enlarged since 1980, especially among those white constituencies most disaffected from the status quo.

No single organization or individual completely dominates the movement. Individuals are frequently members of several different organizations and, despite frequent divisions between groups, the level of ideological agreement and organizational cohesion is actually high.

The white supremacist movement includes both the jack-booted bank robbers of The Order, the Klan and neo-Nazis, as well as the silver-tongued sermonizers of the Christian Patriots. More people are involved in the movement than is commonly believed. Approximately 25,000 activists form the hard core. Another 150,000 to 200,000 people sympathize with the movement, either attending meetings and rallies or buying literature and making donations. The success of veteran racist David Duke at the polls has encouraged other white supremacists to use electoral campaigns to generate funds and draw new supporters. [See Candidate Duke, page 47.]

Today's Racists Have New Strategies

But Duke isn't the only racist with a new strategy. White supremacists have also successfully used AM and FM radio, community access cable TV, and computer bulletin boards to spread their message. Klansmen, neo-Nazis, Christian Patriots and other white supremacists have transformed themselves from a violent vanguard into a political movement with a significant constituency.

Once known primarily by their criminal activities, today they have a noticeable impact on public policy concerning central issues of racism, poverty, crime, reproductive rights, civil rights for gays and lesbians, the environment and more.

Center for Democratic Renewal • P.O. Box 50469, Atlanta, GA 30302-0469 • 404/221-0025

This Klansman participated in paramilitary exercises in north Alabama in the 1980s.

minder of the activity of white supremacists in every corner of our country's life.

The Klan Today

The Ku Klux Klan is the organization most clearly identified with white supremacy. Even in the 1990s, crossburnings and night-riding continue to terrorize communities large and small from one end of the country to the other. Klan marches through small towns polarize residents, often provoking racist violence long after the event.

In 1992 there were dozens of Klan factions, many competing with each other for members. The major groups were:

• The Knights of the Ku Klux Klan, led by Thom Robb and headquartered in Harrison, Arkansas. The Knights have been an active part of the Aryan Nations and have successfully recruited skinheads. Other leaders include K. A. Badynski in Tacoma, Washington; Ed Novak in Chicago; Michael Lowe in Texas and Stanley McCollum from Alabama.

• The Invisible Empire Knights of the Ku Klux Klan, led by James W. Farrands and headquartered in Sanford, North Carolina. Originally from Connecticut and from a Catholic background, Farrands was the first national Klan leader from the North in several decades. Other Invisible Empire leaders include John Baumgardner from Florida; Daniel Carver from Georgia; William Hoff from New York and Tom Herman, a former New Hampshire police department employee.

• The Confederate Knights of America, led by Terry Boyce and headquartered in Huntersville, N.C. Boyce is a self-professed militant and has built a skinhead following in the Southeast. Other leaders include Marcus Blanton and Dennis Mahon.

For example, comparative polling surveys taken during the height of David Duke's political campaigns showed that almost twice as many white people in Louisiana as in the rest of the country were opposed to government efforts to help African-Americans get better job opportunities.

A constant barrage of marches, white supremacist propaganda and political organizing has left a visible mark on the populace. The focus of public policy has shifted to blaming the victims of racism, instead of changing the institutions which perpetuate it.

The shape of the white supremacist movement — at one time dominated by white-robed Klansmen and influenced by uniformed neo-Nazis — has changed considerably in the past decade. Many Klansmen have defected to other, more sophisticated organizations. Only one-quarter, or approximately 6,000 of hard-core white supremacists were Klan members in 1992. The Klan, nevertheless, remains a violent, dangerous re-

The False Theology of Christian Identity

Identity is a quasi-theological movement of small churches, tape and book distribution houses, and radio ministries which seeks to broaden the influence of the white supremacist movement under the guise of Christianity. Because many of its core beliefs are now held by members of different Klan and neo-Nazi organizations, Identity binds the movement across the country. Instead of *Mein Kampf,* Identity uses the Bible as the source of its ideology. It teaches that people of color are pre-Adamic, that is, not fully human and are without souls. Identity followers believe that Jews are children of Satan and that the white people of northern Europe are the Lost Tribes of the House of Israel.

The racial identity of the Israelites in the Old Testament is the central turning point for this quasi-religious movement — hence the name, Identity.

According to Identity believers, their true lineage has been hidden for the past 2,000 years, supposedly since white people migrated out of Biblical Israel. They believe that their racial identity is important because of the fate of various racial groups during the period they refer to as the End Times.

Identity groups also refer to themselves as Kingdom Identity because of their belief that the Second Coming of Christ will occur prior to the establishment of His Kingdom here on earth.

Some Christian denominations believe that true Christians will leave the earth and meet Christ at the time of the Second Coming, escaping a period of war, plagues and disasters known as the Tribulations. This process is known as the Rapture. Unlike these Christians who believe the Second Coming will occur prior to the establishment of the kingdom, the Identity movement considers the Rapture a hoax and a Jewish fable of "marshmallow Christianity."

According to this reasoning, if there is no Rapture, Christians can expect to suffer through the Tribulations in order to reach the Kingdom. Identity teaches that the "elect" people of the Anglo-Saxon nations have a special role to play throughout the period of the Tribulations and until the establishment of the Kingdom. In Identity Christianity, election is determined by race, not by the redemptive grace of God.

Since many Identity believers think that humankind is now in the period of the Tribulations, current events are interpreted as the fulfillment of dire prophecies. Some believe that social security numbers and drivers licenses are the Mark of the Beast, and should not be used.

The Tribulations, they believe, are divine retribution for their sins: they have sinned by allowing the stranger — Jews and others — to live amongst them. They have sinned because society allows interracial marriages. They have sinned by allowing the sodomites (homosexuals) to continue their evil practices. Since Identity followers believe that the Bible commands racial segregation, they interpret racial equality as a violation of God's Law. If Christian ministers advocate racial equality, they are advocating breaking God's Law.

> **Identity teaches that people of color are pre-Adamic, that is, are not fully human and are without souls.**

Identity and the Christian Republic

The creation of a white Christian republic in the United States is a shared goal within the white supremacist movement, from the hard-core neo-Nazis of the Aryan Nations to the many Christian Patriot groups. The Identity movement provides a theological justification for this racism and breach of the constitutionally-mandated separation of church and state.

For example, William Potter Gale, an influential Identity leader who died shortly after being indicted for conspiracy to kill IRS agents, wrote:

"The Church is composed of the many-membered body of Jesus Christ. This Republic was founded as a Christian Republic. The government is nothing but an expansion of the Christian church! It was founded by a compact ... known as the Articles of Confederation, Perpetual which have their source in the Holy Bible. Since the Constitution was lifted from the Articles of Confederation, the source of the Constitution is the Bible."

Identity, like other sections of the white supremacist movement, teaches that an international Jewish banking conspiracy is behind many of the world's events. Sheldon Emry, who led the Lord's Covenant Church in Phoenix, Arizona, before his death, spelled it out for his followers:

"God Almighty warned in the Bible that one of the curses which would come upon His People for disobeying His Laws was: The stranger that is within thee shall get up above thee very high [Deut. 28:44-45]. Most of the owners of the largest banks in America are of Eastern European ancestry and connected with the Rothschild European banks."

Emry's themes are now a staple of Identity theology and form part of the basis of its appeal: America is the new Promised Land; Jews and other non-whites are aliens in this land; the Federal Reserve and interest (usury) are violations of God's law; the price that the true House of Israel pays for violating that law is domination by the Jews.

The same themes are echoed by Pete Peters, a minister of the LaPorte, Colorado, Church of Christ. Peters believes that:

"Once God's laws are obeyed by His people, the body of people shall be healed. Healthy bodies throw off parasites. When there is repentance and obedience to His laws, the porno shop will no longer be on Main Street, the Jewish Hollywood filth will no longer be tolerated...the homosexual

Key Figures in the Contemporary Hate Groups Movement

Thom Robb   David Duke   J.W. Farrands   Tom Metzger

Shawn Slater   Louis Beam   Pete Peters   Richard Kelly Hoskins

Willis Carto   Don Wassal   Ed Fields   Robert Heick

and the murderer will be removed, the Jewish banker will no longer be allowed to charge interest..."

Identity and Mass Influence

During the late 1970s and early 1980s, Identity was used as a rationale to establish paramilitary survivalist camps far removed from the mainstream of society. During the 1990s, some Identity leaders have attempted to rid their movement of its paramilitary image and establish a larger following with broader influence.

Chief among these Identity leaders has been Pete Peters. Peters is developing new methods for the

Identity movement to expand. From his home in LaPorte, he has built a radio ministry with many followers who regularly purchase his literature and taped sermons. Each summer Peters runs a family-style Bible camp in the Colorado Rockies. When he convened the 1990 camp almost 500 adults and small children participated. Similar events were held in 1991 and 1992. Peters also holds a regular camp session in Virginia. He has speaking engagements across the country, and recently purchased 1,000 acres of land in Wyoming.

In 1989, 1990 and 1991, Peters led a delegation of his followers to Washington, D.C., to lobby against gun control and other issues. In November 1989, Peters led the opposition to an amendment to a Ft. Collins, Colorado, ordinance that would have outlawed discrimination based on sexual orientation. The anti-discrimination measure failed.

Although a Clergy Coalition organized to support the anti-discrimination measure, no one challenged Peters's claim to be a legitimate Christian leader or his adherence to the racist theology of Identity. As a result, Peters successfully cast himself as a community leader and gained new adherents. Peters' success has served as a model for other Identity leaders.

The Aryan Nations and the neo-Nazis

The Aryan Nations has been one of the umbrella organizations which seeks to unite various Klan and neo-Nazi groups. Although the main headquarters are in Idaho, Aryan Nations members exist throughout the country. In 1989, the Aryan Nations opened a headquarters for the South in Tennessee.

In the mid-1970s, Identity leader Richard Butler, a former California Klansman, purchased a 20-acre site and settled in northern Idaho. Butler attracted a number of his followers from southern California to northern Idaho and surrounding parts of Washington and Montana.

In 1979, Butler convened the first Aryan Nations World Congress on his property. Klan and neo-Nazi leaders from the United States, Canada and Europe gathered to exchange ideas and strategies. The meetings became an annual event, and resulted in closer cooperation among a wide variety of Klan and neo-Nazi groups.

By 1982, the Aryan Nations annual congress was attracting 200 to 300 white supremacists. The Church of Jesus Christ-Christian was subsumed as an organization, but its Identity theology bound the various organizations together.

Beginning in April 1989, the Aryan Nations began a yearly youth meeting on the anniversary of Hitler's birthday. Skinheads, particularly from the surrounding Northwest, have attended, breathing new life into the organization. More recently, the group has suffered from factionalization and the defection of high-ranking members. Some of the Skinhead leaders that had earlier gravitated towards Richard Butler have also declared their independence.

The Order

Some Klan and neo-Nazi leaders believe that they will never develop a following among the majority of white Christians. They think that white supremacists will come to power by violent revolution and terrorizing their opponents into quiescence.

In 1983, two Aryan Nations leaders formerly associated with Klan groups, Robert Miles and Louis Beam, published a small-circulation newsletter which called for the adoption of a clandestine strategy of violence and terror.

Almost immediately, an underground formed and the activities associated with The Order began. The Order patterned itself after a book called *The Turner Diaries*, by William Pierce, a leader of the neo-Nazi National Alliance. These developments electrified the white supremacist movement and focused public attention on the Aryan Nations compound in Idaho.

In November 1984, former National Alliance member Robert Matthews died in a fiery 24-hour shootout with more than 200 law enforcement officers on Whidbey Island in the Puget Sound area of Washington state. In the six months that followed, over 35 neo-Nazis were arrested for a spectacular series of murders, robberies and counterfeiting. Labeled The Order, the group was described as having split from the Aryan Nations, although the terrorists had been members of several Klan and Identity groups, as well as the Hitleresque National Alliance.

Twenty-one members of the Order were indicted in Seattle for racketeering and those that did not plead guilty were convicted in December 1985. The group's activities became the basis for a subsequent federal indictment on charges of seditious conspiracy to overthrow the government of the United States. Charges were filed against Butler, Beam, Miles and seven others. After a three-month trial in 1988 in Ft. Smith, Arkansas, however, all ten defendants were acquitted by an all-white jury.

Neo-Nazi terrorism and bomb plots continued. In September 1986, a church rectory and government buildings in Couer d'Alene, Idaho, were bombed by Aryan Nations members. Again in 1990, Aryan Nations members attending a Hitler birthday celebration at the compound plotted to bomb gay community targets in Seattle. Three men were indicted in May and convicted in October 1990.

In 1991 a shadowy group calling itself the Phineas Priesthood emerged, continuing the strategy of violence and terrorism.

Although the Aryan Nations operates from coast-to-coast, its leaders have declared their goal is the formation of a Northwest Mountain Republic in the states of Washington, Oregon, Idaho, Montana and Wyoming. The Aryan Nations is also active in Canada.

Tom Metzger and the Third Position

Metzger and the White Aryan Resistance (WAR) assumed national importance because of his use of communications technology, his emphasis on young people — especially skinhead neo-Nazis — and a peculiar political approach known as the Third Position.

Metzger produced more than 45 half-hour segments of a television show he called "Race and Reason." Intended for cable TV, these programs have been broadcast on community access stations in Arizona,

California, Georgia, Idaho, New York, North Carolina, Pennsylvania, Tennessee, Texas, and Virginia. In each case Metzger used local racists to sponsor his program. Other white supremacists are now producing similar programs and airing them on cable TV.

Metzger has used his national platform to promote a variant of Nazi philosophy known as the Third Position. Third Position politics had been popular among European fascists, who professed no allegiance to either the Capitalist West or the formerly Communist East. Instead, they focus their propaganda attacks against white economic and political elites. They often claim to support "national revolutions" by small nationalities dominated by larger multi-national states, i.e., the Welsh in Great Britain. Metzger claims to represent the interests of white working people world-wide in a battle against both race mixing and capitalist exploitation. These anti-capitalist politics are shared by an increasing number of white supremacists.

Metzger often calls for racial solidarity between whites in the United States and Russia. And he has declared that a white civil war against corporate elites is the primary goal of the white supremacist movement.

Metzger is pro-union, claiming that workers who are not unionized are even more vulnerable to the predatory practices of the capitalists than those who are in "corrupt unions." He claims to be pro-ecology.

Although he was fined $12.5 million in connection with the 1988 murder of an Ethiopian immigrant, Mulegeta Seraw, by skinheads, Metzger remains an active influence. Variants of his Third Position ideology have been adopted by others, particularly young skinheads.

The Skinheads

Bands of racist skinheads have mushroomed in more than 35 cities since 1986, growing in membership from just 300 nationwide to a peak of perhaps 3,500 in 1991. They have appeared repeatedly on national television talk shows, projecting an image of rebellion attractive to alienated white youth.

Skinheads are a spinoff from another subculture known as punk rockers and are most easily recognized by their closely shaven heads. Some skinheads are explicitly racist while others have banded together to oppose bigotry, such as the Skinheads Against Racial Prejudice (S.H.A.R.P).

Skinheads and punks both express their general sense of alienation through music and dress. Some punks have also become active in the peace and anti-apartheid movements in contrast to many racist skinheads who have translated their personal code of violence into racist activity and membership in neo-Nazi organizations.

Although small, there has been a punk scene in every major metropolitan area since British punk rockers first introduced their music to the United States in 1976. From the very beginning, many British skinheads were attracted to the racist violence of British neo-Nazi groups like the National Front. British neo-Nazis have had years of experience organizing street-tough skinheads, and a new breed of racist political soldiers has attacked Pakistanis, Indians, Caribbean blacks, Jews and Gays.

At one time Metzger and WAR were the pre-eminent adult influence among the youthful neo-Nazis. In the Southeast, however, neo-Nazi skinheads worked closely with Klan groups. In the Northwest the Aryan Nations increased their influence among skinheads after Tom Metzger, his son John and WAR were fined $12.5 million in damages for their part in the murder of Mulegeta Seraw.

These young neo-Nazis have an uninhibited penchant for raw violence. Dozens have been convicted of hate crimes including murder, assault and arson, in addition to the more frequent vandalism.

Unlike the Klan youth corps groups of the late 1970s, most skinhead neo-

Racist skinheads at a rally in Gainesville, Ga.

Center for Democratic Renewal • P.O. Box 50469, Atlanta, GA 30302-0469 • 404/221-0025

Nazi groups are organized by young people and thus are more successful at attracting their peers.

However, on a number of occasions, they have shown a dismaying sense of solidarity with adult Klan groups. On June 28, 1986, a crowd of over 1,000 young people turned out to hear a Klan rally in Marquette Park in Chicago. After being incited by the Klan, approximately 500 youths attacked a small anti-Klan demonstration across the street.

The Christian Patriots

One of the new breed of racists that has emerged since the late 1970s calls itself the Christian Patriots. They call themselves many names — populists, America Firsters, Identity believers, patriots and Christian Patriots. Ten years ago many of them belonged to the Posse Comitatus (Latin for "Power of the County"). Today they belong to dozens of different organizations. Unlike the highly structured Klan and neo-Nazi organizations, these organizations comprise a semi-anarchic section of the white supremacist movement. The core beliefs are:

- White people and people of color are fundamentally two different kinds of citizens, with different rights and responsibilities.
- The United States is not properly a democracy, but a Republic in which only people with property should vote.
- Democracy is the same as "mobocracy" or mob rule.
- The United States is a Christian republic, with a special relationship between Christianity and the rule of law.
- Internationalists (usually identified as Jews) and aliens (sometimes identified as Jews, sometimes as immigrants and sometimes as people of color) are attempting to subvert the United States Constitution and establish one-world socialism or alternatively, the New World Order.

Candidate Duke

David Duke

In 1989, fringe political figure David Duke moved into the mainstream by winning a seat in the Louisiana House of Representatives. In 1990 he received 605,000 votes — 60 percent of white voters — in a campaign for the United States Senate, and followed that up with a 1991 campaign for governor in which he outpolled both the incumbent governor and the official GOP nominee in Louisiana's open primary before losing to the Democratic nominee in the winner-take-all run-off.

In the primary, Duke again won 60 percent of white voters; in the run-off he got 55 percent of all white votes, despite an unprecedented anti-Duke coalition which thoroughly aired his Klan and Nazi past and attacked the credibility of his new-found Christianity, his claims to have changed his views, and his confessions of mistaken intolerance in his younger days.

Truly, no Louisianan who voted for Duke could have been unaware of his past, his fundamental — and unchanged — philosophy, and the racist aspects of his legislative record as well as his gubernatorial platform. The fact that 55 percent of white Louisiana voters still backed Duke indicates the depth of the appeal that racial politics still holds. Many political scientists who followed Duke's campaign believe he would have done equally well in other states.

Duke's campaign was well-funded by small contributors from across the country, and the Louisiana polls had barely closed before he announced his candidacy for the 1992 GOP presidential nomination.

That campaign foundered due to many factors. Duke may well have believed he might win the Louisiana governorship, but he knew he had no chance of winning the presidency. However, he is now a professional campaigner, and the publicity from his campaigns disseminates the message of the white supremacy movement while it brings in the money to support Duke and his propaganda machine.

The media, of course, continues to find Duke irresistible. [See **Covering the Dukester** in Part 3 of this manual.]

- The Federal Reserve banking system is unconstitutional and a tool of the "International Jewish Banking Conspiracy."

The ranks of the Christian Patriots have grown as some members of Klan and neo-Nazi groups exchange their robes and uniforms for the camouflage of false patriotism.

According to Christian Patriots, in a democracy the majority rules. And, so the reasoning goes, since the majority of people are not wealth producers, but rather are either idlers on the welfare roles or parasites of some other kind, the majority will be able to vote themselves the wealth of the productive minority. In a Republic, they argue, the individual is sovereign, and his rights are not subject to majority rule. According to the Christian Patriots, that essential distinction between a democracy and a republic has been subverted in the United States.

The first wave of Christian Patriot organizing centered in the tax protest movement of the mid-1970s. Christian Patriots agitated against the income tax and the Federal Reserve System, both of which they regarded as unconstitutional. Many Christian Patriots actually began refusing to pay taxes or file returns. They also engaged in barter through gold and silver exchanges such as the National Commodity and Barter Exchange in Denver.

Many of these Christian Patriots became followers of the Christian Identity movement. Some extended their tax resistance and barter economy to a form of survivalism. They began training with weapons and living in communal encampments preparing for nuclear cataclysm, race war, economic disaster, or all three. There has also been a movement among the Patriots to gravitate toward the Republican Party.

David Duke, the Populists and the Ballot Box

Christian Patriots have also become active in the Populist Party. Organized in 1984 as an amalgamation of former Klansmen, neo-Nazis and others on the far-right, the party's first chairman, Robert Weems, was well-known in his native Mississippi as a Klan leader. *The*

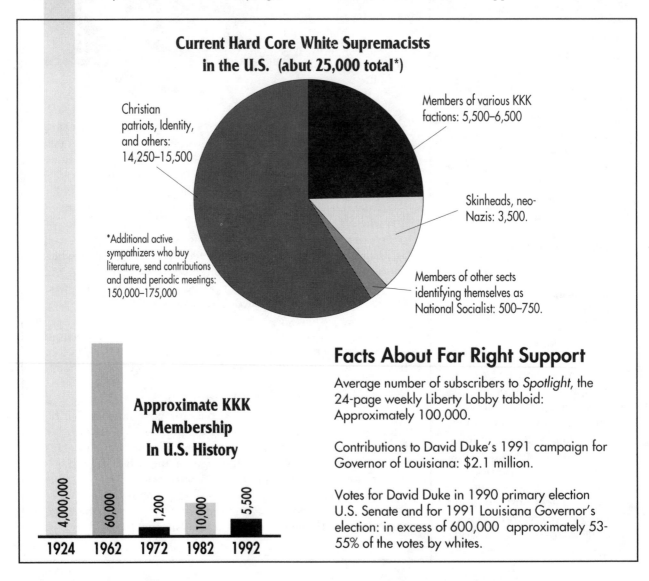

Current Hard Core White Supremacists in the U.S. (abut 25,000 total*)

Christian patriots, Identity, and others: 14,250–15,500

Members of various KKK factions: 5,500–6,500

Skinheads, neo-Nazis: 3,500.

*Additional active sympathizers who buy literature, send contributions and attend periodic meetings: 150,000–175,000

Members of other sects identifying themselves as National Socialist: 500–750.

Approximate KKK Membership In U.S. History

4,000,000	60,000	1,200	10,000	5,500
1924	1962	1972	1982	1992

Facts About Far Right Support

Average number of subscribers to *Spotlight*, the 24-page weekly Liberty Lobby tabloid: Approximately 100,000.

Contributions to David Duke's 1991 campaign for Governor of Louisiana: $2.1 million.

Votes for David Duke in 1990 primary election U.S. Senate and for 1991 Louisiana Governor's election: in excess of 600,000 approximately 53-55% of the votes by whites.

LYNDON LAROUCHE: NO FRIEND OF BLACK FREEDOM

The Lyndon Larouche organization, through the use of front organizations, demagogic ballot initiatives, and perennial political candidacies on the local, state, and federal levels has attempted to gain supporters and money from both the African American and white communities.

The most visible Larouchian front organizations are the Schiller Institute and National Democratic Policy Committee (NDPC). The Schiller Institute has attempted to muster support in the African American community by associating itself with Louis Farrakhan's Nation of Islam and by attacking leading African American civil rights organizations and leaders. Larouche has attempted to portray himself as a strong advocate for black freedom and equality by addressing issues of importance in the African American community such as drugs, AIDS, hunger, etc. One Schiller Institute recruiter at McGill University in Canada even went so far as to assert, "We've basically taken over the civil rights movement in the United States."

This is particularly ironic since an October 7, 1979 article in the *New York Times* reported that the LaRouche organization was paid by the Bureau of State Security of the Republic of South Africa to produce intelligence reports on the United States anti-apartheid movement.

A closer look at Larouche reveals his actual view of the black freedom movement. The Larouche organization issued a barrage of attacks against TransAfrica, the nation's leading anti-apartheid organization. Vicious Larouchian attacks have been directed against Jesse Jackson, former Mayor of Atlanta Andrew Young and his wife Jean, former Georgia State Senator Julian Bond, as well as numerous civil rights activists and organizations. More recently, in 1992, LaRouche operatives infiltrated the national convention of the NAACP, and published character assassinations targeting civil rights activists who discussed Larouche's links to the far right.

The NDPC serves as an arm of the Larouche machine in the political arena. Lyndon Larouche has run for President every election year since 1976. The NDPC has run candidates as both Democrats, Republicans, and Independents for local, state, and federal offices and has attempted to seize control of party central committees, political organizations, and grassroots groups unaware of their very hidden agendas. The NDPC orchestrated the infamous 1985 California ballot initiative, Proposition 64, calling for the quarantine of victims of AIDS. The NDPC urged a round-up of all prostitutes, homosexuals, drug users, and anyone else exposed to the AIDS virus and advocated their incarceration in "special isolation hospitals, under prison guard if necessary."

Both the NDPC and its precedessor organization, the National Caucus of Labor Committees, have used smear tactics and violence to silent their opponents. Operation Mop-Up, launched by NCLC in 1973, was a campaign of violent attacks against political rivals, like the National Welfare Rights Organization.

Though Larouche groups have often attempted to attach themselves to causes and movements such as opposition to the 1991 Persian Gulf war, they have simultaneously attempted to promote extreme right-wingers such as former Ku Klux Klan Grand Dragon Roy Frankhouser and racist and anti-Semitic conspiracy theories. A 1986 study by two Furman University professors found that, "Nearly all" Larouche contributors claim to be either "very conservative" or "extremely conservative" and also have an affinity for organizations such as the John Birch Society.

Spotlight, a weekly tabloid associated with the Liberty Lobby, played a critical role publicizing the Party and attracting members.

In spite of its marginal political status, the Populist Party continues to field candidates. In 1992 the Populists ran Bo Gritz, a Vietnam war hero, as their presidential candidate.

After his election as a Republican to the Louisiana House of Representatives in February 1989, David Duke became the most successful white supremacist leader in the United States. He built a large constituency for his racist views within Louisiana and a substantial base of financial support nationwide. Young people on campuses across Louisiana built student organizations to support his candidacy.

Although Duke has been a Republican since 1989, he entered the 1988 Super Tuesday presidential primaries as a Democrat and ran in the general election as the Populist Party's presidential nominee. Other racists, too, are jumping from the Populist Party to the Republican or

Leading revisionist scholars

The Institute for Historical Review seeks to "prove" that the holocaust is a hoax and has been grossly exaggerated by Jews for their own benefit. The following persons are members of the Editorial Advisory Board of the *Journal of Historical Review.*[*]

George Ashley, Ph.D. - Los Angeles Unified School District (Ret.)

Enrique Aynat, LL.B. - Torreblanca, Spain

Phillip Barker, Ph.D. - Minneapolis, Minnesota

John Bennett, LL.B. - Melbourne, Australia

Friedrich Berg - Ft. Lee, New Jersey

Alexander V. Berkis, LL.M., Ph.D. - Longwood College (Ret.)

Walter Beveraggi-Allende, Ph.D. - University of Buenos Aires, Argentina

Arthur R. Butz, Ph.D. Northwestern University, Illinois

Boyd Cathey, Ph.D. - North Carolina

Robert H. Countess, Ph.D. - Huntsville, Alabama

Albert J. Eckstein Ph.D.

Robert Faurisson Ph.D. - Lyon, France

Georg Franz-Willing Ph.D. - Uberlingen, Germany

Verne E. Fuerst, Ph.D. - Hartford, Connecticutt

Samuel Edward Konkin III - Long Beach, California

R. Clarence Lang Ph.D. - Seguin, Texas

Martin A. Larson, Ph.D. - Phoenix, Arizona

William B.Lindsey, Ph.D.

James J. Martin, Ph.D. - Colorado Springs, Colorado

Carlo Mattogno - Italy

Revilo P. Oliver, Ph.D. - Urbana, Illinois

Henri Roques, Ph.D. - Colombes, France

Wilhelm Staglich, J.D. - Badenweiler, West Germany

Udo Walendy - Germany

Andreas R. Wesserle, Ph.D. - Milwaukee, Wisconsin

published by the Institute for Historical Review; listing is as of Spring 1992.

Democratic parties.

The Liberty Lobby launched a Populist Action Committee in 1991 to support far-right candidates who ran as Republicans, Democrats, Populists or independents. This multi-party strategy was initially devised by Lyndon LaRouche, whose National Democratic Policy Committee has run candidates primarily as Democrats, but also as Republicans and independents.

The LaRouche organizations subscribe to anti-Semitic and racist conspiracy theories which have attracted Klan and neo-Nazi support.

Other white supremacists have followed in Duke's footsteps and will run for public office in the future.

Willis Carto and the Liberty Lobby

Behind the host of former Klansmen and neo-Nazis

who play leading roles in the Populist Party is the shadowy figure of Willis Carto. Carto has been a leader on the Far Right since the 1950s. Posing first as a conservative during the Goldwater years, today he poses as a populist. He is at the center of a web of organizations besides the Populist Party: the Liberty Lobby, the Institute for Historical Review, Noontide Press and the weekly tabloid *The Spotlight.* A 1981 article published by Washington columnist Jack Anderson quoted an editor for the John Birch Society:

"In my opinion, the preservation of anti-Semitism as a movement has occurred because of the activities of Willis Carto." Carto and *The Spotlight* have often denied that they are anti-Semitic, claiming instead to be merely anti-Zionist.

In the past the Liberty Lobby has sued Jack Anderson and the *Wall Street Journal* for libel, but did not prevail in either case.

The evidence of Carto's racist and anti-Semitic views is extensive and long-standing. Carto unabashedly called for a racial view of history in his introduction to *Imperium*, a lengthy racist book written by an obscure Hitler admirer named Francis Parker Yockey. Carto's own Noontide Press has continually reprinted *Imperium*. In the same introduction, Carto wrote: "Negro equality ... is easier to believe in if there are no Negroes around to destroy the concept."

The Spotlight

At the center of Carto's empire is a 32-page weekly tabloid newspaper, *The Spotlight.* The newspaper has carried classified ads for everything from Identity literature and the racist propaganda of countless white supremacist periodicals to display ads for vitamins and health foods. Over the years *The Spotlight* has praised the White Patriot Party as nationalists and attacked Martin Luther King, Jr. as a communist. The paper has taken up the cause of Klansmen and neo-Nazis, Posse Comitatus-killer Gordon Kahl, and praised the British National Front (a neo-Nazi organization in Britain) as populists. *The Spotlight* promotes the denial of the Nazi genocide of European Jewry, often blaming World War II on Jews, President Roosevelt and other "internationalists."

The Spotlight, however, does not contain the crude language of some Klan and neo-Nazi literature. Instead, it codes its bigotry with anti-big government rhetoric.

The number of paid subscribers to the tabloid has been approximately 100,000 since the mid-1980s. Approximately another 50,000 copies are circulated through

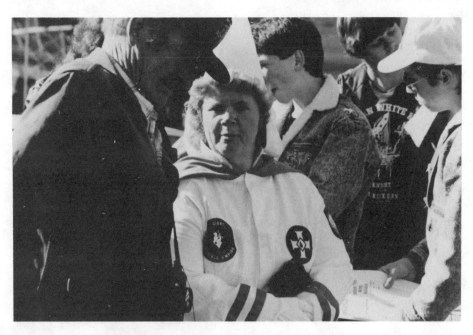

Women & Hate Groups

Despite the white supremacist movement's continuing commitment to (white) male supremacy, women are active members of Ku Klux Klan and neo-Nazi groups—particularly skinheads. In addition to themes such as "traditional family values" which they share with conservatives and others on the far right, white supremacists regard women primarily as "breeders" for successive generations of white people. Organized racists often claim to be "protecting" white women—a false sense of chivalry which has repeatdly ended in lynchings and other racist violence.

In *Women and the Klan*, Kathleen Blee detailed the legions of white women who joined the Klan during the 1920s. In some cases women Klan members served as auxilliaries—appendages to the male Klan chapters which dominated the Klan. In other cases, however, women Klan members and their organizations were equal partners in hate.

During the 1970s, David Duke first opened his Klan group to full-fledged membership by women. Since then, wives of Klan leaders, such as Darlene Carver in Georgia, have taken leadership roles—often as the secretary or treasurer of a local group. Many of the young people at southern Klan marches are women, sometimes with their children in tow.

Among Christian patriots as well, some women are recognized as leaders. Cheri Peters, wife of Identity pastor Pete Peters, organizes other Identity women to fulfill their duties as subordinates of their husbands and fathers. Montanan Peggy Christiansen has established her own career as a well-known advisor on tax avoidance.

But among the new generation of neo-Nazi skineads,
women have been the most visible as leaders and members. Young skinhead women often attend racist marches and rallies unaccompanied by men. Although skinhead groups are dominated by men, women such as Elizabeth Bullis in the American Front and Liz Sherry in the Confederate Hammerskins have become leaders on their own.

Lyn Metzger, daughter of White Aryan Resistance leader Tom Metzger, has organized the Aryan Women's Legaue in several cities. Although the Aryan Women's League is largely an adjunct to W.A.R., it has several programs of its own—including pro-environmentalist propaganda. One male skinhead leader, who calls himself Baxter the Pagan, wrote an article for the W.A.R. newspaper urging his male counterparts to support the Aryan Women's League and other white supremacist organizing by women.

bulk distributors who sell the weekly over the counter or in paper boxes. Assuming an average of three readers for each paper, approximately 450,000 people see *The Spotlight* each week.

The Institute for Historical Review

The Liberty Lobby and Willis Carto have also been at the center of the Institute for Historical Review (IHR). Like the slick monthly magazine *Instauration*, IHR provides the theoretical glue to hold various elements of the white supremacist movement together.

The Institute for Historical Review (IHR) has gained international notoriety for its outrageous efforts to deny the deliberate destruction of European Jewry by Hitler's armies. Since first offering a $50,000 reward to anyone who could prove the Holocaust occurred, the Institute has tried to revise other parts of World War II history.

The Institute publishes a quarterly journal, eight newsletters annually and publishes and distributes dozens of book titles. Each year around 120 revisionists gather for a conference, which is often nothing more than an international gathering of neo-Nazis.

The Institute is not an organization for wild-eyed lunatics sporting jackboots and swastikas. Instead it attempts to put an academic facade on its anti-Semitic agenda. Eighteen of the 25 editorial advisory committee members listed in the IHR journal hold doctorates. (See box on page 50.) Others hold advanced degrees or teach at universities.

White Supremacists and the New Right

At the same time that Klan and neo-Nazi groups were in resurgence, a new right movement emerged. It was composed of Fundamentalist Christians such as Pat Robertson and Jerry Falwell, neo-conservatives such as Irving Kristol and a new generation of leaders such as Richard Viguerie, Howard Phillips and Paul Weyrich.

Both the new right and the white supremacists targeted the social gains of the 1960s, the Carter administration, and women's rights. The new right began as a movement outside government institutions, although it soon established itself in the seat of power in Washington, D.C.

Ronald Reagan was elected in 1980 by only 25 percent of the voting age population. But his ascendancy was the direct result of the mass mobilization by all sections of the right wing. His election was a turning point and there was a sharp pull to the right which was felt in every sphere of national life. But the lack of a common enemy created a breech between the white supremacist movement and the new right.

Pat Buchanan's 1992 presidential primary campaign hardened the distinction in the conservative movement between neo-conservatives and traditional conserva-

Pete Peters speaks in front of the U. S. Capitol.

tives. Since then, there has been a growing rapprochement around new nationalist-nativist themes between sections of the white supremacist movement and sections of the traditional conservative movement—such as Buchanan, *Washington Times* columnist Sam Francis and Llewellyn Rockwell of the Ludwig Von Mises Society.

Pulled into this political re-alignment has been Pat Robertson's Christian Coalition which has a well-developed strategy for taking over the Republican Party "precinct by precinct" by 1996. During the 1992 Republican Convention, over 300 of the 2,000 delegates were members of the Coalition; they controlled the platform committee; and they succeeded in setting the tone for the entire convention. In Louisiana, southern California and other areas, the Christian Coalition is working in open alliance with known white supremacists.

Conclusion

Although numerically small when compared to the size of the United States population, the white supremacist movement has an influence beyond its numbers. It has employed many of the mechanisms of modern mass communications and tailored its messages to appeal to diverse alienated and disenfranchised sectors of the white population. □

Responding to Hate-Motivated Activity

(See more detailed listing on next page)

EXPANDED CONTENTS FOR PART 3

MONITORING, RESEARCH AND SECURITY

Introduction

Documentation, though time-consuming and difficult, is a vital component of countering hate group activity. Properly done, monitoring and research provide solid information which helps end the denial and silence that allows such activity to take place; helps lessen the sense of isolation felt by victims of hate attacks; and helps build coalitions between the groups targeted by bigoted activity.

Documentation is also a strategic aid: it is the primary tool which can be used to spot trends early and shape counter-strategies. Finally, investigative research can pull back the public relations mask to expose the backgrounds and philosophies of far right leaders, thus undercutting their influence and sometimes even exposing illegal activities.

Research Exposes Far Right Philosophies

Not every community organization has the capacity to conduct systematic research and documentation. However, a few national, regional and state organizations have been doing this work for years, and their publications and files offer a foundation from which to begin.

The model projects mentioned below, as well as the tips for collecting information, illustrate the fundamentals of hate group monitoring.

Model Documentation Projects

North Carolinians Against Racist and Religious Violence (NCARRV) annually issues its *Report on Bigoted Violence and Hate Group Activity in North Carolina.* The report, which is sent to 300 media contacts statewide, and then discussed at a state capitol press conference, consists of a 10-12 page chronology, a map, an analysis, and policy recommendations.

The chronology covers both criminal incidents and such constitutionally protected events as marches, rallies, and meetings. Based on the chronology, NCARRV staff map the incidents to show regional patterns. Then the research director writes an analysis of the year's events to determine trends: whether violence is increasing or decreasing, in what sectors, what the history of hate groups has been in the state for that year, what leaders have emerged or left the state, what anti-Klan legal or community actions have been tried (with evaluation of their relative successes). The report closes with a list of policy recommendations.

Reporters Appreciate Valid Documentation

"When we started doing the reports," said Christina Davis-McCoy, NCARRV Director, "media and 'experts' really underplayed the amount of Klan organizing and bigoted violence in the state. An AP reporter would call the State Bureau of Investigation, then do a year-end wrap-up saying things weren't so bad. Now, every year the press has a lot of detailed information on exactly how bad things are, and NCARRV has become recognized as the principal clearinghouse for information on hate violence and the far right in North Carolina."

PrairieFire Rural Action, Inc., became the Midwest center for monitoring far right groups such as the Posse Comitatus when Posse members began coming to PrairieFire meetings to recruit farmers. "We were working directly among constituencies of people targeted by the far right," recalled Daniel Levitas, former PrairieFire research director, who later became executive director of the Center for Democratic Renewal. "We had direct access to far right activists who contacted PrairieFire on a

1991 REPORT:
Bigoted Violence And Hate Groups
In North Carolina

Annual Report
North Carolinians Against Racist and Religious Violence

The annual report produced by NCCARV (North Carolinians Against Racist and Religious Violence) has become a respected and widely used reference for reporters in North Carolina.

routine basis to talk with us, assuming we were allies." Levitas issued a series of "confidential memoranda" to hundreds of key farm and rural activists. PrairieFire worked the press heavily with this information, also sharing it with national networks such as CDR and the American Jewish Committee. When this work became known, Posse sources dried up and PrairieFire became a hate group target. By that time, however, PrairieFire was able to develop innovative outreach to farmers to counter Posse propaganda. [See **Rural Responses**]

The **Coalition for Human Dignity** in Portland, Oregon, a community rocked in recent years by far right and skinhead activity, also emphasizes research. "We are lucky in Portland that the Metropolitan Human Relations Commission documents events in the city and county thoroughly," said CHD member Jonathan Mozzochi. "Our researchers can concentrate on far right organizations — who the leadership is, where they are operating." The Coalition for Human Dignity issued a report on the far right in Oregon that exposed the racist and anti-Semitic underpinnings of the Christian patriot movement, leading to critical television reports. [See **Youth Organizing** and **Christian Patriots**]

The **Arkansas Women's Project** — with a long history of work in the battered women's and rape crisis movements — combines documentation of racist, anti-Semitic, and homophobic violence with tracking violence against women. In 1988, the Women's Project organized a statewide network to be their "eyes and ears for justice." "We bring people together who have never sat together and talked in the same room — black and white, male and female, gay and heterosexual, Jews and Christians," project director Kelly Mitchell-Clark explained. The Women's Project provides education and asks its volunteers to read their local newspapers and pass on relevant information.

The **Northwest Coalition Against Malicious Harassment** serves the five-state region of Idaho, Montana, Oregon, Washington and Wyoming. With over 260 member groups, the NWCAMH provides resources for community-based organizations and produces a yearly report on hate crimes in the region. It organizes an annual conference and other educational forums on white supremacist activity and malicious harassment throughout the Northwest. It frequently provides expert speakers to programs and organizations. And it works to facilitate the development and enforcement of malicious harassment laws in the five state area. The NWCAMH enjoys a close working relationship with the United States Justice Department Community Relations Service and other law enforcement agencies.

Checklist for Information Sources

If you wanted to begin documenting hate activity, what would your sources be? Here's a check list.

1. Newspaper clippings. If your organization can't afford a clipping service, volunteers can provide a good substitute. A little training in advance will save a lot of headaches later. Stress to your volunteer clippers that the date and name of the newspaper must be affixed to every article. If you can persuade the volunteers to paste the clippings on sheets of paper consistent with your filing method, you will be one step ahead of the game (see *Organizing Your Files* below).

For organizations with more resources, most states have "clipping services," businesses that pay its workers to scan all the daily and weekly newspapers (and sometimes transcripts of radio and television newscasts) to clip articles on subjects requested by clients. The fee is often based on the number of clippings found each month. State-wide clipping services are usually better than national services, since the latter rarely subscribes to smaller newspapers. Take care when making out your list of subjects to exclude wire service stories, or you will receive many copies of virtually the same article reprinted in a number of newspapers.

2. Victims' reports. First-person reports and testimonies from those who have been injured or threatened by hate activity are invaluable, both for public education and documentation and for possible evidentiary purposes. Every organization should have a standard "intake" form (see sample, Section 4), and all staff and volunteer workers should have copies at hand and know how to get the necessary information. Victim narratives of their experiences should be tape recorded when possible. Victim testimonies should be supplemented by as much verification as possible — police reports, newspaper clippings or court records. Collecting affidavits is another useful way of documenting what has occurred.

3. Hate group literature and propaganda. Many far right organizations distribute newsletters, tabloid newspapers, magazines, brochures, posters and other printed materials to recruit and indoctrinate members. These publications offer insights into past and future activity, philosophies, and organizational strength and resources. Most publications contain pleas for money and/or subscription information. A less well-known member of your organization, using a post office box can order Klan and neo-Nazi publications to monitor what the hate group leaders are telling their constituents. Subscribe to these publications.

4. Dial-A-Hate lines. If you have a far right "hate line"—an advertised phone number linked to a recording on a hate group's activities as well as diatribes on local or national issues—in your area, call it regularly, even weekly. You may learn about upcoming marches or rallies, or you may hear a threat against someone or an organization. Tape the messages, process any immediate information on an intake form, and label and file the tapes for future educational or evidentiary use.

5. News Reporters. You should identify and introduce yourself to reporters who cover far right activities or particular incidents of hate violence. If you use a professional approach, and establish that you and your organization are a credible, informed source, reporters will call you when they need background information, verification of rumors, or re-

sponses to incidents. You may sometimes learn of incidents when reporters call you, or you may pick up details that you didn't know. But beware of trying to use the media by "pumping" reporters for information.

6. Rallies. When Klan or neo-Nazi rallies are held in public places, you can sometimes send representatives to monitor the rallies — either discreetly or openly, depending on security considerations. Find out exactly what group is marching by getting a copy of the parade permit. Take photographs, when possible, of vehicles and participants. Pick up copies of publications that are handed out, and tape record speeches that are made. (NCARRV monitors taped a speech of one Klan leader in Raleigh, North Carolina, the day after he helped lead an attack on civil rights marchers in Forsyth County, Georgia. In the speech, he bragged about the assault, and the NCARRV tape was later used in his trial to help prove motivation.) All monitors need to be carefully selected and need some basic orientation. The CDR can help set up a simple training session.

Private events on private property are a very different matter; the best advice is to stay away. Leave that to law enforcement, although you are certainly correct to alert authorities if you learn where and when a private Klan rally or neo-Nazi meeting is going to be held.

7. Monitoring agencies. Be sure to subscribe to the *Monitor*, the newsletter of the CDR, and get on the mailing list for other materials. Other helpful publications are available from Klanwatch, the Anti-Defamation League and Political Research Associates. *Searchlight* is a British magazine which keeps up with Nazis in Europe. See **Resources** for subscription information. Your organization may wish to affiliate with CDR to receive special training and more detailed information.

8. Election reports. Candidates in all state and federal and most local elections are required to file

Automobile tags can help identify suspects in hate violence incidents.

Prudent monitoring of white supremacist rallies and other public events will yield much useful information such as names of key leaders of area activity, the extent of local support, the level and type of rhetoric being employed, and the local issues which are being used to boost local membership in Klan and other right-wing groups.

reports about their financial contributions. This information can be helpful in identifying candidates who receive far-right support.

9. Court monitoring. Civil or criminal trials of white supremacists often offer a wealth of information, although a large time commitment is required to monitor court proceedings. Court monitors need training or at least some basic orientation before covering a trial. A sympathetic local lawyer can provide this training and teach your monitors which parts of the trial are most important. See also **Court Records**, below.

10. Court records. Trial and deposition transcripts and court documents in civil and criminal cases can also be gold mines of information about white supremacists. Your access to case files may vary by jurisdiction. Identify the various local courts (municipal, state, federal, divorce, bankruptcy) and go to the respective clerk of court offices. Look up the case number in the chronological or alphabetical index, then ask one of the clerks for it. (The file will be closed if the defendant was acquitted or the charge has been dropped.)

The file may contain all the official information on the case, including indictments, the court docket, motions, and the final disposition. If the case was appealed, you can get a copy of the transcript at a reasonable cost. "Extremists are very litigious," says Dennis King, the investigative reporter who is an expert on Lyndon

LaRouche. "They get into squabbles — divorces, lawsuits, and so forth — and leave an incredible paper trail." A search by plaintiff's or defendant's name in the court clerk's office will tell you if your local white supremacist has sued or been sued. If so, get the case number and ask for the files (including the file of exhibits). Look especially for depositions. Ask the clerk if any other related files exist. You may also want to contact the original attorney and ask to see her or his files. In examining court records, "Look for [white supremacists'] enemies," King instructs. "People who would love to spill their guts." Don't forget to check the records of parking violations, which give the places that violations occurred. You may find the driver's license number, in which case you may be able to get a copy of their driver's license (with address) and driving record.

11. The Freedom of Information Act. If you are not in a hurry, the FOIA can be a potent source of information on far right groups and on individual cases investigated at the federal level for civil rights violations. This 1966 law, amended in 1974 and 1976, applies to all administrative agencies of the executive branch (including the military). Using the FOIA is complicated and labor intensive. *The Reporter's Handbook* contains much helpful and detailed advice. In summary, however, know that there are nine exemptions to FOIA, and the one most relevant to your search will probably be Exemption (b) (7), which prohibits disclosure of "investigatory records compiled for law enforcement purposes" — if, for instance, disclosure would interfere with law enforcement procedures, or jeopardize a fair trial, or reveal a confidential source, or constitute an unwarranted invasion of privacy. You probably can't get information on any ongoing investigation. And the Privacy Act requires permission of any individual to get information on that individual. However, a request for information on organizations will include some information on individuals within or connected to an organization. Before you begin a FOIA search, get exact information on which government office has what you need, by calling them on the phone. Then write to that agency, preferably on organizational letterhead, citing the FOIA statute and requesting the information as precisely as possible.

You may want to set a limit on copy fees, or ask to be informed first about copy and search fees. If you can demonstrate public benefit, fees can be waived. On the envelope's lower left corner, write "Attention FOIA Officer." By law, the agency has ten days from receiving your request to acknowledge it. Then, agencies take months to reply fully. According to the Reporters' Committee on Freedom of the Press, the FBI takes an average of 320 days to fulfill an FOIA request. Follow-up calls and letters may expedite the process. If your request is denied, you can appeal and even sue. Refer to *The Reporter's Handbook* for details.

12. The Hate Crimes Statistics Act (HCSA). On April 23, 1990, Congress enacted the HCSA requiring the United States Attorney General to establish guidelines and collect data "about crimes that manifest evidence of prejudice based on race, religion, sexual orientation, or ethnicity, including where appropriate the crimes of murder; non-negligent manslaughter; forcible rape; aggravated assault, simple assault, intimidation; arson; and destruction, damage or vandalism of property." The data is collected as part of the federal Uniform Crime Report (UCR) and will be published annually by the FBI in a summary report. Nearly all 50 states have law enforcement agencies responsible for compiling crime statistics, and those agencies should be submitting reports to UCR. If your state has such an agency, ask for the data (you may or may not get it). Call the UCR (202-324-5037) and ask how you can get access to the data collected for the Hate Crimes Statistics Act. If you are collecting information yourself, compare your data with the officially reported data to see how thoroughly state or local law enforcement is cooperating with hate crimes data collection.

13. Directories and references. The teaching of investigative techniques is outside the scope of this brief checklist of sources, but the courthouse and the local library contain many references which are helpful in tracking down elusive individuals. Names and addresses can be found and cross-checked in driving records, phone books, voter registration lists, and various criss-cross and city directories and indexes. Biographical indexes list thousands of names from hundreds of "who's who" and biographical dictionaries. Your local reference librarian or, perhaps even better, a private investigator or a lawyer who does debt collection work, can help you and other members of your organization learn how to use library and court references effectively. Also check the clip file (sometimes called the "morgue") in your local newspaper's staff reference library, if public access is permitted. For more detailed information, see *The Reporter's Handbook*.

If you need advice getting any of this monitoring and research in place, call CDR. Similarly, call CDR if you have advice or information to share. "Sharing information created a synergistic effect," Levitas explained of his work at PrairieFire. "Our local information increased knowledge of regional trends, and CDR sharpened our ability to understand what it was we were seeing."

Organizing Your Files

Establishing a well-ordered filing system is an important part of the documentation process. Several helpful hints are:

1. Be sure that every item in your files has either a publication name and date or a filing date and a source.
2. Leaflets and other literature gathered from marches, demonstrations, rallies, etc., should be annotated with the date and location where the material was acquired.
3. Think long and hard about your file categories before you begin. Categories should be consistent. For example, if you establish an Aryan Nations file for 1990, 1991 and 1992, their labels should read:
   Aryan Nations 1990
   Aryan Nations 1991
   Aryan Nations 1992
   not
   Aryan Nations 1992
   1991 Aryan Nations
   Neo-Nazis: Aryan Nations 1990.
4. Newspaper clippings and faxes should be photocopied for storage onto plain copier bond paper. This not only makes them easier to handle — because they're all the same size — but they won't turn yellow and begin to crumble in a few years. Although the rest of your filing cabinets may be letter-sized, you might want to consider legal-size cabinets for your newspaper clippings. The reason is that an article spanning the entire width of a newspaper page will fit on a legal sheet, which

means less cutting, pasting and folding for you or your file clerks.

5. A computerized database index of your files will help minimize duplication of materials. A logical set of key words in a "comments" field of your database will speed up searches.

6. One useful filing method for photographs, if linked to a database, assigns a unique number to every photo. This number can be written at the bottom or edge of the photo with a special non-smearing pen, or on a small label affixed to the photo. The number is typed into the database along with other relevant information, and then the photos are filed in numerical sequence. To find a photo, look it up on the computer by date, location, subject or other keyword. A similar numerical system also works for newspaper clippings, and, when thousands of clips have accumulated, is often more efficient than a system which, for example, puts a copy of a clipping in one folder and then another copy of the same clipping in another folder on a different subject that is also mentioned in the article.

Security Tips For Activists

Monitoring and exposing hate groups can pose serious risks. It is important for activists to realize that they may become the recipients of harassment and threats designed to discourage their efforts. In the past some people have been the victims of beatings, arson and even murder.

A few simple security precautions may help reduce the risks associated with opposing hate groups.
Careful documentation is required. Photographs, physical evidence, personal notes or telephone logs, affidavits and statements from witnesses are examples of evidence that should be gathered.

1. Secure your office and home. This step includes duplicating computer disks and important documents and storing them away from the primary office site. If possible, keep your exact physical location inaccessible to hate groups.

2. Keep a camera loaded with film at your home and office. This will enable you to take quick photos of suspicious visitors or damaged property if a break-in occurs.

3. Be aware of and record suspicious phone calls. Some hate groups will pose as reporters or potential volunteers in an attempt to gather information about you or your organization. If you receive a phone call that you think is suspect: 1) ask for the name and address of the person to whom you are speaking; 2) tell them you have to call them back in a few minutes; 3) hang up and call directory assistance to verify the number as well as the address; 4) call back to the number given to you by directory assistance. If you keep a recording

Georgia Klansman Danny Carver videotaping the monitors at a white supremacist event.

device attached to your phone system, it may be possible to record harassing phone calls that may be used later as evidence.

4. Set up call tracing. The phone company can assist you in setting up call tracing to track harassing callers. This service is available in most areas and usually costs less than $10 a month, after an initial installation fee.

5. Maintain a log. A log of suspicious calls and incidents can be used as evidence in civil litigation or as part of a criminal prosecution; to provide factual background to the media; as a consciousness-raising tool to educate and inform others; to provide important information about the pattern of incidents which may give you valuable clues to identify the perpetrator.

6. Report all incidents. Law enforcement authorities should be informed of any harassing incident, no matter how minor. This will enable them to provide increased police protection and be aware of patterns of attacks. Personal contact with law enforcement personnel can also be an important tool in helping to expedite effective responses. In some situations you may want to choose the alternative of hiring an independent private investigator, but this can be an expensive option. □

LEGISLATIVE RESPONSES AND ISSUES

Introduction

Hate crimes — violence, threats of violence, and harassment motivated by prejudice based on race, religion, ethnicity, or sexual orientation — must be dealt with using a variety of strategies. Recognizing that prejudice cannot be legislated out of existence, communities around the country have responded by passing criminal and civil laws designed to deter and punish perpetrators of hate crimes. There have also been many innovative legal strategies which have proven to be effective tools for combatting hate activity.

This section will examine existing federal and state hate crime laws and offer guidance about the possibilities of passing similar legislation in your community. A table of state hate crime penalties and remedies is presented at the end of this section which you may consult for specific information.

Hate Violence Deserves Special Remedies

Hate violence is unique in nature and deserves distinct treatment by federal, state and local laws and agencies. It injures the dignity and self-respect of the victim as well as the community in which the violence occurred.

Community Involvement in Stopping Hate Violence

Community involvement in stopping hate crimes can ensure that:

1) Statutes are passed protecting *all* groups of hate crime victims, including, but not limited to, bias based on race, sexual orientation, religion, ethnic/national origin, and gender;

2) Local officials, either law enforcement or government representatives, are monitored to ensure compliance with the statutes;

3) Positive working relationships are developed between the community and law enforcement officials to effectively respond to hate violence;

4) Long-term coalitions and alliances are developed to address hate violence and other forms of racism and bigotry in the community;

5) The local community and potential victims know about the law in case they or someone they know is targeted;

6) Victims of hate violence have a supportive community when hate incidents occur; and

7) Strong messages are sent to potential perpetrators that the community will not tolerate such acts without immediate and severe penalties.

Prompt Responses Help Keep Problems In Check

Like a burglar looking for a home without an alarm, those who would practice hate may be deterred by a community with visible mechanisms of defense.

Legal Definition of Hate Crimes

What exactly is a hate crime, and how should it be treated legally? According to the United States Department of Justice Uniform Crime Report, hate crimes are those:

"…crimes that manifest evidence of prejudice based on race, religion, sexual orientation, or ethnicity, including where appropriate the crimes of murder, non-negligent manslaughter; forcible rape; aggravated assault, simple assault, intimidation, arson; and destruction, damage or vandalism of property."

State and local officials bear primary responsibility for law enforcement and the prosecution of hate crimes. These officials must have available to them effective legislation which will allow a vigorous response to such crimes, consistent with constitutional considerations.

Because of the alarming rise in hate-motivated crimes, state and local lawmakers and communities are working to pass legislation to track, deter, and punish these acts. At least 46 states have some sort of hate crime legislation and at least eight states have statewide reporting systems. However, the prosecution of the perpetrators of hate violence has lagged far behind the pace at which these crimes are committed. Additionally, many of the states that prohibit certain hate crimes — for example, Georgia's statute prohibiting terroristic threats — are missing other important components.

Overview of Existing Federal Legislation

In a political climate where the federal government is deferring to state legislators important civil rights decisions, too few federal remedies are available for the victims of hate violence. Nationally, the civil rights movement is portrayed as "being over" and racism, discrimination, and prejudice are seen as remnants of the last decade which are no longer a problem for the average citizen. Such a political climate has made it difficult to enforce existing civil rights legislation and even more difficult to pass new legislation dealing with racism and bigotry.

Federal Hate Crimes Statistics Act

The national Hate Crimes Statistics Act (HCSA) was passed in April 1990 and requires the Justice Department to spend five years gathering data on crimes motivated by prejudice based on race, religious, ethnic background, or sexual orientation. As part of this effort, the Justice Department established a toll free number — 1-800-347-HATE — for the public to report hate crimes. The United States. Attorney General has delegated other hate crime data collection responsibilities under the act to the Director of the FBI. The FBI's Uniform Crime Report (UCR) Section has been assigned the task of developing the procedures for and managing implementation of the collection of hate crime data.

Hate crime statistics will be collected along with existing UCR crime data, which is gathered by local and state law enforcement officials.

The Department of Justice is implementing a National Incident-Based Reporting System (NIBRS). This new unit-record reporting system will replace the UCR Summary Reporting System which was created in 1930, and will provide for expanded collection and reporting of offenses, arrests and their circumstances. Currently, information is collected from local law enforcement on a quarterly basis and in many cases involves reams of paperwork. The new system is computer-based, and will rely much more heavily on computer records and magnetic tapes.

There are several areas of concern to activists regarding this new law. First, according to representatives of the FBI, the Justice Department will only be able to collect hate crime data that is voluntarily provided by state and local agencies. Because the UCR is a voluntary reporting system, those local agencies that do not document hate crimes or perceive the documentation as too burdensome, will not be represented in the official statistics.

In states where hate crime legislation does not exist at all, underreporting will probably distort the national statistics. However, underreporting is a serious deficiency with all data collection efforts.

In those states where existing legislation does not include crimes motivated by prejudice based on sexual orientation, it will again be difficult for the FBI to gather accurate statistics. Some gaybashing statistics are kept by the National Gay and Lesbian Task Force and these hate crimes can be reported by calling 1-202-332-6483. The Task Force issues a yearly report on anti-gay violence, which may be obtained from the address listed in the Resource Section of this manual.

Before the federal Hate Crimes Statistics Act can be considered truly effective, Congress must fully fund data collection efforts, direct federal agencies to study and remedy America's hate crime problem, provide much-needed funding for police training at the local level, and perhaps most importantly, make support for hate crime victims a top priority.

State and Local Hate Crimes Legislation

Forty-six states and the District of Columbia have passed various types of hate crime laws. A chart listing these states and their legislative penalties and remedies is at the end of this section.

State and local hate crime legislation is usually designed to do five things:

1) Give prosecutors and law enforcement agencies the tools they need to enforce stiffer penalties for those who commit hate crimes;

2) Bring the state into compliance with the HCSA by requiring the collection of data on hate crimes within the state;

3) Give law enforcement officers valuable training in how to track hate crimes and respond appropriately;

4) Allow the states to bring independent civil actions to protect the civil rights of hate crime victims. Individuals could also bring civil suits against those who damage their property or injure them because of their status; and

5) Send a strong message to those who would commit acts of bigoted violence and harassment that the state will not tolerate hate violence. To the extent

Heavily armed Klansmen pose special problems for law enforcement, and increase the risk of injury and intimidation of citizens.

to which criminal penalties deter crimes, these laws may help prevent individuals from committing acts of hate violence if they know that stiffer penalties (higher fines and tougher sentences) are likely to result.

Existing state statutes are made less effective by the lack of enforcement. For example:

1) The lack of citizen monitoring of hate crime prosecutions can result in the dismissal of the cases; and

2) Judicial racism or homophobia by prosecutors and judges creates the presumption that hate crime victims, particularly if they are black or gay, are not credible witnesses. For example, in 1988 in New York City, a city with chronic and highly-publicized hate crime, only 33 hate crimes were prosecuted out of the estimated 800 incidents that were brought to the attention of the New York City Police Dept. Bias Unit. All of the current state statutes overlook this crucial problem.

The failure of state hate crime statutes to address the problems of enforcement due to prosecutorial discretion requires that citizen advocacy groups develop a pro-active approach to the entire judicial process. People should systematically monitor hate crime prosecutions, challenge seemingly unfair plea bargains, and confront inaction on the part of prosecutors, or improper behavior of judges.

1. Enhanced Penalties

A major feature of most hate crimes legislation is the enhancement of penalties for offenders. For example, a person convicted of a simple misdemeanor such as assault or trespass motivated by the status of the victim (race, religion, national origin, sexual orientation, etc.) can receive a stiffer sentence consistent with that of a felony or aggravated misdemeanor. Persons who commit felonies motivated by the status of the victim can be made to pay increased fines, serve minimum sentences, or both. Enhanced penalties are not new in the legal system; they have historically been used in cases of child abuse and more recently to deal with drug offenders. Additional penalties are available on both the state and federal level for persons who threaten, assault or murder law enforcement officers, judges, and members of Congress, for example.

Nearly 20 states have passed enhanced penalty statutes, including Illinois, Massachusetts, California, Florida, Idaho, Washington, West Virginia, Montana, Maryland, Pennsylvania, Michigan, and Oregon. Although there have been instances in which lower state courts have ruled such laws are unconstitutional (Michigan, for example), most states with hate crime legislation have not had problems obtaining convictions. However, with the June 1992 ruling of the United States. Supreme Court invalidating a St. Paul, Minnesota, hate crime law,

Constitutionality of hate crime laws threatened

As this handbook went to press, a recent ruling by the United States Supreme Court had the potential to undermine existing state hate crimes laws and federal efforts to collect statistics. In *R.A.V. vs. City of St. Paul Minnesota*, 60 U.S.L.W. 4667 (June 22, 1992) the United States. Supreme Court ruled that crossburnings are a form of protected speech. In the case, a white juvenile burned a cross in the yard of a neighboring African American family. Evidence showed the youth was trying to intimidate the family into moving from the neighborhood.

The youth was tried under a recent St. Paul municipal hate crimes ordinance. A lower state court ruled that the law was unconstitutional because it was vague and overbroad. On appeal, the Minnesota State Supreme Court upheld the law, but narrowed its construction. The case was then appealed to the United States. Supreme Court which unanimously found the St. Paul ordinance unconstitutional. But there was sharp disagreement between Justice Scalia, who wrote the majority decision, and Justices Blackmun, White and Stevens, who wrote minority opinions. Many legal scholars feel that Scalia attempted to set new guidelines for First Amendment cases, but are not certain what those guidelines are.

Justice Scalia's majority decision held that it is not necessary to curb "speech" to protect specific categories of people in order to fulfill the government's duty to "ensure the human rights of members of groups that have historically been discriminated against." Scalia argued that other laws protect against violence and intimidation. It was the "content" prohibition in the St. Paul ordinance—against racial, religious, and gender based bias—which Scalia found objectionable.

In contrast, Justice Blackmun wrote, "I see no First Amendment values that are compromised by a law that prohibits hoodlums from driving minorities out of their homes by burning crosses on their lawns, but I see great harm in preventing the people of St. Paul from specifically punishing the race-based fighting words."

Justice White argued that Scalia had placed "fighting words...on at least equal constitutional footing with political discourse."

Although the majority decision invalidated the St. Paul municipal ordinance, there are hate crimes laws which are still intact. Among those are penalty enhancement laws which increase the penalties for already existing crimes if they are motivated by bias.

In June 1992, however, the Supreme Court of Wisconsin ruled that state's penalty enhancement law unconstitutional. In *State of Wisconsin v. Todd Mitchell*, the court distinguished between "intent" to commit a crime and "motive." The Wisconsin court decided that motive—the reason a crime was committed—could not be punished, but that intent could. It ruled that penalty enhancement laws were based on punishing motive.

The *R.A.V. v St. Paul Minnesota* and *State of Wisconsin v. Todd Mitchell* decisions will result in a new round of litigation which is certain to redefine many of the constitutional issues related to both the First Amendment and hate crimes legislation. Users of this handbook should contact the CDR for periodic updates. Call 404-221-0025.

the constitutionality of enhanced penalty statutes is highly questionable. (See Constitutionality of Hate Crime Legislation.)

Unfortunately, enhanced penalties have sometimes backfired when judges are reluctant to have their judicial sentencing flexibility limited by the statutes.

Some prosecutors report being stymied at times by judges who give lenient sentences, particularly with juveniles. Judges in most jurisdictions are reluctant to saddle young offenders with a criminal record. In addition, judges may not believe young people realize the seriousness of their hate violence. Many young offenders are given only a slap on the wrist, even though they commit the majority of hate crimes. As a result, prosecutors and judges can appear to be sending a message to the community that nothing should be done to young people who commit hate crimes.

2. Data Collection

Although the federal government has mandated that the Justice Department prepare an annual report on hate violence throughout the United States, little data will be available from those states that do not have data collection laws, except from those cities in a state which have passed local ordinances. This is because law enforcement agencies in states without hate crime laws are not required to collect information on which rapes, robberies, assaults, arsons, and murders are hate-motivated. Unless local law enforcement agencies are required under state law to collect this information — and unless police are given adequate training on how to recognize and respond to hate crimes — the federal law will be less helpful to the people in the state. Policymakers at the state level will have no way of knowing whether the problem is getting better, worse, or staying the same. Nineteen states have such laws.

3. Training

Law enforcement officials need continuing training to deal with hate crimes. This includes training for prosecutors and, when possible, judges. Because of turnover, simply training all the officers, or sheriffs, in a given police department once is not enough. The training should be incorporated into the ongoing training new officers receive, and should be required for the veterans as new legislation is enacted. Only seven states mandate police training.

4. Civil Remedies

Forty states that prohibit hate violence in one form or another through their criminal codes have not statutorily empowered a victim to obtain compensation from the offender in a civil suit for damages.

Under some hate crime laws, prosecuting attorneys or attorneys representing municipalities or individuals may bring a civil action for injunctive relief (temporary or permanent restraining orders) to protect the rights of victims of hate crimes or to receive damage awards. Civil remedies can also include compensatory money damages, including but not limited to those for emotional distress, and punitive damages, attorney's fees, and costs of litigation. This allows victims to sue the perpetrator(s) and redress under the law.

5. Sexually-Oriented Violence

While violence motivated by homophobia (fear or hatred of homosexuals) is covered more extensively in Part 1 of this manual, it is mentioned here because of the importance of including violence against lesbians and gay men in local hate crimes statutes. As of February 1991, only 12 states included sexual orientation in their hate crime data collection laws. Those states without sexual orientation in their protected categories suffer from both significant underreporting and a diminution of the importance given to homophobic violence by the

law enforcement agencies and the communities concerned.

6. Anti-Klan Statutes

Statutes have been enacted in many states aimed at prohibiting activities commonly engaged in by various factions of the Ku Klux Klan. For example, the state of North Carolina absolutely prohibits secret political and military societies and secret societies organized to violate laws. The state statute also regulates signs, passwords, handshakes, and disguises used to further illegal purposes and disallows the use of private property to host prohibited secret societies. Similar legislation exists in Virginia and Oklahoma.

In other states such as Illinois, anti-Klan statutes increase the punishment for assault, kidnapping, and battery when the crime is "aggravated" for a number of reasons, including the wearing of hoods, robes, or masks in such a manner as to conceal the identity of the perpetrator. Several states prohibit or regulate certain secret societies, particularly secret military societies.

7. Wearing Hoods and Masks

The most common anti-Klan statute prohibits persons from wearing hoods or masks in public or on the private property of another without that person's permission. For example, a 1951 Georgia ban on the wearing of masks or hoods was drawn up to keep Klan members from inflicting terror anonymously. Although the statute was declared unconstitutional by a state court in May 1990, it was later upheld by the Georgia Supreme Court. At issue was whether the Klan was a "persecuted group" whose members' First Amendment rights to free

Michigan

The Michigan hate crimes law was declared unconstitutional by a Washtenaw County judge November 28, 1990, after a 21-year-old white man was convicted of destroying an African American couple's apartment in a fit of racially motivated hate. Even though it is likely that the offender will be convicted of arson, civil libertarians joined with right wing opponents in characterizing the Michigan law as unlawfully punishing offenders for constitutionally protected speech.

The greatest problem, according to the Michigan ACLU, is that the hate crime law creates two sets of penalties for the "same" offense. This oversimplification ignores the fact that plain arson is different from hate-motivated arson, in that the motivation is to terrorize not only individuals but entire communities. The primary effect of these constitutional challenges to hate crimes laws has been to portray the offenders as the victims, while the rights

and needs of the actual victims are diminished. Just as society recognizes the need to provide greater penalties for pre-meditated murder as opposed to manslaughter because of the especially heinous nature of the crime, so should we provide higher penalties for hate crimes.

Grupe

Another constitutional challenge to a hate crimes law occurred in the state of New York in 1988 when Peter Grupe was convicted of aggravated harassment because he attacked a Jewish man while shouting anti-Semitic obscenities. Grupe alleged that the law unduly restricted his freedom of expression and unfairly penalized him with an enhanced sentence, as mandated by the New York statute.

The County Court upheld his conviction, denying that First Amendment protection of free speech extended to those who commit or incite violence. States have the right to prohibit "fighting words," words by which their very utterance inflict injury or

tend to cause a violent reaction. Despite Grupe's claim that he was being prosecuted for making an anti-Semitic statement, the Court held that he was being prosecuted for his commission of violence and that the obscenities were incidental in establishing his motive, but not the basis on which he was being convicted. It was his violent conduct that was being regulated, which the state of New York has the constitutional right to legislate and prosecute.

Grupe also challenged the law as violating his equal protection rights under the 14th Amendment due to the enhanced penalty the hate crimes law mandated. The court held that disparate treatment of two classes of offenders (bias-assault and simple assault) had a rational basis in that the New York state legislature had determined that victims of hate crimes had a special vulnerability because of historical discrimination. Special classes of people, such as children or the elderly, also can be protected by the state with enhanced penalties as a deterrent. Thus enhanced penalties for hate crime offenders was upheld by the Court.

Center for Democratic Renewal • P.O. Box 50469, Atlanta, GA 30302-0469 • 404/221-0025

speech might depend on anonymity. The Georgia Supreme Court held that the law does not infringe on the Klan's right to free speech and free association, and that instead, the Klan's history of anonymous violence makes the mask a form of intimidation subject to government control. Due to the anonymity that a mask affords, the identification and apprehension of perpetrators of hate crimes would be difficult for law enforcement agencies.

Sixteen states have banned the wearing of masks or hoods by the Klan in particular, and by other demonstrably violent individuals (criminals) or groups in general, like paramilitary organizations.

8. Burning Crosses

As with the anti-mask statutes, 18 states have prohibited the placing of burning crosses or other symbols on public or private property. Some states prohibit the activity on public property, whereas most others proscribe it if done on private property without the consent of the owner or occupier.

Some states focus on the perpetrator's motive. It may be a crime only if the offender acts with the intention of intimidating, terrorizing another, or in "reckless disregard" of causing any person or group of persons to be terrorized.

9. Paramilitary Training

As of August 1991, 24 states had legislation prohibiting paramilitary training activities, usually in response to white supremacists who have threatened the peace and security of the state's residents.

Free speech or harassment? How will the courts decide?

Generally speaking, paramilitary training laws prohibit persons from assembling as a "paramilitary organization," a group which plans or engages in military exercises, training, or warfare, usually dressing in uniform or carrying real or simulated weapons. The precise definitions of paramilitary training, as well as the proscribed activities, vary from state to state. In some states the group must be engaging in the activity "with the specific intent of committing civil disorder," in order to be prosecuted successfully. Statutes regulating paramilitary organizations can be used to curtail the planning of violence by white supremacist groups. Unfortunately, their effectiveness is minimized if the courts punish the offense merely as a misdemeanor.

As a result of such legislation, there have been convictions in Florida and North Carolina and the widespread Klan paramilitary training that existed in those states in the early 1980s has been drastically reduced. The focus of the paramilitary activities has moved West — as discussed in Part 2.

10. Local Municipal Ordinances

Montgomery County, Maryland, is one of the few counties that began collecting data on hate crime incidents in the early 1980s. In 1982, the County had collected evidence on more than 185 hate violence incidents for that year alone. The Montgomery County

Council, faced with a startling increase in the number of crossburnings, swastika paintings, and other incidents motivated by racial or religious hatred, passed emergency laws in 1982 that created a $50,000 "tipsters fund" to aid in arrests and established civil fines for hate crime perpetrators.

Perpetrators are fined $2,000 if convicted of a hate crime; half of that fine is paid to the victim and the other half goes to the County's anti-hate violence fund to pay rewards to tipsters who give police information for apprehension of hate crime suspects. The law also made parents liable for civil damages for juveniles who commit hate crimes.

State Coalition Efforts

California

In 1984, the California legislature added sexual orientation, age, and disability to an existing law that enables victims of violence and intimidation to sue assailants for compensatory damages plus $10,000 in punitive damages. Threats and violence based on race, religion, sex and political ideology were already covered by existing law, but escalating hate crimes in the state forced a re-examination of the issue.

The California Attorney General's Commission on Racial, Ethnic, Religious, and Minority Violence published its final report in 1986, based on a one-year study of bias motivated crimes throughout the state and a series of public hearings it had sponsored.

Recommendations were made calling for the collection and dissemination of data on incidents, a new comprehensive civil rights statute including criminal penalties, the expansion of victim assistance programs, changes in criminal justice policy, and increased training for both criminal justice officials and the general public.

The Attorney General's office played a central role in efforts to pass new legislation, AB 63, which included sending out updates to community based organizations on the bill's status and appeals for constituent

lobbying. The Attorney General and advocates of the bill viewed support from law enforcement as critical, and obtained endorsements from key criminal justice agencies, including the California Peace Officers Association, the Highway Patrol Board and influential chiefs of police. The bill also received support from a range of religious and civil rights groups, as well as human rights commissions.

In 1987, the legislature passed AB 63 which authorizes local district attorneys and the State Attorney General to seek injunctions necessary to prevent crimes motivated on the basis of race, color, religion, ancestry, national origin, and sexual orientation. It also raises certain misdemeanor hate crimes into felonies.

There was little organized opposition to AB 63. The ACLU initially opposed the bill, fearing it could limit First Amendment rights, but changed its position after language was added stating that the bill in no way limits the exercise of free speech. While the bill was generally unopposed, there was some lobbying against its "sexual orientation" clause. A conservative group urged removal of the gay provision and persuaded one legislator to drop his co-sponsorship of the bill because it included protections for gays and lesbians.

To minimize controversy, supporters downplayed

Most jurisdictions place some limits on paramilitary activity by private individuals or groups.

Center for Democratic Renewal • P.O. Box 50469, Atlanta, GA 30302-0469 • 404/221-0025

the gay aspect of the bill. No gay groups testified at the hearing, but a number of witnesses discussed anti-gay violence in their testimony and gave examples of such violence. The Attorney General made it clear that if anti-gay violence was not addressed in the legislation, he would withdraw his support for it. Tom Banes, the primary sponsor of the bill, also let it be known that he would pull the bill from consideration if sexual orientation was deleted.

When AB 63 came up for a vote, there was no amendment offered to remove the sexual orientation clause, and the bill passed the Assembly by a vote of 53-20. It subsequently passed the Senate 25-1.

Iowa

After a third crossburning in Dubuque in 1988, a meeting was convened by the Iowa Civil Rights Commission and the Association of Human Rights Agencies to discuss the rising incidence of hate crimes in the state. Approximately 25 civil rights, religious, and human rights organizations formed the Iowa Coalition Against Hate Crimes to propose legislation and provide more information and develop strategies to counter hate violence. The Coalition was chaired by the Association of Human Rights Agencies and the Jewish Community Relations Commission of Greater Des Moines.

Hate crime legislation was passed overwhelmingly in the Iowa House of Representatives in 1989, but was defeated in the Senate. Because of the inclusion of sexual orientation in the legislation, the Governor had threatened to veto the bill anyway. In the fall of 1989, the Coalition delivered a report to the governor that presented findings and recommendations and called for the state to establish a Task Force on hate crimes. The governor appointed the Task Force, that included officials of the Dept. of Public Safety, the Dept. of Education, the Dept. of Human Rights, leaders of the two organizations co-chairing the Coalition, and two citizen representatives.

Comprehensive hate crime legislation passed both Houses in July 1990, and was signed by the governor. The bill also mandated reporting of hate crime statistics.

Political tensions existed within the state from the beginning of the effort. In the first year, sexual orientation was kept in the bill defeated by the Senate. The

> Coalitions require the cooperation of groups committed to civil rights, women's rights, gay and lesbian rights, and human rights. They should include representation from law enforcement, religious groups, civic associations, business leaders, and others who all need to be treated equally and with respect.

opposition came mainly from the evangelical community. The Coalition changed its tactics the second year, keeping in sexual orientation, but packaging the bill as a crime bill, a law and order tool.

The Iowa Civil Liberties Union expressed concerns about first amendment issues, but did not publicly oppose the law. The evangelical community was largely silent in the second effort, but homophobic hate mail flooded the governor's office. Ironically, for the opposition, this tactic backfired because this open demonstration of hatred actually helped change the Republican governor's mind about the extent of bigotry which was amply proven by the hate mail.

Georgia

In 1990 and 1991, a coalition of over 40 civil rights and community groups, with the support of State Representative Nan Orrock and other legislators, attempted to pass a hate crimes bill in Georgia.

Public support for the legislation was strengthened in December 1990 when Alabama Federal Judge Robert Vance and Savannah civil rights attorney Robert Robinson became the victims of mail bomb assassinations. A resident of Rex, Georgia, Walter Leroy Moody, was convicted of the crimes in 1991.

In 1990, the bill was stalled in the House Rules Committee by legislative leadership that was hostile to the concept of hate crimes legislation in general and protection for lesbians and gay men in particular. In 1991, the bill was defeated by a 103-64 vote on the floor of the House of Representatives. Opponents of the legislation claimed they were against giving "special rights" to gay men and lesbians. But when sexual orientation was removed from the bill by legislators, they still opposed it.

The legislative failure to pass a hate crimes law gave the Georgia Coalition Against Hate Crimes new insight into the strengths and weaknesses of its own coalition effort.

Although many groups signed on to support the legislation, too few actually had the resources to devote to the effort. In addition, the organizing work focused on the metropolitan areas of the state, primarily in Atlanta, while the opposition targeted ultra-conservative, predominantly white suburban counties surrounding Atlanta and the more numerous rural representatives, deluging them with letters and hysterical phone calls.

The Coalition focused its efforts on lobbying and public education, but the opposition disdained visits to state legislators. Instead, they circulated fliers to lawmakers that read, "While homosexuals grab all the headlines, all the African Americans, Jews and others will seem less and less unfairly victimized by comparison."

This was a cynical attempt to divide the civil rights coalition using inflammatory and homophobic language. It did not split the coalition, but the opposition did generate over 100 calls a day to the state legislature. This created the false impression that Georgians did not want to deter hate crimes.

Major state newspapers wrote editorials supporting the legislation, but they often failed to link brutal pictures of the victims of hate violence and the endless stories about the Ku Klux Klan to the need for the legislation. Several editorials were focused on the free speech/First Amendment aspects of the law, rather than seeing it as a tool for law enforcement and community protection.

The Governor, the Georgia Bureau of Investigation and several police departments supported the bill but did not lobby aggressively enough to ensure its passage. And the Coalition did not use its considerable influence to reach out to other legislators and gain more support for the bill.

Several key strengths were developed during the coalition campaign. Members resisted the effort to divide the coalition over the inclusion of sexual orientation. Each coalition member supported and reinforced each other. Thus, the American Jewish Committee spoke out against hate crimes targeting Arab-Americans (particularly because of the increased attacks during the Gulf War), while the NAACP supported the sexual orientation provisions of the bill. This solidarity sent an important message to people in Georgia, and has resulted in closer working relationships between the groups to pass other civil rights legislation.

How to Pass a Hate Crime Law in Your State

1. Use Reports to Define the Problem

Document the existence of hate crimes in your state as efforts are launched to pass a hate crime law. Reports of hate crimes will be available from many sources, including victim reports, newspapers, law enforcement and media sources. Collect as many of these as possible, if you don't already do so. Assembling them chronologically or by victim category will allow you to publicize the hate crimes and draw public attention to the problem.

The National Gay and Lesbian Task Force publishes an annual report on anti-gay hate crimes which may be useful. Similarly, the Anti-Defamation League publishes an annual "Audit of Anti-Semitic Incidents."

Incident reports are also available from the Center for Democratic Renewal, the Southern Poverty Law Center, the National Institute Against Prejudice and Violence, as well as statewide anti-violence organizations such as North Carolinians Against Racial and Religious Violence, the Portland Coalition for Human Dignity, the Northwest Coalition Against Malicious Harassment, and others.

Find out which agencies in your state keep anti-violence statistics. There may be existing resources to help you assemble an overview of your state or city's hate violence problem.

2. Build Statewide Coalitions

Statewide (or citywide for municipal ordinances) coalitions are critical to the passage of hate crimes legislation. The most successful efforts have been based on gaining the cooperation of a wide cross-section of the community. This will mean contacting representatives of civil rights, women's rights, gay and lesbian, and human rights organizations as well as law enforcement, religious groups, civic associations, business leaders, and a host of other key people who will join you in wanting to deter hate crimes.

Coalitions will be most successful if every partner is treated equally and with respect. Coalition tensions arise most frequently when some members bring more resources to the effort, and then exert a controlling interest in the process. Since coalitions are usually underfunded and understaffed, these resources can be welcomed; however, each coalition partner must make some contribution to the overall effort and their views must be respected.

Statewide coalitions are important because legislators in every part of the state must be influenced. Efforts that focus on the larger cities while ignoring the smaller, rural communities are jeopardized because the rural vote (usually more numerous and conservative) can kill the legislation. Rural communities have just as much to gain from successful legislation and emphasis should be placed on including them in the statewide effort.

To make the most of constituent lobbying efforts, set up a network with contacts in as many legislative districts as possible. One person from your organization should be responsible for maintaining a complete list of contacts that can be mobilized rapidly as activity on the bill develops.

Identifying key contacts in each district of your state is important — they are the people who will be responsible for direct contact with the legislator in that district. These key contacts should be people who are willing and able to meet with legislators as constituents or as supporters of the legislation. It is important to diversify, as much as possible, the key contacts. They should be representative of your coalition, so that your coalition is not perceived as being "only" women, or "only" gay, or "only" African American.

Key contacts should identify and organize other supporters in their district. Seek out local affiliates of the national organizations who support hate crimes legislation. A list of such national groups is contained in the appendix of this manual.

3. Find Sponsors and Lobby

Lobbying is a crucial part of any campaign to pass hate crime legislation. During lobbying, identify representatives to sponsor the legislation and influence votes. A bill sponsor is that legislator who takes the leadership to get the bill passed.

As many sponsors as possible is helpful. After a sponsor has been identified, it is important to work closely with that legislator, ensuring that s/he has the most up-to-date information available. They should be an integral part of your coalition effort and kept fully informed of all developments. They will be important advisors to your coalition, and their advice should be solicited concerning other legislators necessary to a successful effort.

It is important to be prepared for your meetings with legislators and to do good follow-up. In addition to good lobbying skills you will also need to be prepared for questions from your legislator. Many legislators will not understand the need for hate crime legislation, believing that existing laws already meet that need. Some will be resistant to certain provisions, such as enhanced penalties or including lesbians and gays, and you should be prepared to answer their concerns with accurate information.

To have the most impact on the legislature, organize a lobby day: a day when your organized influence is felt. Arrange for transportation to take supporters to the state capitol. Make appointments with legislators in advance.

It may be useful to prepare a briefing book, a collection of material outlining the nature of the legislation and the impact it can have. It can be long or short, but should be well-organized and neat. A briefing book can be important in providing legislators with concrete information.

The briefing book can include articles on topics such as the experience of other states and local governments in passing hate crime legislation. It might include information on issues most frequently subject to stereotyping, such as homosexuality and free speech. It may list the organizations that support the legislation and include letters of support from important sectors, such as law enforcement. It should include a copy of the bill, because there is no guarantee that the legislator has actually seen the bill.

- Arrange a meeting. Any voter in a legislator's district should be able to meet with the legislator or one of her/his staff to discuss issues. Call ahead to arrange a meeting. You may want to take another constituent with you to show additional support for the bill.

- Know your facts. It is important to present a clear argument to your legislator. Know what the hate crime bill says and what it will and will not do. For example, will it outlaw free speech? Be able to answer your legislator's questions in an informed and direct manner. Bring support materials with you to give to him/her.

- Eliminate stereotypes. Your legislator will have the same stereotypes about supporters of hate crimes legislation as the average citizen. Your most important task may be to eradicate stereotypes. Be prepared to answer questions about who is victimized by hate crimes; how it affects all people, not just minorities. Bring information about how a "non-stereotypical" person was victimized; i.e., a white male attacked by skinheads. This will help address the concern that "special privileges" are contained in the bill. Remember, everyone who has a racial definition, gender, sexual orientation, and religious preference will be protected by the legislation. That leaves very few people out.

- Listen as well as talk. Your legislator will have things to say about the bill and information to share with you. Listen carefully. Sometimes what is not said is just as important as what is said.

- Look for opportunities. Look for opportunities to add more information. Remember that your legislator considers many bills each session and cannot possibly keep up with all the facts for all the bills. If a question arises which you cannot answer, promise to get back to him/her with the answer — and do send the information. The legislator will appreciate having your information. Find out if your legislator has an assistant who will be working on this bill and talk with them as well.

- Don't argue. If you and your legislator disagree on a point, do not argue. It will put him/her on the defensive. Even if they won't vote for the bill, it might be possible to have them abstain or be absent at the time of the vote. In the long run, it will be more productive to avoid confrontations.

- Discover their position. Try to get your legislator to clarify her/his position. Be persistent but not pushy. If your legislator will not state his/her position, offer to send additional information that may clarify any questions. Be sure to recognize the difference between a lobbying meeting and a vote count meeting. In an initial meeting, avoid getting a "no" — this leaves the door open for further lobbying efforts.

- Follow-up. Write your legislator after the meeting and thank them for talking with you. Supply any

Visible citizen support can help pass a good bill or defeat a bad one.

information that you promised to send.

4. Build Grassroots Support

Grassroots support is one of the most essential elements to ensure passage of the legislation. Your coalition can prepare sample letters to state representatives urging support of the bill. These should be distributed as widely as possible through community groups, religious institutions, and businesses, asking them to sign the letters and send them to their legislator. It would be helpful to have a copy sent to the coalition as well.

Letter writing and phone call campaigns help because legislators must know what constituents want. Others who would be against the bill are most likely to say so, loud and clear. For every letter a legislator receives against the bill, there must be many more in favor of the legislation.

It is important to work with your local media. Newspapers can often be persuaded to write editorials supporting the legislation, particularly if the bill is cast as a "law and order" tool. Work to ensure that media interest does not focus on the free speech/First Amendment aspects of the bill, but rather focuses on the victims of hate crimes and what law enforcement needs to apprehend the perpetrators. Victim testimony can be very influential, so try to support your arguments with examples from actual victims. However, do not put undue pressure on victims to testify or tell their stories.

Many victims fear additional exposure because of the risk of retaliation.

Letters to the editor are also an important tool in influencing the media. Letters should be brief and straightforward and come from a variety of supporters. An organized letter campaign should include all of the aspects of the proposed legislation, and can be used to debunk the stereotypes associated with hate crimes legislation.

Avoid using form letters that use the same stock phrases, however. Editors are sensitive to the fact that interest groups may try and manipulate them.

Public rallies, marches, and demonstrations can be useful. These should always be peaceful and the proper legal permits obtained. Attacks on specific legislators or other elected officials should be avoided, if possible; you may need their votes later on. However, if your local prosecutor has refused to prosecute a particularly vicious hate crime, a public rally may be the opportunity to draw attention to the fact that legislation is needed to make him/her do their job. ■

Overleaf, chart depicts various hate crime statutes in effect throughout the United States.

Center for Democratic Renewal • P.O. Box 50469, Atlanta, GA 30302-0469 • 404/221-0025

State-by-state listing of hate crimes laws

	Bias Crime[1]	Data Collection	Police Training	Cross-burning	Mask, Hoods, Robes, Disguises	Institutional Vandalism/ Desecration of Place of Worship/Burial	Paramilitary Training	Parental Liability
AL						Y		
AK								Y*
AZ		Y,D,G,SO	Y,D,G,SO	Y[2]		Y		
AR				Y[3]		Y	Y	
CA	Y,A,C,D,E,G,SO[4]	Y,D,SO		Y,NS,OS	Y	Y	Y	Y
CO	Y[5]					Y	Y	
CT	Y,C,SO	Y,SO		Y,D,G[6]	Y,D,G	Y,D,G	Y	
DE					Y	Y		Y*
DC	Y,A,C,D,G,P,SO[7]	Y,SO	Y	Y,NS,OS		Y[34]		
FL	Y,C,E,SO[8]	Y,SO		Y,OS	Y,E	Y	Y	Y*
GA[35]				Y,OS	Y	Y	Y	
HI						Y		
ID	Y,C[9]	Y		Y,OS		Y	Y	
IL	Y,C,E,G,P,SO,D[10]	Y	Y		Y	Y,C,P	Y	Y
IN[39]						Y		Y
IA	Y,A,C,D,E,G,SO[11]	Y, SO		Y				Y
KS						Y		
KY						Y		Y*
LA					Y,C	Y,C	Y	
ME	Y,C[12]	Y, SO	Y			Y		
MD	Y	Y, SO		Y,OS		Y[13]		Y
MA	Y,C,SO[14]	Y,D,SO	Y			Y		Y
MI	Y,C,G[15]	Y,G,SO			Y		Y	Y*
MN	Y,D,G,SO[16]	Y,A,D,G,SO	Y		Y			
MS						Y		
MO	Y,C[17]					Y,C	Y	Y*
MT	Y,E[37]			Y,OS		Y[38]		
NE[18]							Y	
NV	Y,E,G,SO					Y		
NH	Y,E,G,SO[19]							
NJ	Y,SO	Y[36],SO		Y,NS, OS		Y	Y	
NM					Y	Y		
NY[20]	Y					Y	Y	Y*
NC[21]				Y,OS	Y	Y	Y	Y
ND[22]								
OH	Y,C,E,P				Y	Y,C,P		Y
OK	Y,C,D[24]	Y			Y	Y	Y	
OR	Y,C,P,SO[25]	Y,A,D,SO	Y			Y	Y	
PA	Y,C,E[26]	Y	Y			Y	Y	Y
RI	Y,C[27]D,SO	Y,SO		Y,NS,OS		Y,C	Y	
SC[28]				Y	Y	Y	Y	
SD[40]								
TN	Y,C[29]				Y	Y	Y	
TX		Y,SO				Y		
UT	Y,E	Y						
VT	Y,D,E,G,SO			Y				
VA	Y,C[30]	Y		Y,NS	Y	Y,C	Y	Y
WA	Y,C,D[31]			Y,C,OS		Y		
WV[32]					Y		Y	
WI	Y,D,E.SO					Y,D,SO		
WY								

A = age included in statute
G = gender included in statute
SO = sexual orientation included in statute

C = civil action provided by statute
NS = Nazi swastika covered by statute
Y = state has such a statute

D = disability included in statute
OS = other symbol covered by statute
# = applies to particular crimes

E = enhanced penalty provided by statute
P = parental liability imposed by statute
* = applies to property damage only

Note to Readers

Because of fast-changing developments — including not only the passage of new laws, but the repeal of existing or old ones — this chart may contain errors. Discrepancies also exist between this compilation and those of other civil rights organizations. This is most likely because of differing interpretations of particular statutes. This chart is the product of original and extensive legal research funded jointly by the Center for Democratic Renewal and the National Lawyers Guild Summer Projects Committee.

The research was conducted by Nelson S. T. Thayer Jr.

Annotations to Chart

1. The "Bias Crime" column contains statutes which are sometimes referred to as "ethnic intimidation laws" or "malicious harassment laws." All of the laws in this category are aimed specifically at bias or hate crimes. Some of the laws in this category are generic civil rights statutes which can also be used to prosecute perpetrators of hate crimes; some are merely penalty enhancers.

2. Arizona's crossburning statute is ambiguous in that it applies to "entering or remaining unlawfully on the property of another and burning, defacing, mutilating or otherwise desecrating a religious symbol or other religious property of another." For the purpose of this chart, we have interpreted this law to cover situations in which the "religious symbol" burned (i.e., a cross) is not necessarily the property of the person whose property has been entered. It is unclear whether the religious symbol needs to be "the religious property of another." In any case, the statute applies only to action on the property of another person.

3. The Arkansas crossburning statute applies in "public places" only.

4. The Bane Civil Rights Act also authorizes the state attorney general, the local district atorney, or city attorney to seek injunctive or other equitable relief. California also has a law requiring training in racial and cultural diversity for peace officers."

5. Colorado's bias crime law is an ethnic intimidation statute.

6. Connecticut's crossburning and desecration statutes are included under the "Discriminatory Practices" section of the Human Rights title.

7. The District of Columbia also has a Human Rights Statute that bars coercion and retaliation.

8. Like California, Florida has a "Street Terrorism Enforcement and Prevention" legislative finding which seems to be aimed at both drug gangs and racist activity. Regardless of the original intent of the legislation, the law offers a potential remedy for hate crime victims.

9. In addition to this malicious harassment statute, Idaho also has a civil rights law which establishes that "freedom from discrimination" constitutes a civil right. Another Idaho law establishes a Commission on Human Rights.

10. Illinois' hate crime law also applies to "mob action."

11. Iowa's statute speaks of "infringement" on or "violations" of the rights of the individual. Laws prohibiting crossburning and paramilitary training are included in this statute.

12. Maine's statute refers to harassment "based on characteristics." The law is group-neutral and does not identify which categories or classes of persons are protected.

13. Maryland's desecration statute is included in its law covering "Religious and Ethnic Crimes."

14. The Massachusetts Civil Rights Act also authorizes the state attorney general to seek injunctive or other equitable relief. Massachusetts also has a law barring 'disguises to obstruct execution of law, performance of duties, or exercise of rights.'"

15. Michigan's bias crime law is an ethnic intimidation statute.

16. The Minnesota law is actually composed of several separate statutes, each containing subparts which enhance the penalty for crimes committed out of bias. Minnesota also has a "Declaration of Policy" under its Human Rights section.

17. Missouri's statute is an ethnic intimidation law.

18. Nebraska does not have any "bias crime" statutes, but does have a law providing a civil remedy for "deprivation of constitutional and statutory rights, privileges, or immunities."

19. New Hampshire has a statute establishing a Commission for Human Rights.

20. New York has a statute outlawing discrimination with respect to places of public accommodation and amusement, and another establishing a Commission on Human Rights.

21. North Carolina has a statute outlawing certain secret societies and another creating a civil cause of action for "interference with civil rights."

22. "North Dakota has laws barring 'discrimination in public places', 'preventing exercise of civil rights or hindering or preventing another aiding third person to exercise civil rights', and 'concealing, aiding, compelling, or inducing unlawful discrimination.' North Dakota also has a 'state policy against discrimination'."

23. In addition to this ethnic intimidation statute, Ohio also outlaws "interfering with civil rights" by public servants.

24. Oklahoma's "malicious intimidation or harassment" statute also applies to telephonic transmission and distribution of a message "likely to incite or produce imminent violence against another because of race, etc." Oklahoma laws also outlaw organizations that take "oaths against the state."

25. Oregon's bias crime law is a simple intimidation statute with a bias provision.

26. Pennsylvania's statute is an ethnic intimidation law which includes "harassment by communication or address." "In addition to the ethnic intimidation law, Pennsylvania has another law which authorizes the state attorney general, or county district attorney to institute a civil action for injunctive or other equitable relief if needed to protect any person or property."

27. In addition to this "ethnic or religious intimidation" statute, Rhode Island also has a law establishing a "Commission on Religious, Racial and Ethnic Harassment."

28. Although it does not have any "bias crime" or "malicious harassment" laws, South Carolina has laws establishing a State Human Affairs Commission and outlawing "conspiracy against civil rights."

29. In addition to this malicious harassment statute, Tennessee also has a statute outlawing "civil rights intimidation," which includes wearing a mask or disguise. The Tennessee crossburning ban was repealed in 1989.

30. In addition to this statute creating a civil cause of action for "racial, religious, or ethnic harassment, violence or vandalism," Virginia also has statutes outlawing lynching (under "Crimes by Mobs" — see also, Illinois), picketing or disrupting "tranquility of home."

31. This malicious harassment statute also outlaws crossburning and desecration. Washington's desecration statute also outlaws "threats to bomb or injure property." Washington also has statutes which create a Human Rights Commission, and require the Administrator for the Courts to "develop a curriculum for a general understanding of hate or bias crimes, as well as specific legal skills and knowledge of [Washington State malicious harassment law], relevant cases, court rules, and the special needs of malicious harassment victims."

32. Although it does not have any bias crime statutes, West Virginia has an anti-paramilitary training law, which is contained in a statute "prohibiting violations of an individual's civil rights." West Virginia also has a statute establishing a Human Rights Commission.

33. Wyoming has a statute which holds "discrimination prohibited."

34. The District of Columbia desecration statute applies only to "tombs" and "cemetery railings," not the desecration of houses of worship.

35. Georgia also has a law prohibiting terroristic threats and acts, in addition to barring paramilitary training.

36. New Jersey's data collection law is mandated by the Attorney General, not by law.

37. Montana's enhanced penalties statute specifically protects "civil rights workers."

38. The language of Montana's prohibition against institutional vandalism is contained within that state's bias crime/sentence enhancement law.

39. "Indiana has a 'Civil Rights violation' law which protects against discrimination in public services and accomodations and public housing. The law covers disability and gender."

40. "South Dakota has a law barring 'interference with religious practices'."

The following are fragments from the chart (left margin):

on account of ...e, creed or color.

...ns which tend to expose ...rsons to hatred, contempt ...ridicule prohibited

...publication of false written or ...nted material with intent to ...aliciously promote hatred ...cause of race, color or religion.

...imprisonment or fine for malicious ...rassment of immigrants.

...ng to incite one race to ...surrection against another race. ...r theatrical act reflecting upon ...y race or class of citizens; penalty.

Center for Democratic Renewal • P.O. Box 50469, Atlanta, GA 30302-0469 • 404/221-0025

LEGAL REMEDIES AND ISSUES

Introduction

Private civil lawsuits can be a valuable tool for combatting hate group activity or forcing hate groups to compensate their victims. Litigation — in a process called "discovery" — can also be used to learn important inside information about a particular group. Lawsuits can also hit individuals or groups where it often hurts the most: their wallets. Litigation can effectively focus community attention on the problem of hate activity by providing an opportunity for media coverage or community organizing. It can also be used to force a local government to publicly state its opposition to hate group activity. This section focuses on a variety of issues related to litigation and legal remedies.

Litigation and legal proceedings are obviously not the most effective tools to use in every situation. Some judges are conservative in their views and have scant sympathy for community activists or hate crime victims. The same problem may exist concerning prosecutors or law enforcement officials.

Litigation Is Not Always the Most Effective Tool

Cost is another drawback. The expenses of litigation in court costs, deposition fees, attorney's fees and expert witness fees can quickly mount up.

Assessing the potential benefits of litigation is complex. Often the questions become very technical and turn on seemingly small points. Most often, there will be several alternatives available. A group can choose to use one or several of these alternatives, depending on the drawbacks and potential benefits of each.

Litigation can also be a two-edged sword. It is often used by hate groups to secure the right to demonstrate or the right to use public facilities. But communities facing such litigation by hate groups can blunt these efforts with a bit of planning. In some situations, hate group litigation can be avoided or checked by ensuring that local officials don't make needless mistakes, such as arbitrarily denying permit requests for hate group marches or rallies without doing their homework. In other situations, private individuals or community groups may wish to enter the litigation and argue against the hate group position. Sometimes the most effective response is to secure passage of a state or local ordinance which undercuts the hate group's effort. A community should not simply throw up its hands in defeat when a hate group invokes First Amendment, free speech arguments. All persons, particularly those against whom the hate group's venom is directed, have a constitutional right to enjoy the rights of residency and citizenship free from intimidation.

Pursuing Civil Actions for Money, Court Injunctions, and Declarations of Rights

A civil action is a lawsuit in which an individual or group (plaintiff) seeks something from another party (defendant) which will cure a wrong the other party has allegedly done them. The types of remedies which may be sought in a civil action are: an award of money; a court injunction; or a court declaration of rights between the parties. A successful plaintiff can: recover a monetary award for any damages she or he can show were caused by constitutional deprivation; obtain any appropriate injunctive or declaratory relief; receive an award of attorney fees; and, in appropriate cases, obtain an award of punitive damages.

Money Damages Can Be Recovered in Some Cases

There is one cluster of federal statutes which was originally adopted during Reconstruction with the intention of suppressing Klan activity and protecting the rights of African American citizens: the Civil Rights Acts, 42 U.S.C. 1981-1985. Although these statutes have never lived up to their full promise, they remain some of the most effective litigation tools in combatting hate activity. They authorize civil actions for damages when certain requirements are met.

42 U.S.C. 1981 & 1982

Section 1981 prohibits racial discrimination in the making or enforcement of contracts, in access to the courts, in "the benefit of all laws and proceedings for the security of persons and property," and in "punishment, pains, penalties, taxes, licenses and exactions of all kinds." Section 1982 prohibits racial discrimination in the inheritance, purchase, lease, sale, retention, or conveyance of real or personal property. These statutes prohibit racial discrimination not only by government entities or officials, but also by private individuals. An individual who can prove a claim under section 1981 or 1982 can recover damages from the persons that have discriminated against him or her.

In order to prove a claim under sections 1981 or 1982, a plaintiff must show that he or she was discriminated against on the basis of race in regard to one of the activities covered by these statutes. These activities can include the refusal by a private school to admit African American students, the refusal of a company to sell a franchise to a qualified African American entrepreneur, the refusal by a business to serve customers of a certain race, the refusal of an employer to hire a person of color, disproportionate police harassment of African American citizens, and racially-motivated surveillance or malicious prosecution. Some courts have also held that Section 1981 protects against racially-motivated physical assaults. Activities which have been considered covered by section 1982 include racially motivated refusals to sell property, racial discrimination in renting or leasing property, racial discrimination in the use of subdivision-owned recreational facilities, and even racial discrimination in the sale of such personal or intangible property as caskets or life insurance contracts. Some courts have even found that 1982 offers protection against public actions which greatly impeded the ability of African American property owners to use their property and against racially motivated retaliation experienced by white property owners who entertain African American guests.

The plaintiff in a section 1981 or 1982 case must not only show that the defendant's actions fall within the coverage of these statutes, he or she must also show that the defendant's action was motivated by racial discrimination. These statutes only offer protection against racial discrimination: they do not protect against discrimination on the basis of sex, age, religion or national origin. Courts have determined that Congress intended to protect African Americans, persons of Arab descent, Jews, Japanese, Vietnamese, Koreans, Haitians, and Caucasians. It is unclear, however, whether discrimination against Latinos is covered. The plaintiff must show that the defendant would not have taken the challenged action but for her or his racially discriminatory motive.

These statutes can be used to force businesses that discriminate against people of color to pay for their discrimination and to change their ways. They can also be used against persons who have committed racially-motivated assaults. In recent CDR-sponsored litigation, Section 1981, along with other anti-discrimination statutes, was used to force the resignations of three employees of the Blakely, Georgia, fire department. Blakely's fire chief and several of its firefighters were members of the Klan and it was alleged that the fire department had failed to give equal fire protection to African American residences and persons. The suit resulted in the resignation of the fire chief, the termination of the Klan fire fighters, and the institution of policies for equal fire protection.

42 U.S.C. 1983

The most commonly used statute involving cases of police brutality is 42 U.S.C. 1983. Section 1983 provides a vehicle for the vindication of the federal rights which are conferred in other places. In order to prove a section 1983 claim, a plaintiff must both show that a defendant violated one or more of the plaintiff's federal statutory or constitutional rights and that the defendant did this "under color of state law." Persons are considered to act "under color of state law" when they are the employees of any government entity and are purporting to act under the authority granted to them by that government entity, when they are private persons who are acting in conjunction with government employees, or when they obtain their authority to act from a government-instituted rule or procedure.

Some of the wide-ranging claims brought under section 1983 include police brutality claims and First Amendment claims. A section 1983 claim is often appropriate when a government entity or employee has discriminated against someone, as Section 1983 can be used to enforce the 14th Amendment's guarantee of equal protection of the law. Ironically, hate groups often use Section 1983 to challenge restrictions local governments place on their ability to demonstrate or organize.

42 U.S.C. 1985

This statute provides specific penalties when two or more individuals engage in *conspiracies* to deprive persons of their federally protected civil rights. This section has been particularly useful in cases involving joint action between government agents and private individuals in contrast to section 1983 which is limited only to government actors. This statute also covers purely private conspiracies where no government agents are involved. Section 1985 provides no substantive rights itself but offers a means to enforce other rights (such as the 14th amendment right to equal protection) guaranteed elsewhere. For example, some abortion rights advocates have used Section 1985 to assert that abortion opponents illegally conspired to deprive women of their right to interstate travel in seeking to obtain an abortion.

In another case involving a brutal, fatal attack on an African American man, Samuel Spencer, the victims' parents brought suit against the four white perpetrators (*Spencer vs. Casavilla* 903 F.2nd 171 2nd Circuit 1990) alleging that the assailants had violated Spencer's federally protected right to travel when he was attacked while staying at his sister's home in New York.

State Remedies

In considering litigation possibilities, hate group opponents should not overlook some valuable causes of action under state law. The types of causes of action which are available will vary from state to state. Some of the ones which are most frequently used against hate groups are described below.

- **Assault or Battery Claims.** Persons who have been subjected to direct, threatening encounters with hate group members may be able to recover damages on claims of battery or assault. In order to recover damages for battery, a plaintiff must typically show that the defendant intended to harmfully or offensively touch another person and that the defendant's actions resulted in a harmful or offensive touching of the plaintiff. A touching is considered offensive if it offends a reasonable sense of personal dignity. Assault claims have similar burdens of proof. A defendant is ordinarily held liable for assault if the defendant takes an action with the intent to cause a harmful or offensive touching of another and the defendant's action puts the plaintiff in imminent apprehension of such a harmful or offensive touching. The basic difference between the tort of battery and the tort of assault is that a battery requires that an actual touching occur; it is sufficient for a plaintiff in an assault claim to show that he or she was put in imminent apprehension of such a touching. For example, a person who points a gun at another and either intends to shoot or threatens to shoot may have committed the tort of assault, even if he or she never fires the gun. Threatening words alone are not typically considered sufficient to hold the speaker liable for assault; the words must be accompanied by other circumstances which put the listener in reasonable apprehension of an imminent harmful touching.

- **False Imprisonment.** A tort claim of false imprisonment should be considered in instances in which hate group members have restricted the mobility of others. State laws concerning false imprisonment claims often provide that a defendant is subject to liability to the plaintiff if the defendant intended to confine someone within certain boundaries, the defendant's action directly or indirectly resulted in the confinement of the plaintiff within these boundaries, and the plaintiff was aware of the confinement and was harmed by it. It is usually not sufficient to show that the defendant blocked one means of exit; the plaintiff must show that the defendant forestalled use of all readily usable means of exit which were known to the plaintiff. The confinement may be accomplished by physical barriers, by physical force, by the threat of physical force, or by the use of other types of threats.

- **Intentional Infliction of Emotional Distress.** Many states recognize a tort of intentional infliction of emotional distress. The plaintiff asserting such a claim is typically required to prove that the defendant's actions were extreme and outrageous,

A victim of a beating can file state criminal charges and can bring a civil suit against his or her attackers. The specific remedies vary from case to case and from jurisdiction to jurisdiction.

Vandalism and racist and/or anti-Semitic grafitti are common forms of harassment.

that these actions caused severe emotional distress to the plaintiff, and that the defendant either intended to cause this emotional distress or was recklessly indifferent to the probability that this distress would ensue. The use of racial slurs, particularly by an employer or supervisor, has been recognized by some courts as sufficient to sustain a cause of action for intentional infliction of emotional distress.

- **Trespass.** An action for trespass can be helpful in situations in which hate group members walk across or use someone's private property without the owner's consent. To prevail on a trespass claim, a plaintiff should show that the defendant, without the consent of the plaintiff, either came onto land which is owned or possessed by the plaintiff, caused an object or a person to come onto the plaintiff's land, remains on the plaintiff's land, or fails to remove from the plaintiff's land an object which the defendant is under a duty to remove. The plaintiff need not show that the defendant has caused any harm to the plaintiff's property; it is sufficient to show that the defendant caused an unauthorized entry onto the property. Thus, if a hate group member throws rocks at another person's house, one of the torts he or she has committed was a trespass.

- **Nuisance.** A few cases have explored a possible cause of action against hate groups for the tort of public nuisance. A public nuisance is generally defined as "an unreasonable interference with a right common to the general public." Some cases

have argued that racially or religiously motivated harassment, or the denial of equal protection of the laws, constitutes such a public nuisance.

- **State Civil Rights Statutes.** Do not overlook the possibility that your state may have civil rights laws. Some states have anti-discrimination laws which have broader coverage or offer more extensive relief than the federal civil rights remedies. In Massachusetts the Attorney General's Office used civil injunctions against perpetrators to prohibit them from continuing racially motivated acts. The Attorney General's office also filed a complaint under the Massachusetts Civil Rights act against an offender who had allegedly twice attacked Vietnamese residents. By this and similar lawsuits, the Attorney General said, "my office seeks to assure the members of the Vietnamese, Cambodian and Laotian communities the same basic civil rights as all residents of the Commonwealth."

Pursuing Criminal Prosecutions

A criminal prosecution is significantly different from a civil court suit. Criminal prosecutions can only be brought by such public officials as prosecutors, solicitors, district attorneys, United States Attorneys, or Attorneys General. The primary purpose of a criminal action is to protect society by punishing or imprisoning those who have failed in some way to confine their conduct to the limits prescribed in the criminal laws. The immediate goal of a criminal prosecution is to impose a term of imprisonment, probation, and/or a fine on the person who has allegedly committed the crime.

Center for Democratic Renewal • P.O. Box 50469, Atlanta, GA 30302-0469 • 404/221-0025

The fact that a criminal prosecution can only be brought by such officials as public prosecutors can be frustrating when public officials do not take hate crimes seriously. In such communities, human rights advocates may need to lobby and organize to push the prosecutor to pursue these cases.

Sometimes community groups can influence the prosecutor by providing information regarding the criminal activities of local hate groups, as was done in a case involving an attack by Klansmen on civil rights marchers in Decatur, Alabama. In the Decatur case, the FBI investigated potential criminal charges against the Klansmen but closed the case on the basis that it could not find sufficient evidence to prosecute. The Southern Poverty Law Center subsequently brought a civil action against the Klansmen and, in pursuing that suit, gathered a great deal of information concerning the facts of the attack. This information was passed on to federal prosecutors, who then prosecuted a number of the Klansmen.

In determining whether it may be appropriate to pursue criminal prosecutions of hate group members, community groups should consider the full range of criminal laws available. Laws prohibiting terroristic threats, assaults, arson, vandalism, and public disorder are often helpful in combatting hate group activity, as is stringent enforcement of weapons regulations. Some common types of laws which most specifically target hate group activity are described below.

The KKK Acts: 18 USC 241-243, 245-47

During Reconstruction, Congress passed a set of criminal statutes which were intended to curb the terroristic actions of the Klan. These statutes, now codified — as amended — in 18 U.S.C. 241-247 (West 1969 & Supp. 1991), impose criminal penalties on persons who deprive others of federal civil rights under specified circumstances. The provisions of each of these statutes is briefly described below.

Section 241 prohibits conspiracies to intimidate any United States resident in the free exercise or enjoyment of any federal right or privilege or because that resident has exercised a federal right or privilege. It also prohibits groups of two or more persons from going, "in disguise on the highway, or on the premises of another, with intent to prevent or hinder" a United States resident's exercise or enjoyment of any federal right or privilege.

Section 241 was recently used to prosecute a man who burned a cross on land adjacent to his apartment complex. The man, Lee, was convicted on the basis that he had conspired to deprive the black tenants of the apartment complex of their civil right to be free from racial discrimination in housing, in that he had used the burning cross to attempt to intimidate these tenants. Lee argued that his conviction violated his free speech rights. In upholding his conviction, a federal appeals court found that this application of section 241 had not abridged Lee's free speech rights. It held that because of the historic use of a burning cross as a "precursor to or a promise of violence against black people," Lee's conduct had been the equivalent of an intimidating threat that violent retribution could follow. It found that Congress's decision to outlaw such conduct did not impermissibly abridge the First Amendment.

Section 242 provides criminal penalties for any person who, under color of state law, willfully subjects a United States resident to a deprivation of a federal right or privilege. It also prohibits persons acting under color of state law from subjecting any resident to "different punishments, pains, or penalties" on the basis of his or her color, race, or status as a non-citizen. To act "under color of state law" means to act under the real, purported, or claimed authority of any state or local law, regulation, position, or custom. Section 243 prohibits the exclusion of persons from jury duty on the basis of race or color.

Section 245 forbids the interference with or intimidation of any person because of that person's exercise of certain specified federal rights, as well as retaliation because of the exercise of these rights. The rights specified are the right to vote, to run for office, to receive the benefit of any program administered by the federal government, to apply for or enjoy employment with the federal government, to serve as a juror in federal court, and to receive the benefit of any program receiving federal financial assistance. The section further prohibits interference with, intimidation of, or retaliation against a person because of his or her use of a public school, receipt of any benefit from a program administered by any state or local government, application for employment, service as a state court juror, use of interstate travel facilities, or enjoyment of restaurants, hotels, or places of entertainment, on the basis of that person's race, color, religion, or national origin. The statute also punishes intimidation of or retaliation against persons on the basis that they participate on a non-discriminatory manner in the enumerated benefits or have assisted others to participate in them. Section 246 prohibits attempts or threats to deprive persons of federal employment benefits or relief benefits on the basis of political affiliation, race, color, sex, religion, or national origin.

One recent use of section 245 arose out of the 1984 murder of a radio-talk show host, Alan Berg. In the case, a jury found that Berg was murdered by white supremacists David Lane and Bruce Pierce because he was Jewish and because he ridiculed certain hate groups on the air. The convictions were held to be proper under section 245, as Berg's murder interfered with his enjoyment of his employment as a radio talk show host and was motivated by his religion and statements he made over the air. Section 245 has also been used on several occasions against Klansmen who attacked demonstrators.

Section 247 sanctions any actual or attempted defacement, damage, or destruction of religious building or grounds — if the acts were prompted by the religious character of the property and if the resulting damage to the property is in excess of $10,000. It also prohibits the use of force or threat of force to obstruct or attempt to obstruct persons in the exercise of their religious beliefs.

Each of these federal criminal statutes may be valuable tools to use in combatting hate group activity. They can often be used in tandem with state criminal charges, as many of the acts they cover are also covered by more general state statutes. The availability of federal criminal remedies can be particularly important in situations where local officials are unwilling to prosecute hate crimes: they give the community another potential avenue of relief — the federal prosecutor.

Community Organizing for Legal Cases

Community support for legal cases, whether they are being fought in criminal or civil court, is important to the success of the case and to the health of the community. District attorneys, police, juries, and judges respond to the political climate. Knowing that neighbors or constituents are concerned can make them take hate violence more seriously. Bigoted attacks are meant to terrorize entire communities, but mobilizing for justice can help turn fear into empowerment.

The Harvey Case: Kansas City, Missouri

In the early 1980s, the murder of African American jazz musician Steve Harvey in Kansas City, Missouri, so outraged his community that their organizing forced the Justice Department to expand its definition of federal civil rights. On April 15, 1981, Harvey, who had gone to a city park at night to play his saxophone, was attacked in a restroom by bat-wielding white men who had come to the park looking for gay people to beat up. One of the men, Raymond L. Bledsoe, beat Harvey to death with the bat in the company of two white friends. Three months later, Bledsoe's housemate informed on him to get a plea bargain in an unrelated burglary charge. In August 1981, an all-white jury in Kansas City found Bledsoe not guilty, in spite of the eyewitness accounts of the friends who had been with him that night.

The next day, Harvey's widow, Rita, and a friend, Alvin Sykes, began an extensive organizing effort that eventually brought Bledsoe a life sentence for murder. When the Civil Rights Division of the United States Department of Justice initially denied their request for an investigation on the basis of a legal technicality (no official of the state was involved in the assault), they did their own legal research to find sections of the 1968 Civil Rights Act that prohibited interference with the rights of people to use public facilities regardless of race, showing that these provisions had been used successfully four times. They convinced the Justice Department that prosecution might be possible, but the Department required a determination that the public's interest was involved and that the case would achieve substantial justice.

The Steve Harvey Justice Committee then began to mobilize public support to demonstrate this interest, fueled by the community's outrage. It sent a formal request for an investigation to the Assistant Attorney General in Charge of Civil Rights, William Bradford Reynolds, with a supporting letter from the NAACP. They launched a petition drive and traveled to Washington to deliver the first 3,000 signatures (by that time, a preliminary investigation was underway) and requested that they be notified immediately if the Justice Department was about to drop the investigation. They gained support of the city's political, business and religious leadership. On the first anniversary of Harvey's death 700 people called the United States Attorney's office in Kansas City to support the investigation. Then Harvey's mother and others went back to Washington with another 3,500 signatures to meet with federal attorneys.

The Justice Department established the case as a priority, and the Committee contacted the Department every ten days to monitor the progress of the investigation, informing the community about its status. The Committee also joined in supporting a bill to expand the jury pool beyond its current base of registered voters, a measure that passed, enhancing the possibility of minorities on the jury.

Eighteen months after the original acquittal, Bledsoe was indicted on civil rights charges. He was convicted in April 1983 by an all-white jury, and the judge sentenced him to life imprisonment, the maximum possible penalty, noting the vicious, brutal, senseless nature of the murder.

The Chin Case: Detroit, Michigan

One inevitable goal of organizing around legal cases is to try to see that the assailant serves time or pays monetarily, as a deterrent to other such acts. But favorable verdicts are never guaranteed. The organizing around the Vincent Chin case shows how much can come from community mobilization and education, even in the face of an unfavorable verdict.

When Chinese-American Vincent Chin was murdered in Detroit by two white auto workers angry at the Japanese the Asian community expected it to be an open-and-shut case. After all, there were 30 witnesses to the brutal attack. When a judge gave the assailants a suspended sentence and light fine, the outrage — and the organizing — was immediate. In Kansas City, the African American community was a sizeable portion of the city's population. But the various Asian nationalities

Community support can be crucial to the outcome of a case with reluctant prosecutors.

which turned it down. The federal strategy eventually resulted in two trials.

Early on, the coalition held a successful press conference, sponsored by the Chinese Consolidated Benevolence Association, and paid careful attention to educating the media about the cultural significance of the first local protest by the Chinese community. Then came meetings with judges and prosecutors. When evidence accumulated of official stonewalling, the coalition picketed, with plenty of public-

in Detroit, taken together, amounted to approximately one percent of the population.

"Since it was such a small community, we all knew from the beginning that getting justice in the Chin case would have to be a coalition effort," said Helen Zia, a Detroit resident at the time and a member of the American Citizens for Justice coalition that emerged. Community involvement built rapidly, with usually two meetings a week in different parts of the city in places that reflected the various national and class constituencies of Asians in Detroit: the more established restaurateurs in Chinatown (who were largely Mandarin-speaking), the Cantonese-speaking restaurant and laundry-workers, professionals such as attorneys (most of them Asian-Americans), scientists and engineers (many of them immigrants from Taiwan and other parts of Asia, college-educated, many with Ph.Ds). Then there were links to the Japanese-American and Philippino communities, later Korean and South-Asian. The coalition skillfully avoided potential splits, such as strong feelings for or against Taiwan or the People's Republic of China. The American Citizens for Justice also reached out to other civil rights groups, the African-American community and the United Auto Workers union.

The strategy was two-fold: pursuing legal options and building community response. "We saw that it wouldn't be enough just to go through the legal system. We wanted to make as much noise as possible," commented Zia. The attorneys gathered information and brainstormed, settling on two legal strategies — pressing the state Attorney General for resentencing, and pressuring for federal prosecution. The appeal of the sentence went to the Michigan Supreme Court,

ity. Over a two-month period, they organized a major demonstration at the federal building, calling for the Justice Department to pursue the case.

The Chin case received national attention in the Asian media, and interest in Japan and China stirred international coverage as well. A massive letter-writing campaign to the Justice Department, according to William Bradford Reynolds, resulted in more letters than any other case in which he had been involved. The coalition printed thousands of fliers with the names, addresses, and phone numbers of officials to whom letters should be addressed. It also initiated a petition drive, and people all over the country also initiated their own petitions. Fundraising was viewed as an organizing and publicity strategy as well, and the coalition arranged with other cities to have joint demonstrations on selected days. They raised $180,000, much of which went for legal fees in the state appeal.

Mrs. Chin, Vincent's mother (a naturalized citizen who had emigrated from China in the 1940s), was an informed, active and visible participant from the beginning. "It meant a lot for people to know she was there," Zia said. "Even though it was painful for her, she spoke to the media often, and it helped to make the tragedy of the case real for people." Her moral authority also helped to head off challenges to the coalition's credibility when less-than-principled "allies" claimed access to the money. The coalition took delegations to Washington to visit the Justice Department and to speak to their representatives in Congress.

When the federal trial came, the coalition organized court-watches, deciding to pack the courtroom only on selected days, since they didn't want to intimidate the jury. They held meetings to inform court-watchers how to act, to take notes, and what to look for. The jury found Ebens guilty, and he appealed, citing pretrial publicity, prosecutor's errors, and challenges to some of the judge's rulings. Ebens won the appeal, and the Justice Department scheduled a second trial, this time in Cincinnati in 1987.

"Change of venue hurt our chances tremendously," remembered Zia. "The awareness in Cincinnati of racism against Asians was almost non-existent." During jury selection, only 19 of 200 prospective jurors could answer that they had ever "known any Oriental people"; and those who did were questioned closely, implying bias. The jury foreman was a 50-year-old white factory worker who had recently been laid off. The jury found Ebens not guilty.

"It was a very big disappointment," Zia recalls, "though from the beginning, we had been careful to educate people about the criminal justice system, and not tie success to a particular sentence. Afterwards, we worked with the community in Detroit to show how much progress we had made getting anti-Asian violence acknowledged as a trend and on the national civil rights agenda. The verdict also showed us all how far we had to go."

Organizing around the Chin case produced a national hearing on anti-Asian violence by the United States Civil Rights Commission, a report by the same body, and two new Asian organizations, Break the Silence Coalition in the Bay area and the Committee Against Anti-Asian Violence in New York. It also helped to consolidate Asian political work nationally. "We were able to establish coalitions and networks across groups that had never worked together so closely before," Zia explained. "Asians all around the country, from many different backgrounds, saw what happened to Chin as an extension of what they encountered every day."

Chattanooga, Tennessee

When an all-white jury found two of the three Klansmen not guilty after they had opened fire on four elderly African American women on the streets of Chattanooga in April 1980, the National Anti-Klan Network and the Center for Constitutional Rights launched the first federal civil rights lawsuit filed in the twentieth century based on post-Civil War Ku Klux Klan acts. At that time, the Justice Department was refusing to prosecute 1979 Klan attacks in Greensboro, North Carolina, and Decatur, Alabama, as well. "Such abdication of their duties to protect all citizens from violence compels private attorneys to do the work of the Justice Department," said attorney Randolph Scott-McLaughlin.

The National Anti-Klan Network (later the CDR) took on much of the community mobilizing for the case. For three months, its Religious Task Force members traveled to Chattanooga, speaking in churches and

rallying the African-American community. Nationally, the Network initiated a "Women's Appeal for Justice in Chattanooga," supported by prominent women around the country such as Coretta Scott King, Ruby Dee, and NOW president Eleanor Smeal. When the case came to trial, community members were there to monitor the proceedings and express their concerns by their physical presence.

At the same time, CCR commissioned the National Jury Project, specialists in jury selection, to survey the community for information that would aid in picking a jury. As CCR attorney Scott-McLaughlin recalled, "When the white survey respondents were asked what they knew about the Klan, the majority said that the Klan enforced the moral code of the community…. Approximately one-third of the white respondents stated that they felt blacks were too aggressive and were opposed to any further advancements for blacks. A similar group was opposed to black, out-of-town civil rights lawyers handling cases in Chattanooga."

When jury selection began in February of 1982, this survey information turned out to be too accurate; almost all of the white jurors believed that the Klan protected community morals. The judge refused to allow defense attorneys to eliminate black jurors automatically ("for cause"), and one black woman did make it onto the jury. "This was extremely important," Scott-McLaughlin explained. "For either side to prevail, the verdict had to be unanimous or plaintiffs would have the right to a new trial. There was no way that a black woman, after she heard the evidence, could possibly find the Klansmen innocent of all charges."

The CCR lawyers were able to introduce convincing testimony that the women had indeed been seriously injured, that a conspiracy had caused the injury, and that the conspiracy was motivated by racism. On February 26, 1982 the jury found all three Klansmen guilty and liable to the plaintiffs for $535,000. Three days after the verdict, the judge issued an injunction against the Klan. The Chattanooga case pioneered the legal strategy that proved so successful in the 1980s of bringing Klan members into civil court.

Scott-McLaughlin concluded, "The judgment in the case sent a clear message to the KKK that they can and will be brought to justice for their evil and violent deeds. The verdict, from a Southern jury composed of five whites and one black, also sent a message to those battling against the forces of retrenchment that we can win."

Blakely, Georgia

In February 1990, a black resident of Blakely, Georgia called the CDR answering machine: "It's a matter of life and death," the message said. The call was from Ben Cawthon, president of the Concerned Black Citizens Committee of Blakely, organized to deal with issues such as allegations of police brutality and unfair costs for municipal services. Cawthon told CDR that the African American community suspected that the fire chief Franklin Brown was a Klan member, and that the fire department's unequal fire protection had led to the deaths of two African American children in 1986 and 1987.

Blakely, a town of 6,000 residents, 42 percent of whom are African-American, had never had a black representative on the city council, and although the school system was 65 percent black, only one of five school board seats was held by an African-American.

CDR encouraged the committee to formally incorporate and also put them in touch with professional legal counsel. African American leadership in Blakely recognized from the beginning that Klan control of the fire department was a symptom of a larger problem of black disenfranchisement.

The legal strategy they crafted addressed both the symptoms and the root causes of the problem. They first filed a voting rights suit against the city, which the city settled rapidly, by creating two majority black districts. After extensive investigation by CDR, Atlanta attorney Brian Spears filed a federal class action suit against Brown and the city, alleging that city council members had known about Brown's Klan membership and done nothing about it and that Klan control of the fire department had violated the constitutional rights of Blakely's African American residents.

By failing to remove Brown as fire chief after learning of his Klan affiliation, the all-white city council was also charged with "maintaining a public nuisance" in violation of state law.

A mass meeting for the black community in Blakely, billed as a "Freedom Revival," helped kick off the campaign, bringing Rev. Mac Charles Jones of the CDR Board in to preach. A high profile press strategy focused on getting the word out to surrounding counties, statewide, and nationally.

When Spears and CDR were able to present evidence — including secret Klan documents and subpoenaed phone records — that Franklin Brown was indeed in the Klan, he resigned, citing health reasons. In April 1991, the city settled, forcing two other fire department employees who had been in the Invisible Empire to resign as well. The city also agreed to upgrade training for all firefighters and to require public safety employees to take community relations training. The Concerned Black Citizens Committee has gone on to address other issues such as the discriminatory way that discipline is applied in the school system and school board appointments are made. An active campaign for voter registration resulted in the election of two African Americans to the previously all-white city council — a first in the more than 100 year history of Blakely.

And in June 1992, the United States Justice Department issued criminal indictments against five Blakely Klansmen (one of whom was the fire chief's son) for their alleged role in criminal crossburning activities which violated the civil rights of white women who had African American friends.

Portland, Oregon

When the Southern Poverty Law Center announced it was suing White Aryan Resistance (WAR) leader Tom Metzger for his role in instigating the Skinhead murder of Ethiopian immigrant Mulegeta Seraw, the Coalition for Human Dignity moved to respond.

Its members didn't want to predetermine the agenda for action so they called a meeting of a broad range of community groups. With strong participation from the African-American, Latino and Native American communities, plans emerged for a march and rally.

> **The day before the Portland trial opened, 3,000 people turned out for a rally and march. Only 25 skinheads showed up, and they gave people no trouble.**

The planning group decided that their main speakers would be grassroots-based community leaders, not public officials. They made the march call very broadbased, adding issues such as Indian treaty rights and violence against women.

"We immediately had to deal with sensationalist press coverage," remembered Jonathan Mozzochi. "Police began saying that 300 Nazi Skins would be in town. We wanted to make it safe for people, so we organized carefully." The Metropolitan HRC encouraged the mayor to march, adding an element of safety for the rest of the participants, and proclaimed the entire week "Dignity and Diversity Week." The day before the trial opened, upwards of 3,000 people attended the rally and march. Only 25 Skinheads showed up, and they gave people no trouble. "Some people said it was the largest anti-racist march they had ever been in," Mozzochi recalled. The Coalition also organized a court watch and small lunchtime rallies that drew anywhere from 25 to 75 people.

The jury found Metzger guilty and levied a $12.5 million fine. "The legal front is one front," explained Mozzochi, "but we wanted to give meaning to the case by continued grassroots activism."

Center for Democratic Renewal • P.O. Box 50469, Atlanta, GA 30302-0469 • 404/221-0025

The Function of the First Amendment

Many hate groups use public rallies and demonstrations to gain visibility and provoke public controversy, which in turn can increase the media coverage they receive. Such events can also give the hate group the opportunity to flaunt its views publicly and intimidate a wide range of groups using inflammatory rhetoric. When faced with such demonstrations, many communities wonder why they must tolerate them. After all, the views espoused by hate groups have been soundly rejected in anti-discrimination laws and civil rights legislation. Why can't a community just "ban the Klan?"

The answer lies in our constitutional guarantees of free speech. These guarantees, found in the First Amendment to the United States Constitution, provide vital protection for those who wish to dissent from the status quo. They also, however, impose significant restrictions upon a community's ability to shield itself from the harmful effects of hate speech.

The First Amendment Guarantees an Open Marketplace of Ideas

The basic idea which underlies First Amendment guarantees of free speech is that public debate functions like a large, multi-faceted marketplace of ideas. The theory is that all persons must be permitted to publicly state their views, even if their views are wrong. If a stated opinion is wrong, the theory goes, other speakers will expose its errors by responding to it and arguing against it. Only by allowing open debate can the truth emerge.

This theory of the marketplace of ideas means that no topic is considered off-limits. Other speakers in the "marketplace" can expose the inequity of racial discrimination by arguing against it and exposing the fallacies upon which it rests. The First Amendment reflects a belief that, with time and open debate, we will reach the truth.

Must All Places Be Open For Public Debate?

Where does this open debate occur? Does the First Amendment require individuals to open their homes to unlimited debate on issues of public concern? No, it does not. The only places which must remain open to speakers in the "marketplace of ideas" are those which are considered *public fora* or *nonpublic, limited fora.*

These fora are places that have been designated by either traditional use or government announcement as places where people gather to exchange views or to express their views to the public at large. In order to be considered a public forum or a nonpublic, limited forum

Demonstrations and marches can be limited by time, place and manner restrictions.

Center for Democratic Renewal • P.O. Box 50469, Atlanta, GA 30302-0469 • 404/221-0025

a site must ordinarily be owned and managed by a government entity. In a few states, though, state courts have held that such places as shopping malls should be considered public fora.

The Public Forum

A public forum is a place which is either a traditional public forum or a place which the government has designated as a public forum. Places such as public streets, sidewalks, and parks are considered traditional public fora because, as the Supreme Court held in the labor organizing case of *Hague v. CIO*, 307 U.S. 496 (1939), the "[u]se of the streets in public places has, from ancient times, been part of the privileges, immunities, rights and liberties of citizens." The Court further explained in *Schneider v. State*, 308 U.S. 147, 163 (1939), that "streets are natural and proper places for the dissemination of information." Thus, under this reasoning, the Court held in *Clark v. Community for Creative Non-Violence*, 468 U.S. 288, 293 (1983), that the National Park was a public forum. Similarly, in *United States v. Gilbert*, 920 F.2d 878 (11th Cir. 1991), a federal appeals court held that most of an unenclosed plaza surrounding a federal office building and courthouse was a public forum.

In *Flower v. United States*, 407 U.S. 197 (1971), the Supreme Court held that the commander of Fort Sam Houston in San Antonio, Texas, could not prohibit the distribution of "unauthorized" literature because the Fort was essentially a public street. The Court noted that the Fort had:

> "no sentry post or guard at either entrance or anywhere along the route. Traffic flows through the post on this and other streets 24 hours a day. ... The street is an important traffic artery used freely by buses, taxi cabs and other public transportation facilities as well as by private vehicles, and its sidewalks are used extensively at all hours of the day by civilians as well by military personnel."

The Court therefore concluded that the fort should be considered a public forum.

In *Frisby v. Schultz*, 487 U.S. 474, 481 (1988), the Court held that residential streets and sidewalks, as well as those in business districts, are public fora. These decisions, and many others, demonstrate that public streets, sidewalks, and parks will ordinarily be considered public fora in the context of First Amendment activity.

As the Supreme Court explained in *International Society for Krishna Consciousness, Inc. v. Lee*, 60 U.S.L.W. 4749, 4751 (1992), a designated public forum is "property that the state has opened for expressive activity by part or all of the public." One example of such a forum is a public building which is intended to be used as a meeting place for community groups.

The Thirteenth and Fourteenth Amendments: Limitations on the Klan's Exercise of First Amendment Rights

In theory, the Thirteenth Amendment is a limitation on the power of pro-racism groups — especially the Klan — to exercise traditional First Amendment rights. The Thirteenth Amendment, passed in the wake of the Civil War, outlawed the practice of slavery. It prohibits depriving black persons "of the basic rights that the law secures to all free persons." The amendment was intended to not only eliminate state laws establishing or upholding slavery, but also to eradicate the "badges of slavery."

Situations in which hate groups are using demonstrations to attempt to intimidate non-whites cannot simply be viewed as involving the exercise of First Amendment rights in a vacuum. These situations involve a clash of rights: the freedom of speech rights of the hate group on the one hand versus the rights of the people targeted by the hate group to the equal protection of the law. The United States Supreme Court has long recognized that there are some forms of "speech" that are "inseparably something more [than] and different" from simple communication. Where the purpose of a demonstration is to coerce a segment of society to refrain from exercising its civil rights, and where there are other, non-coercive (or less coercive) forums in which the ideas may be communicated, the First Amendment permits a prohibition on the coercive communications.

The constitutional limitations the amendment imposes on the operations of the Klan have been reaffirmed in recent years. In 1981, for example, a federal judge prevented Klansmen from engaging in activities designed to intimidate Vietnamese fishermen. Among the Klan actions which prompted the injunction were ones which would be considered traditional First Amendment activity. The court, however, found that these activities had the predictable effect of interfering with the rights of the Vietnamese fishermen and that the statements made by the Klansmen constituted intimidation and prohibited any further such activity by the Klan. The case may provide a model for community groups to use in countering hate-group intimidation efforts.

First Amendment Issues–

Hate Groups and Public Access

Hate groups have shown an increasing tendency to spread their message and recruit new members using public buildings, such as schools, and over the public airwaves.

When first confronted with this phenomenon, many people will ask whether or not public schools must allow student hate groups to use their facilities?

Increasingly successful efforts by hate groups to recruit teenagers also pose the threat that some student hate activists may seek to hold their meetings at public schools. School officials can be more effective preventing such occurrences if they consider the potential problem and take action to check it before they are presented with a direct request by a hate group to use their facilities.

> School officials have good reason to fear that Klan activities will interfere with the ability of their students to learn.

There is a special statute which must be considered in terms of public school use by a hate group: the Equal Access Act, 20 U.S.C.A. 4071-4074, which provides that any public high school which receives federal financial assistance and which has allowed itself to have a "limited open forum" may not "deny equal access or a fair opportunity to, or discriminate against, any students who wish to conduct a meeting within that limited open forum on the basis of the religious, political, philosophical, or other content of the speech at such meetings." Id. at 4071. Under the Act, a school is considered to have a "limited open forum" if it "grants an offering to or opportunity for one or more noncurriculum related student groups to meet on school premises during noninstructional time." Id. The Act requires not only that the student group be given meeting space, but also that it be given equal access to any school bulletin boards, newspapers, or other fora which the school makes available to other noncurriculum related groups.

Although the Act thus stringently limits the extent to which a school can control the types of student groups which use its facilities, it does authorize schools which have a "limited open forum" to adopt certain uniform rules: e.g., the meetings must be voluntary and student-initiated; and, the meetings must not "materially and substantially interfere with the orderly conduct of educational activities within the school." The Act further states that it should not be construed to authorize any government entity "to sanction meetings that are otherwise unlawful" or "to abridge the constitutional rights of any person."

It appears there are two ways in which a school system could attempt to insulate itself from a hate groups's attempt under the Act to gain access to a school: the school system could prevent itself from being classified as a limited open forum — a very difficult and restrictive proposition — or it could muster evidence to show that permitting access by the hate group would greatly interfere with the orderly conduct of educational activities within the school. A school system which attempts to prove that recognition of student hate groups disrupts the educational processes of a school should note such factors as whether students who do not participate in the hate group feel intimidated by it, whether there is any history of racial disturbances at the school, and whether the hate group is harassing other students. This can be verified, for example, through the collection of signed, sworn affidavits or statements from students. Schools should remember that they have an obligation to protect the ability of all their students, of whatever race, to obtain an education unimpeded by the threat of racial, religious, sexist, or homophobic terrorism.

School officials have good reason to fear that Klan activities will interfere with the ability of their students to learn. In 1986, Klan activity near public schools in Madison County, Georgia, caused serious disturbances in the schools. Klansmen demonstrated near the school, made inflammatory remarks to students going to or from school, and handed Klan literature to students on school buses. In a lawsuit sponsored by the Center for Democratic Renewal, the parents of some of the children who attended the school argued that the Klan activity was terrorizing their children and disrupting their ability to obtain the public education to which they were entitled. The parents were successful in obtaining a court injunction which barred Klansmen from demonstrating within 500 feet of the schools, using intimidating or provocative language in the presence of students going to or leaving from school, or distributing inflammatory literature near school grounds or on school buses. ■

Center for Democratic Renewal • P.O. Box 50469, Atlanta, GA 30302-0469 • 404/221-0025

The Limited, or Nonpublic, Forum

The courts have recognized another category of government-owned property: property that is only open to the public for a particular use or to a limited extent. Such sites are sometimes called nonpublic fora. Some examples of such sites are the advertising space in city transit vehicles, see *Lehman v. City of Shaker Heights*, 418 U.S. 298, 303 (1974); an intra-office mail system for public employees, see *Perry Education Ass'n v. Perry Local Educators' Ass'n*, 460 U.S. 37, 45 (1983); and a fund-raising drive for federal employees, see *Cornelius v. NAACP Legal Defense and Educational Fund*, 473 U.S. 788, 800 (1985).

In *United States v. Kokinda*, 110 S.Ct. 3115 (1990), the Supreme Court explained some of the factors that should be considered in determining whether a particular site is a public or nonpublic forum. One factor is whether the government owns the property in the capacity of a lawmaker (a party that regulates and licenses) or simply as a proprietor which is running a government-sponsored business. Another factor is whether the property in question shares many of the characteristics of the "traditional" public fora, e.g., streets, sidewalks, and parks. A third factor is the extent to which the government has opened the property to expressive activity.

The *Kokinda* Court assessed these factors in the context of a sidewalk which led from a post office's parking lot to its door. It concluded that the sidewalk was a nonpublic forum, noting that the government's operation of the post office is done in its capacity of proprietor, rather than that of lawmaker, and "[t]he postal sidewalk was constructed solely to assist postal patrons to negotiate the space between the parking lot and the front door of the post office, not to facilitate the daily commerce and life of the neighborhood or city." The Court used similar reasoning more recently in *International Society for Krishna Consciousness, Inc. v. Lee*, 60 U.S.L.W. 4749, 4751 (1992), to reach the conclusion that an airport was a nonpublic forum.

Thus, under the current Supreme Court, such traditional demonstration sites as parks, streets, and sidewalks are considered public fora while all other sites are limited, nonpublic fora — unless the government entity which controls a particular site has expressly opened it to First Amendment activity.

Public Forum / Nonpublic Forum Distinction Impacts Demonstrators

What is the significance of whether a particular forum is considered to be public or a limited, nonpublic forum? In essence, the classification has an impact on the types of expressive activity that must be permitted there. Public officials have relatively broad latitude in regulating First Amendment activity at a limited, nonpublic forum. In contrast, they are given much narrower discretion in regulating such activity at a public forum.

In general, any regulations which seek to restrict demonstrations at public fora must be content-neutral, must be narrowly tailored to serve a significant governmental interest and must leave open ample alternative channels for communication of the intended message. Regulations of First Amendment activity in limited, nonpublic fora can be much broader: as the Supreme Court said in *United States v. Kokinda*, such regulations need only, "be reasonable and not an effort to suppress expression merely because public officials oppose the speaker's views."

The issue of whether a particular regulation is reasonable in a particular nonpublic forum must be assessed in light of the primary purpose for which the forum is used. For example, in *International Society for Krishna Consciousness, Inc. v. Lee*, 60 U.S.L.W. 4749, (1992), the Supreme Court considered the constitutionality of an airport's stringent restrictions on First Amendment activity. The Court ultimately upheld the airport ban on solicitation but struck down its ban on distributing leaflets. The decisive concurring opinion of the Court drew a distinction between distributing leaflets and soliciting money because, "solicitation impedes the normal flow of traffic" in the airport, while distribution of leaflets was consistent with the other, permitted usages of the airport terminal.

This opinion indicates that restrictions on First Amendment activity in a limited, nonpublic forum will be tied very closely to whether the activity would interfere in the smooth functioning of the normal business of that forum. Regulations which are reasonably related to protecting the normal flow of business will be permitted. In a public forum, however, restrictions on First Amendment activity will not be upheld unless they are tailored to match an established problem, are not unnecessarily broad, and leave open alternative ways for demonstrators to communicate their message.

Allowable Public Forum Restrictions on First Amendment Activity

The fact that a particular site is a public forum for First Amendment purposes does not mean that a speaker can use the site for a demonstration or march on whatever terms the speaker chooses. For instance, the First Amendment does not require a city to shut down its most-congested street for a parade at rush hour, just because a potential demonstrator wishes to conduct a parade at that place and time. Communities have the right to impose reasonable time, place, and manner restrictions on First Amendment activity, even in their public fora.

Time, Place, and Manner Restrictions

Time, place, and manner restrictions can be properly used by a community to accommodate such needs as regulating traffic flow, safeguarding public safety, and insuring adequate access to places of business. They cannot, however, be used as a pretext for stifling or overly burdening First Amendment activity. Time, place, and manner regulations must be narrowly tailored to serve a significant governmental interest and must leave open ample alternative channels for communication of the intended message.

The Supreme Court recently gave some guidance on how far a community may go in regulating public forum First Amendment activity in a case called *Ward v. Rock Against Racism*, 109 S. Ct. 2746, 105 L. Ed. 2d 661 (1989). *Ward* concerned municipal regulation of the sound amplification equipment used at a municipally-owned bandshell. A wide variety of musical groups were permitted to use the bandshell and its open-air amphitheater for concerts. The city had had considerable problems regulating the sound levels of music in the bandshell.

In response to these problems, the city decided to require all groups using the bandshell to use the sound equipment and sound technician provided by the city.

The Supreme Court held that the city's requirements concerning the use of bandshell sound equipment was a proper time, place, and manner regulation. It rejected the idea that government regulation of expressive activity can only utilize the least restrictive means which a reviewing court can possibly conceive, saying, "restrictions on the time, place, or manner of protected speech are not invalid simply because there is *some imaginable* alternative that *might* be less burdensome on speech." *Id.* (emphasis supplied). The Court explained:

> "[A] regulation of the time, place, or manner of protected speech must be narrowly tailored to serve the government's legitimate content neutral interests but ... it need not be the least-restrictive or least-intrusive means of doing so. Rather the requirement of tailoring is satisfied ... so long as the ... regulation promotes a substantial government interest that would be achieved less effectively absent the regulation. ... So long as the means chosen are not substantially broader than necessary to achieve the government's interest, however, the regulation will not be invalid simply because a court concludes that the government's interest could be adequately served by some less-speech-restrictive alternative."

The Court found that the bandshell's sound equipment regulation met this standard.

A case from Washington, D.C., illustrates the way in which appropriate time, place, and manner restrictions can be used with regard to parades by hate groups. In

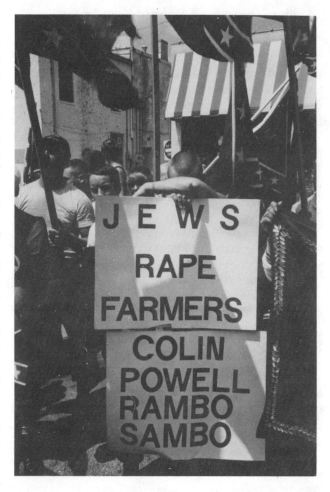

Christian Knights of the Ku Klux Klan Invisible Empire, Inc. v. District of Columbia, 919 F.2d 148 (D.C. Cir. 1990), a Klan group wished to parade along an 11-block route on Constitution Avenue in Washington, D.C.. The city refused to grant the group a permit for the full route requested, but granted them a permit for a route that was four blocks long. The city argued in support of its rejection of the eleven-block route that the size of the Klan's parade contingent would be relatively small, that the parade posed an grave risk of violence, that they lacked sufficient public safety staff to police the requested parade, that securing the requested route would impose great expense on the city, and that the requested event would cause great disruption along the route. The four block route proposed by the city reflected the city's "best estimate of the area they can reasonably secure with the resources available to them."

The court of appeals held that the District of Columbia could limit the parade to four blocks. It reasoned that the restriction was, under the circumstances presented, a reasonable time, place and manner restriction. It held that the city could properly require the parade to operate in such a way that it could be adequately secured with the personnel the city had available. As Judge Randolph stated in a concurring

Center for Democratic Renewal • P.O. Box 50469, Atlanta, GA 30302-0469 • 404/221-0025

opinion:

"[T]he Supreme Court has long recognized that the place and manner of presenting speech can be regulated in light of the probability that it will provoke a violent response."

"The short of the matter is that safety must be taken into account in regulating the time, place and manner of parading and marching .... The case would be different if there were evidence that the authorities discriminated against the Klan on some improper basis. But there is not such evidence. The record before us shows instead government officials conscientiously trying to perform their duty to preserve the peace while accommodating those who could not exercise their freedom to march without the government's protection. ... The First Amendment demands no more."

Thus, even in such a traditional public forum as the city streets, a community may impose restrictions on First Amendment activity in order to serve such other legitimate concerns as traffic flow and public safety. When it imposes such restrictions, however, they must be narrowly tailored to serve a significant governmental interest and must leave open ample alternative channels for communication of the intended message.

Restrictions Not Based on the Content of the Speech Involved

One of the fundamental principles of the First Amendment is that, with very few exceptions, restrictions on speech cannot be based on the content of the speech. A government is prohibited from imposing more stringent restrictions upon speakers of one topic or viewpoint than those it imposes on those of another. In the words of the Supreme Court in *Regan v. Time, Inc.*, 468 U.S. 641, 648-49 (1984), "[r]egulations which permit the government to discriminate on the basis of the content of the message cannot be tolerated under the First Amendment." Restrictions on demonstrators must therefore be "content-neutral".

There are a few, very narrow, exceptions to this rule of content neutrality. These exceptions are in the areas of obscenity, defamation, and "fighting words". Exceptions are made for speech of these types because the value of their expressive content is felt to be outweighed by the harm they do to society. As the Supreme Court said in *Chaplinsky v. New Hampshire*, 315 U.S. 568, 572 (1942), they are "of such slight social value as a step to truth [in the "marketplace of ideas"] that any benefit that may be derived from them is clearly outweighed by the social interest in order and morality." Government entities are accordingly permitted to prohibit such speech or impose more onerous restrictions on it than they could apply to speech that is outside these categories.

As noted above, one of these categories of less

protected speech is defamation. In 1952, in the case of *Beauharnais v. Illinois*, 343 U.S. 250 (1952), the Supreme Court upheld a state law which prohibited defamation of any particular racial or religious group. Subsequent cases in the intervening decades, however, have undercut some of the arguments relied on in that case, and it is unlikely the Court would reach the same result if a similar case were brought today. In 1978, a federal appeals court considered a law which prohibited the dissemination of material which intentionally promoted and incited racial or religious hatred. The measures had been adopted by the Village of Skokie in response to a threatened march by a Nazi group. The appeals court ruled in *Collin v. Smith,* 578 F.2d 1197 (7th Cir. 1978), that the holding in *Beauharnais* no longer applied and the Supreme Court declined to consider the case. In dissenting from the Supreme Court's refusal to consider the Collin case two Justices argued that the *Beauharnais* holding had never been overturned or limited in subsequent decisions.

First Amendment jurisprudence also holds that a government may prohibit the utterance of what are called "fighting words", in part because the courts have recognized that governments have a legitimate interest in keeping the peace. The United States Supreme Court reasoned in *Chaplinsky v. New Hampshire*, 315 U.S. 568, 572 (1942), that "fighting words," those words "which by their very utterance inflict injury or tend to incite an immediate breach of the peace," are not protected by the First Amendment. Subsequent cases have narrowed this "fighting words" exception and have demonstrated that it must be defined very narrowly. Constitutional scholar Laurence H. Tribe suggests in *American Constitutional Law* (2d ed. 1988) at 849-52, that the term "fighting words" could perhaps be adequately defined as statements or words which have a direct tendency to cause acts of violence by the person to whom, individually, the remark is addressed.

A very troubling, recent decision of the Supreme Court has placed severe restrictions on the ability of communities to restrict hate activity. The decision, *R. A. V. v. St. Paul Minnesota*, 60 U.S.L.W. 4667 (June 22, 1992), concerned a law which prohibited displaying a symbol which one knows or has reason to know "arouses anger, alarm or resentment in others on the basis of race, color, creed, religion or gender." The law had been used to punish a juvenile who had burned a cross on the lawn of an African American family. The Supreme Court ruled that the law created an impermissibly content-based restriction on speech.

The advocates for the law argued that "fighting words" were not entitled to First Amendment protection and could therefore be barred. They argued that cross-burning and similar activities were a particular type of "fighting words" which is particularly invidious, and it could accordingly be specifically targeted by an ordinance. The Supreme Court rejected this idea. It held that if a city chose to restrict "fighting words", it could do so; it could not, however, single out certain "fighting words" on the basis of their content and treat them differently than other types. (See Constitutionality of Hate Crime Legislation).

Officials Administering the Regulations May Not Be Given Broad Discretion

Demonstration regulations may not delegate overly broad discretion to the government officials who will be applying them. As the Supreme Court said in the civil rights-era case of *Shuttlesworth v. Birmingham*, 394 U.S. 147, 150-51 (1969), such regulations must contain "narrow, objective, and definite standards to guide the licensing authority."

The delegation of standardless discretion to public officials is considered dangerous in the context of First Amendment activity because it creates an unacceptable risk that the official may grant or deny demonstration permits on the basis of his or her opinion of the views of the demonstrators. The Supreme Court has struck down many restrictions of First Amendment activity on this basis, including a regulation which gave a mayor unbridled discretion in granting a newspaper machine permit (*City of Lakewood v. Plain Dealer Publishing Co.*, 486 U.S. 750 (1988)), a vague "in the best interest of the community" standard (*Southeastern Promotions Ltd. v. Conrad*, 420 U.S. 546, 548 (1975)), a parade permit ordinance permitting denial because "the public welfare, peace, safety, health, decency, good order, morals or convenience [so] require" (*Shuttlesworth*, 394 U.S. at 150-51), and an ordinance giving a police commissioner unbridled discretion over granting permits to speakers (*Kunz v. New York*, 340 U.S. 290 (1951)).

The United States Supreme Court most recently addressed the issue of overly broad discretion of a licensing authority in *Forsyth County v. Nationalist Movement*, No. 91-538 (1992). That case involved the discretion of a County Administrator to determine the amount of a march permit fee. Under the ordinance at issue, the Administrator was to base the fee on the "expense incident to the administration of the ordinance and to the maintenance of public order." Despite the fact that the Administrator was to consider certain factors in assessing a fee, the Court held that those standards were far from sufficient:

"The decision how much to charge for police protection or administrative time — or even whether to charge at all — is left to the whim of the administrator. There are no articulated standards either in the ordinance or in the county's established practice. The administrator is not required to rely on any objective factors. He need not provide any explanation for his decision, and that

decision is unreviewable. Nothing in the law or its application prevents the official from encouraging some views and discouraging others through the arbitrary application of fees. The First Amendment prohibits the vesting of such unbridled discretion in a government official."

It is thus clear that restrictions on First Amendment activity cannot delegate broad discretion to the public officials who administer the restrictions. Demonstration and licensing regulations must accordingly be drafted in such a manner that they give the administering officials very specific rules concerning the types of activity that will be permitted and the types of activity that will not.

Restrictions Which are Consistent with the First Amendment

When a community wishes to discourage hate groups from staging large demonstrations it should consider whether modifications in its parade and demonstration ordinances can foster this goal. They often can. A community must, however, be careful that the regulations it uses are consistent with First Amendment restrictions.

1. Avoid Becoming Mired in an Unnecessarily Divisive First Amendment Debate on the Rights of Hate Groups

When community groups consider the problems posed by hate group demonstrations and parades, they often become embroiled in a debate over the free speech guarantees of the First Amendment. A Coalition may find itself increasingly divided, with some of its members arguing that restrictions aimed at limiting the public activities of the hate groups should be adopted while others argue that the public display of hate groups and hate speech is part of the price we pay for our constitutional guarantee of free speech. Unfortunately, this debate often saps the energy of the civil rights community and prevents it from formulating an effective response to hate group activity.

Although some thoughtful disagreement on the finer points of the First Amendments is inevitable, divisive and lengthy debate can be avoided if the group can agree that it is going to do what it can to oppose and restrict hate group activity, but is not going to propose any action which is inconsistent with current court interpretations of First Amendment restrictions. Under such a composite approach, the faction of the group which sought to impose stringent restrictions on hate groups would agree to focus on creative community advocacy and decline to advocate new regulations which would be likely to be ruled unconstitutional anyway. Those who have been arguing that the First Amendment prevents any restrictions would, on the other hand, agree to utilize those court decisions which have permitted certain restrictions on speech, even if they disagree with the reasoning in those decisions.

When considering which approach to take, it is helpful for a group to consider the probable consequences of adopting sweeping restrictions on demonstrations. Although such provisions may restrict the ability of the Klan to demonstrate, they also dramatically impede the ability of all citizens in the community to exercise their First Amendment rights. Such broad provisions are also likely to provoke a lawsuit against the local government — if not by a hate group then by some other organization. If a hate group brings this type of lawsuit, it may ultimately enrich them by generating more publicity and making the city liable for monetary damages and attorney fees. Thus, the adoption of sweeping restrictions on demonstrations is a dangerous and unproductive tactic.

On the other hand, persons who argue for a very broad interpretation of the First Amendment rights of hate groups should consider that the guarantee of free speech is only one of the rights guaranteed in the U. S. Constitution and by statute. Other rights, such as the rights to freedom from discrimination based on race, sex, and religion, and the right to be free of the badges and incidences of slavery, are equally important. A well-founded fear of hate group activity, or the painful emotional impact of hate speech, intimidates many persons in historically oppressed groups, keeping their voices from being heard in the so-called "marketplace of ideas." Our national discourse is thus deprived of the insights we would have gained from these voices _

voices which have been disproportionately excluded in the past. In this respect, allowing unrestricted hate speech undermines the proper functioning of our First Amendment framework. A free speech purist, thus, fails to give adequate weight to the negative impact of untrammeled hate speech and hate group activity.

The community should focus on its common ground, rather than its differences in theory. It should agree that it will be mindful of both the demands of the First Amendment and the injury hate speech inflicts on equality. The group should not permit this debate to distract it from formulating a strong and effective response to hate activity.

2. Some General Examples of Permissible Restrictions on Demonstrations

There are many types of restrictions or regulations which are consistent with both the free speech requirements of the First Amendment and the public safety needs of the community. A few examples of such regulations are listed below.

- Demonstrators can be prohibited from blocking entrances, obstructing the sidewalk, or interfering with persons who wish to enter or leave a picketed business or home. In general, however, a city cannot impose a flat numerical limitation on the number of demonstrators which will be permitted. Such ordinances have in the past been struck down, on First Amendment grounds, in such cases as *LaFlore v. Robinson*, 434 F.2d 933 (5th Cir. 1970)

Center for Democratic Renewal • P.O. Box 50469, Atlanta, GA 30302-0469 • 404/221-0025

and *Davis v. Francois*, 395 F.2d 730 (5th Cir. 1968).

- A city can deny a permit for a particular site or facility if the number of participants that are anticipated could not be safely accommodated at the requested place. Alternatively, the city could condition the granting of a permit on a numerical restriction on participants.

- A city can impose reasonable restrictions on noise near residential areas and such institutions as schools, hospitals, and nursing homes. It cannot, however, ban all demonstrations at a place that is a public forum, except perhaps to create a very limited buffer zone around places whose operations could be disrupted by demonstrations. For instance, in *Pickens v. Okolona Municipal Separate School Dist.*, 594 F.2d 433, 434-35, 437-38 (5th Cir. 1979), a federal appeals court agreed that a raucous group of protesters could be temporarily barred from demonstrating within a block of a school. It reasoned that the demonstrators had actually caused material disruption in operation of school. It refused to permanently impose such a restriction on the demonstrators, however.

- A city cannot ban all demonstrations in residential areas, but can prohibit sustained picketing at an individual residence. The Supreme Court reached this question in the case of *Frisby v. Schultz*, 108 S. Ct. 2495, 2502 (1988). It reasoned that cities have a compelling interest in protecting the well-being, tranquility, and privacy of the homes of its residents and in protecting persons who are within their homes from being compelled to sustain exposure to communications which are objectionable to them.

- A city cannot ban leafletting or door-to-door canvassing, but can place reasonable regulations upon it. Several Supreme Court decisions, such as *Schneider v. Irvington*, 308 U.S. 147 (1939), indicate that any regulation of the distribution of leaflets must be very narrowly limited.

- A city can, to a limited extent, impose time restrictions on demonstrations. In *Beckerman v. City of Tupelo, Mississippi*, 664 F.2d 502, 512 (5th Cir. Unit A Dec. 1981), a federal appeals court struck down a time restriction — but indicated that a provision which limited demonstrations to the hours between dawn and dusk would in all likelihood be upheld. A restriction on night-time demonstrations can be of significant assistance in undermining the intimidating effect of a demonstration by a hate group, as well as in making such an event easier to secure.

- A city cannot condition a demonstration permit upon payment of a substantial fee. The Supreme Court made this clear in the case of *Forsyth County v. Nationalist Movement*, No. 91-538 (1992).

- A city cannot require a group to obtain insurance or post a bond in order to obtain a demonstration permit.

- A city can require groups that wish to conduct parades to go through an application procedure, as long as such a procedure is done on a content-neutral basis. The application can require the event sponsors to identify the leaders of the group and the persons administering the event, as well as a reasonable amount of information about the nature of the planned event.

- A city can deny a group's request to use a particular parade route if the use of the route proposed by the group would cause serious disruption of traffic in the surrounding area, cause disruption of the provision of fire protection services or emergency medical services to the surrounding area, or greatly increase the difficulty of providing proper security, crowd control, and traffic control for the parade. The city should have well-defined standards it can apply to a particular request to determine whether the proposed event should be permitted: it must not permit officials to exercise broad discretion.

Regulations such as these have been held to represent a proper balance between the right of demonstrators to convey their message to the public and the demands of public safety.

When developing responses to hate group activity don't overlook the importance of influencing local authorities. Officials responsible for reviewing and approving parade permit applications should be approached and encouraged to restrict the amount of time a hate group requests for their march or demonstration. When officials in Atlanta, Georgia, were approached by Klan leaders with plans to rally at the State Capitol, a strict timetable for activities was agreed to which limited the possibility for a lengthy gathering.

The Problem of the Heckler's Veto

A more complex problem is presented by situations in which government officials seek to restrict a demonstration because they fear that spectators observing the demonstration may react in a violent manner. The courts have consistently recognized that any expression of a politically unpopular view creates a risk of disorder; it is necessary to take such risks, however, in order to foster full and open debate on topics of public concern.

As the Supreme Court said in *Cox v. Louisiana*, 379 U.S. 536, 551-52, 85 S. Ct. 453, 462-63 (1965), "constitutional rights may not be denied simply because of hostility to their assertion or exercise." Gagging the lawful, albeit controversial, speech of a demonstrator because his or her views are unpopular amounts to a heckler's veto. Decisions, such as *Glasson v. City of Louisville*, 518 F.2d 899 (6th Cir. 1975), hold that government bodies have the responsibility to provide

protection for demonstrators.

As the federal appeals court indicated in *Christian Knights of the Ku Klux Klan Invisible Empire, Inc. v. District of Columbia*, 919 F.2d 148 (D.C. Cir. 1990), a city is not required to grant a permit for an event that, if held, is sure to produce an uncontrollable riot. The city can assess the resources it has available for crowd control, the anticipated security needs of the event involved, and restrict the event to one which is not reasonably likely to either cause physical injury to persons or property or to incite spectator violence which cannot be satisfactorily prevented by means of reasonable crowd control techniques. In crafting such a response, however, a city should be mindful of the Supreme Court's finding in *Forsyth County v. Nationalist Movement*, No. 91-538 (1992): the Court found that an ordinance which required government officials to set permit fees on the basis of the anticipated reaction of spectators was unconstitutionally content-based.

Demonstrators Who Violate the Law or Impede the Rights of Others

Some groups of demonstrators pose special public safety concerns because they seek to use demonstrations as a means to violate the law or to intimidate others in the exercise of their rights. Some courts have held that a local government can legitimately impose additional restrictions upon a group of demonstrators who have in the past engaged in unlawful conduct during demonstrations. Such a provision might consider whether any leaders of the sponsoring organizations have been convicted of a criminal offense or ordinance violation arising out of a demonstration, picket line, or parade — whether they had a track record of illegal behavior at demonstrations.

In *Hirsh v. City of Atlanta*, 110 S. Ct. 2163 (1990), the United States Supreme Court indicated that a city could impose restrictions upon such demonstrators which would be considered impermissibly restrictive if imposed in a general demonstration ordinance. It explained:

"this injunction imposes time, place, and manner restriction upon a class of persons who have presently and repeatedly engaged in unlawful conduct in the jurisdiction imposing the injunction. It is not an injunction that constitutes a naked prior restraint against a proposed march by a group that did not have a similar history of illegal conduct in the jurisdiction where the march was scheduled."

The Court noted that government "may infringe upon protected expression if it furthers an important governmental interest, if the governmental interest is unrelated to the suppression of speech; and if the invalidated restriction of speech is no greater than essential to the furtherance of that interest." In *Hirsh v. City of Atlanta*, 261 Ga 22, 401 S.E.2d 530 (1991), the Georgia Supreme Court adopted similar reasoning in upholding the restrictions placed on the same group of demonstrators.

A federal trial court reached a similar result in *Vietnamese Fisherman's Ass'n v. Knights of the KKK*, 518 F. Supp. 1001, 1016 (S.D. Tex. 1981). It enjoined Klansmen from engaging in activities designed to intimidate Vietnamese fishermen. Among the Klan actions which prompted the injunction were ones which would be considered traditional First Amendment activity. The court, however, found that these activities had the predictable effect of interfering with the rights of the Vietnamese fishermen and that the statements made by the Klansmen constituted intimidation. It prohibited any further such activity by the Klan.

It is arguable, although not clear, that an applicant for a parade permit could be required to supply information regarding any prior events sponsored by the group. The theory behind such a requirement is that if a group has a history of using demonstrations to incite violence or engage in lawless behavior, this history could legitimately be taken into account by city officials in assessing the security needs of the event.

Some Additional Strategies to Consider When Facing Hate Group Demonstrations

A community confronted with hate group demonstrations should be as creative and thorough as possible in formulating its responses. One avenue which should not be neglected is that of providing a skillful, energetic defense to any First Amendment litigation by the hate group.

When a hate group is denied a demonstration permit, or punished for violating a demonstration ordinance, it often seeks relief by bringing a First Amendment claim in federal court. Some hate groups do not have enough funds, legal support, or membership to pursue this litigation in a vigorous manner. In such cases, an aggressive defense may prompt them to drop the litigation, or could lead to an adverse decision. Such an adverse outcome will also make it more difficult for them to raise the same claims in any future litigation they may bring in that community.

Another alternative which should be considered is the privatization of certain public events. Such a course of action consists of shifting government-sponsored parades and festivals over to non-government organizations to sponsor. For instance, governments in many communities sponsor annual Christmas parades. Some have been forced to permit hate group floats to participate in the parades, because of the First Amendment requirement of content neutrality. If the event is sponsored by a non- government organization, however, that organization can ban hate groups from participation. As a federal trial court explained in *Gay Veterans Ass'n Inc. v. American Legion*, 621 F. Supp. 1510 (S.D.N.Y. 1985), a private sponsor of a parade is not required to use content neutral criteria in deciding who may participate in the event.

One issue bearing further exploration concerns the imposition of civil liability for injuries caused by hate speech. Most states already have some remedies for persons who sustain emotional damage due to the malice of others, in the form of such torts as the intentional infliction of emotional distress. It would seem reasonable to hold hate groups liable for the emotional injury they intentionally cause members of the groups they target.

Such an approach would permit hate speech to enter the marketplace of ideas, but would require the speaker to pay the cost of the damage he or she has imposed. This type of structure would be consistent with the way in which we respond to libellous speech, as well as to speech which provides evidence of impermissible discrimination in the workplace. A course of action which refrains from criminalizing hate speech, while compensating those who are intentionally and directly harmed by it, may perhaps provide an appropriate balance between the competing rights of free speech and freedom from invidious discrimination. ∎

RESPONSES BY RELIGIOUS INSTITUTIONS

Introduction

This section suggests various ways that lay people and clergy in a range of faiths can respond to hate activity. In predominantly white churches, clergy face particular difficulties; here, the contradictions within congregations about racism, anti-Semitism, homophobia and hate groups are sharpest. And here, possibly, the most dramatic blows can be effected against the influence of the far right, particularly against the pretense of many groups to be "Christian organizations." With more local congregations than the United States Postal Service has post offices and reaching into more communities, the predominantly white church has had an impact far less than its potential. The issues in generating response to hate activity in African-American churches, Jewish synagogues, Moslem mosques, or Latino churches — both Catholic and Protestant — are different, but crucial. Vocal action on the part of those most affected by hate violence is usually necessary to **The Role of the Local** prompt the predominantly white church to respond. **Congregation Is Crucial**

In many small towns, the church is the only human rights commission, the only social welfare agency, the only community-based organization in the area. In larger communities, churches and synagogues often are the backbone of the human rights network. This places religious institutions in a special position of responsibility on issues of hate activity.

The governing bodies of all the mainline Protestant denominations, as well as the Roman Catholic Church, have spoken out forcefully against the Klan and racism and have issued calls for action. (Some of these resolutions are included at the end of this handbook.) These statements are vitally important. But the challenge remains to convert resolutions passed at national conventions into deeds at the local level, and this remains a central dilemma of anti-hate ministry.

For centuries the Bible has been used to justify slavery, anti-Semitism, and homophobia. This chapter also includes three theological views of these issues. More recently, the Christian Identity Movement has developed an explicitly neo-nazi "Christian theology" of hate (see Part 2). Religious groups have a vital role to play in making sure that hate groups have active opposition and in providing real political, organizational and spiritual alternatives to the people to whom hate mongers appeal.

Responses by Religious Institutions

Responses by religious institutions to hate violence and hate groups should take different forms, depending on the situation. At times, the response might come from within a single congregation or one denomination; at times it might be an ecumenical response by Christian churches; and times, it might be interfaith. The broader and more unified the response, the better.

For example, in 1986, the leaders of major Protestant and **Responses Should Be** Roman Catholic religious organizations joined the American **Broad and Unified** Jewish Committee to announce the publication of CDR's pamphlet on the Christian Identity Movement, published by the Division of Church and Society of the National Council of Churches. Speakers at the event denounced the neo-nazi "theology" as "a threat to a pluralistic and democratic America, a perversion of authentic religious values, and a source of bigotry, racism, and anti-Semitism." Such an interfaith effort sent the broadest possible message that neo-nazi "theology" is unacceptable.

Opposition to Klan or other organized hate activity at the local level is crucial.

Center for Democratic Renewal • P.O. Box 50469, Atlanta, GA 30302-0469 • 404/221-0025

Other situations show a range of responses, with varying degrees of effectiveness.

A poignant example from western North Carolina illustrates what sometimes amounts to benign neglect on the part of church people in response to hate violence. In a small, rural community a cross was burned at the trailer of an interracial couple on a Saturday night. The next day, when people in the community got out of church, they got in their cars and drove down the road in front of the trailer to view the cross. From the long line of cars on the dirt road, not one person stopped to offer assistance or sympathy, even though the white woman had lived in the community all of her life. The couple and her two children lived in terror and isolation for another year, before representatives of CDR and North Carolinians Against Racist and Religious Violence organized a support group for cross burning victims in the county.

• • •

In 1982 the KKK appeared in LaGrange, Georgia, a textile town of about 45,000 people, one-third of whom are African American, an hour's drive southwest of Atlanta. When the Klan began to organize, most of the town's white ministers, like their counterparts in local government, hoped to ignore it, apparently believing the KKK would disappear if no one seemed to take notice. But this was no isolated incident; Klan activity in that part of the state was rampant at the time.

Residents in Marietta, Ga., counter Klan rally with a prayer service.

A core of African-American ministers, however, were determined not to ignore the Klan's presence. Klan recruiters began handing out fliers and collecting money in downtown LaGrange, and law enforcement refused to respond. Rev. Mac Charles Jones was the first African American minister to act, and he began what was at first a lone vigil beside the Klansmen, handing out his own leaflets. Soon he was joined by upwards of 40 African Americans. The police, fearing a riot, cleared the center of town of both groups. "We upped the ante," explained Rev. Jones. "Whenever a white person took a flyer or gave the Klan money, they had to do so looking us in the eye."

The African-American church in LaGrange became the center for strategizing, meeting, and leading its people to action. "We sang Bill Wilkinson out of a meeting," Rev. Jones recalled. "Clergy went through town calling people to come, and they followed us to Wilkinson's meeting." Regular sermons on the sin of racist violence were an important part of the strategy, preaching that framed the issue of racist violence as a sin. "If it's a sin," Rev. Jones explained, "then the problem the church has to address is how to root it out. Opposing it becomes central to the church's major concern of transforming the world." Such a theological grounding to the LaGrange campaign also helped the activist ministers with more conservative or frightened colleagues who might otherwise have undercut their efforts.

Opposing the Klan was also framed for congregants as an issue of empowerment, an opportunity to bring people together to work against the racism in the community and the society. "What was it about LaGrange that let the Klan come in there?" Jones asked, pointing to the fact that the only African Americans in city hall were the janitors. They began to look at other issues, such as voting rights and the curriculum in the schools.

"Of course, these strategies include terrible risks," Rev. Jones commented, remembering the early morning when police brought him to the station to tell him that his name was on a hit list. They advised him to change his patterns of behavior and to wear a bullet-proof vest. His church was searched several times for bombs. These dangers frightened the congregation, but they held strong. "We also had to hold law enforcement accountable," Jones said, explaining that at the time, the LaGrange Police Department was under a major suit for police brutality brought by local African American citizens.

African-American ministers also pressed white clergy to respond. Under this pressure, both the city council and the ministers of the town's four downtown white churches took public positions against the Klan. The council refused the KKK a permit to march in the city, was taken to court by the Klan and the ACLU, and lost. The four principal ministers condemned the Klan in a letter-to-the-editor of the local newspaper, and later amplified their views in a news conference on the steps of city hall. But on the day the Klan finally marched, none of the four came to an educational meeting on the KKK held at a black church and attended by 400 African American people.

In LaGrange, as in many communities across the country, the crisis over the Klan was one of the first instances that black and white leaders had sat down and talked, and it was a perfect time to begin to heal divisions, but most of the white ministers showed little interest in doing so. A small interracial group of ministers met twice in the year after the first Klan march, but nothing tangible resulted, and the opportunity was lost. Suggestions by black leaders that the group work to introduce anti-racism instruction in the schools and to tackle other issues of prejudice symbolized by the Klan apparently fell on deaf ears. The only white ministers willing to talk about the interrelatedness of economic exploitation and racism were three ministers of rural or mill-village white churches, although they voiced concerns that some of their members might be Klan or sympathizers.

Ministers of the "downtown churches," whose members include most of the city's establishment figures and powers-that-be, were faced with the choice of preaching the gospel and risking their careers or promoting the status quo. In the end, says one of the black LaGrange ministers, it comes down to the demands of the gospel versus the security of the pastorate.

• • •

In Western Kansas in 1987, Jim Wickstrom, a Posse leader and Identity "pastor," showed up in the town of Oakley to recruit distressed farmers into Posse ranks. When the white Ministerial Alliance was approached to speak out against his brand of religion, it refused to act. "At least he is getting people to read the Bible," one white minister responded. It was two years before any religious or government agencies in the town responded to the farm crisis. This vacuum, as well as the irresponsibility of religious leadership, allowed Wickstrom to gain a following.

On the other hand, white ministers who take the hate mongers on head-on, can have important successes. In Wichita, Iowa, Rev. Charlotte Reif thwarted efforts by Populist Party members to take over a meeting at the Wichita United Methodist Church, where she is a minister. She had called the meeting to organize farmers, to educate them on borrowers' rights and to show them how the farm crisis was not their fault. At the meeting, fifty local people attended, and then twenty members of the Posse showed up. Rev. Reif found herself "toe to toe" with Betty McConkey, top Populist leader, Rev. Reif told the *United Methodist Reporter*.

"They wanted to use our meeting as a forum, but I said no, and my congregation said no. We wouldn't let them talk, so they left," making threats to a member of the PrairieFire staff on hand for the meeting. "My congregation got the chance to see the Populist Party for what it is, a bunch of pushy, racist bullies." Rev. Reif already had an active ministry of advocacy for farmers in crisis, probably a key factor in her success at turning the Posse away. She says that the trick is to first make it clear that hate groups like the Posse are wrong in their beliefs, then next to give people an alternative, to "enable them to care for each other as a church community." When she hears that a farm is being sold, she is there to stand by the family and help them respond, legally and with other strategies. When the Posse arrives, the farmer already has support and doesn't want the Posse's venom.

• • •

The community of Washington, Pennsylvania, a town of 38,000 people 30 miles from Pittsburgh, was able to counter active Klan organizing and is in the process of building an ongoing, broad-based anti-racist organization. In 1989, media in the area carried stories that in nearby Taylorsville, a black professional football player was starting a "home for wayward boys." A local Klan organization, seized on the event, picketing and marching against the project and making it hard for the home to locate property to begin construction. Shocked by the increased Klan presence, local ministers and other citizens held a "Witness for America Rally." It drew five hundred people. "Pretty amazing," as one of its organizers explained, for a rural community with no public transportation.

Community Action Southwest, a local community agency, got involved in helping the steering committee create the Committee for Racial Equality, which meets regularly to deal with issues of racism in the community. When a professor at a local college began writing racist articles denigrating the ability of black students, the committee met with the president of the university to discuss the situation. They also pulled together college professors to take a strong stand for affirmative action and to look at racism on the area's college campuses.

Center for Democratic Renewal • P.O. Box 50469, Atlanta, GA 30302-0469 • 404/221-0025

The second year, CRE held its Witness for America rally at an African Methodist Episcopal church. In 1991, it was held at a synagogue. The Committee has also sponsored workshops on racism, and spent some time looking at their own internal dynamics to counteract intragroup racism.

"It's the first interracial group that's ever taken on anything in Washington, Pennsylvania," Elizabeth Beck, an organizer with Community Action Southwest, reported.

• • •

In South Chicago, the scene of Martin Luther King's march in Marquette Park, the Religious Coalition to End Racial Violence forged interfaith solidarity against hate attacks. South Chicago had long been the scene of bias crime; year after year, the Human Relations Commission chronicled the attacks, and a neo-Nazi group organized openly in the area. The religious community decided it was time to respond when a neo-Nazi group got a permit to protest a "Dream Day" celebration in Marquette Park commemorating the anniversary of King's famous speech. Led by United Methodist ministers, an ad-hoc group held a worship service and marched to the park to counter the white supremacist demonstration. "It was quite memorable," remembers United Methodist minister Marti Scott, one of the pastors of Emanuel Parish, a cooperative ministry of three churches. "There were 300 of us, 800 police, and 1,000 white supremacists. After that, we saw the first action had been only a beginning."

The core of United Methodist ministers were operating in a predominantly Roman Catholic area, so they began dialogue with Catholics. When they realized the level of anti-Semitism involved, they also began to include synagogues. A large Arab population and anti-Arab activity brought inclusion of mosques. They held press conferences, raised money for victims, put together school curricula, began to shape a hate crimes network, interfacing with the Chicago police and the HRC. When the Persian Gulf conflict brought an upsurge of anti-Arab attacks in 1990 and 1991, the coalition printed a poster, "Arab-Americans are our neighbors, not our enemies."

The two factors that seemed to hold ministers back from responding to hate activity were fear of negative response from their congregations and fear of retaliation from people acting out of hatred. "I got people from the congregation involved from the get-go," Scott explained. "I also made a clear Biblical statement that we can't tolerate this kind of activity as Christians." Scott also attributes the solidarity of religious leadership in South Chicago to their ability to respond in an ongoing way. The United Methodist District Superintendent was solidly behind the efforts, and all nine UMC churches in their cluster were unified in opposition to hate activity. "We sent a signal that this is what it meant to be a United Methodist," Rev. Scott explained. "There was no place for people in our congregations to go if they left here."

The activism was not without a price. Rev. Scott remembered the vandalism to the church soon after she arrived. Someone from the congregation had apparently let the vandals in, and congregants and ministers arrived to find swastikas behind the pulpits and hymnals defaced. A couple of years later, she received death threats on the answer machine and through the mail. Vandalism at her home let her know that would-be attackers knew where she lived. Her white, working-class congregation stood behind her and offered a reward for information leading to the arrest of persons committing bias crimes. "Members of my congregation were astonished at the threats. They got angry," Rev. Scott explained . "I had some sleepless nights and some nights I went to sleep with friends. We increased security precautions at the church and put in a security system at home. But it was also a kind of spiritual awakening. I realized that I had to either believe harder in my faith or give it up."

Like Rev. Reif, Rev. Scott and her parish twere

Homosexuality and Religion

For most of human history, gay men and lesbians have been viciously persecuted. Today, homosexuals are a favorite target of the religious right, whose members frequently quote scripture to justify anti-gay bias and even violence. There are even those who claim that AIDS is God's punishment on homosexuals.

In an August 17, 1992 op-ed piece in the *New York Times*, Peter J. Gomes, an American Baptist Minister and professor of Christian morals at Harvard University, observed that nine Biblical citations are customarily invoked to condemn homosexuality. Four (Deuteronomy 23:17, I Kings 14:24, I Kings 22:46 and II Kings 23:7) simply forbid prostitution by men and women. Two (Leviticus 18:19-23 and Leviticus 20:10-16) explicitly ban homosexual acts. These bans, appear alongside a longer list of biblical injunctions against such things as eating raw meat, wearing garments made of different yarn and planting two different kinds of seed in the same field. Tatoos, adultery and sexual intercourse during a women's menstrual period are similarly outlawed by this Holiness Code.

According to Gomes, three references from St. Paul are frequently cited as scriptural evidence of the evils of homosexuality (Romans I:26-2, I Corinthians 6:9-11 and I Timothy 1:10). "St. Paul was concerned with homosexuality only because in Greco-Roman culture it represented a secular sensuality that was contrary to his Jewish-Christian spiritual idealism. He was against lust and sensuality in anyone, including heterosexuals. To say that homosexuality is bad because homosexuals are tempted to do morally doubtful things is to say that heterosexuality is bad because heterosexuals are likewise tempted. For St. Paul, anyone who puts his or her interest ahead of God's is condemned, a verdict that falls equally upon everyone," writes Gomes.

Felicia Fontaine, a lesbian minister with Universal Fellowship of the Metropolitan Community Church, says the religious right is misusing the Bible. "I don't read the same Bible as other people," she said. "I read John 3:16 'Whosoever believes in Jesus Christ shall have eternal life.' That passage does not specify race, sex or sexual orientation."

Fontaine believes the Biblical quotations cited against homosexuals are misinterpretations. For example, Ezekiel said the sin of Sodom and Gomorrah was greed — not sex. "Even the use of the word sodomite in the King James version of the Bible refers to prostitution, not homosexuality," Fontaine said. So, when St. Paul condemned a sin, he was referring to

prostitution, not homosexuality.

Gomes's column offers a similar observation: "...the story [of Sodom and Gomorrah] is not about sexual perversion and homosexual practice. It is about inhospitality, according to Luke 10:10-13, and failure to care for the poor, according to Ezekiel 16:49-50: 'Behold this was the iniquity of thy sister Sodom, pride, fullness of bread, and abundance of idleness was in her and in her daughters, neither did she strengthen the hand of the poor and needy.' To suggest that Sodom and Gomorrah is about homosexual sex is an analysis of about as much worth as suggesting that the story of Jonah and the whale is a treatise on fishing."

According to Gomes, there is no mention of homosexuality in the four Gospels of the New Testament. "The moral teachings of Jesus are not concerned with the subject," he writes.

Biblical interpretations that are used to condemn gay men and lesbians are used in much the same way that other readings of scripture have been to justify the perceived inferior status of other minority groups. This is, in part, because the Bible itself contains many opportunities for potentially controversial interpretations.

For example, after literally centuries of debate over the portrayal of the role of the Jews in the crucifixion of Jesus Christ, the Catholic Church and most Protestant denominations have officially renounced earlier interpretations which held the Jews responsible. Supporters of segregation and white supremacy have also often invoked the story of the Children of Ham as a way of explaining the existence (and inferior status) of people of color. Today those interpretations are not regarded as either credible or morally just.

Those who interpret scripture to justify the persecution of gay men and lesbians are misusing the Bible in exactly the same way that segregationists and anti-Semites manipulated scripture to justify the oppression and victimization of blacks and Jews. □

engaged in active ministry for their own white congregations. At Emanuel, there were legal programs to help elderly whites on fixed incomes deal with Social Security claims and landlords. There were food programs and work with youth during the summer. "After the sanctuary was defaced it took five years of intense service programs to get that congregation to trust us again. They came to see that we were in favor of an open political process, but we also cared about them."

Clergy-Sponsored Trainings and Activities

Many denominations are undertaking to offer trainings for their clergy and lay leaders in countering hate groups. This is a good way to build a widespread response in a state or region, as well as to build support for activism within congregations, so that activist clergy and lay people do not become isolated.

To counter anti-Semitic organizing in the Midwest, leadership training sessions were held in nearly a dozen states under the auspices of agencies such as the North Dakota Conference of Churches, the Missouri Interfaith Coalition, PrairieFire Rural Action, the United Church of Christ Board for Homeland Ministries, the Jewish Community Relations Bureau of Kansas City, the American Jewish Committee and CDR.

Another tactic by which religious institutions assist local communities in struggles against hate violence is by putting pressure on local clergy and congregations. The Racial Justice Working Group of the National Council of Churches has often sent delegations to monitor trials of individuals accused of racist violence. These interdenominational delegations meet with local ministers and lay people to discuss events in the community. Such visits can help generate publicity as well as to show national concern for what townspeople may think is only a local issue.

Working with African-American and Jewish Religious Institutions

The Catholic Church and mainstream Protestant denominations are hierarchically organized, with national offices and staffs and regional organizations as well. Multi-million dollar budgets and policies flow from national decision-making bodies composed of local church representatives, with disciplinary structures to enforce church doctrine. Neither Jewish congregations nor many African-American churches are organized in such an hierarchical way, but allow for far greater local autonomy.

The historical Black church is centered in Baptist and Methodist traditions — African Methodist Episcopal, African Methodist Episcopal Zion, Christian Methodist Episcopal, National Baptist Convention of America Inc, National Baptist Convention USA Inc, Progressive National Baptist Convention, and the National Missionary Baptist Convention of America. The Black Methodist denominations are more hierarchical than the Baptist, but the African-American church is grounded in the local context. The congregation's money stays there, and Black denominations do not have the multi-million dollar national budgets and staffs that the mainline predominantly white Protestant denominations and the Catholics do. Within the Black Methodist denominations, the Bishop has an important role and can often determine the direction of a whole region. But his power is balanced by the power accrued by the local preacher.

Black Baptist churches are autonomous. No out-

A Christian Theological Perspective on Racism

All oppressed people experience themselves being defined by others as "less than" and "inferior to" within the American and world context. As a result, racial and ethnic minorities are pushed towards concern for self-esteem within their communities and must constantly struggle to affirm the unique value of their own lives.

Is the cultural, social, political and economic definition of people of color the same as God's evaluation of us in the matter of creation? Is the historic suffering of racial and ethnic people punishment for the sin of being born who we are? Can we turn that suffering into redemption for the world? Are there unique insights that racial and ethnic people can offer about handling diversity? What does it mean for African Americans and Native Americans to still be here, in spite of slavery, lynchings and every kind of impediment, including attempted genocide?

The persistent struggle and continued existence of people of color speaks to a practical, real life dimension of the resurrection, of life beyond crosses.

The power of God is made known in a particular way through the Bible. Within the pages of the Bible is disclosed who God is, what God is about and God's acting in human history. This word of God speaks to the questions, hopes and aspirations present in the experience of all oppressed and exploited people. It is through the Word that we are reminded that God shows up and is made known in our daily experiences.

We are the sons and daughters of God. As mild as that statement appears, when placed in a context where people are defined as less than others because of race, this affirmation takes on revolutionary dimensions. When people begin to see themselves as valuable, worthy of being loved, it not only raises self-esteem, but also makes us less likely to destroy others who are of equal value.

To assert that we are all sons and daughters of God, just a little lower than the angels, is to combat the sin of racism. It moves us towards the preservation of life because we are all precious in God's sight.

This basic concept is Biblically undergirded. The Bible is the story of God's continuous action in history to free us from the negation of one another. God sends Moses to tell Pharoah, "Let my people go." The Prophets call the nation to repentance for its mistreatment of the poor, the orphans, the widows, the least of the land. Jesus comes as evidence of God's love for humankind and the whole creation and brings good news for those who are the least valued within society.

Whomever he touches, they are restored, made whole and they see themselves in a new relationship with God and their brothers and sisters. Paul later reminds the church that because of the new relationship there is no male nor female, slave or free, Gentile or Jew with unequal value.

The church has to be about the calling of individuals, peoples and all of humankind, back to an essential understanding of who we are in relationship to each other and the eternal. The content of sermons should be balanced so that one is convinced about the power of sin in life and at the same time reminded of how precious is the gift of life and love that God bestows upon the human family. The story of the Bible is the story of a God of love and power who seeks to call humankind to a new world order where the dehumanization of persons or communities is out of order. The Bible begins with an understanding that the image of God has been stamped on humankind making all of us special and unique in our freedom, understanding and responsibilities as caretakers and stewards of the entire creation.

The creation stories highlight the Creator's gift of stewardship and dominion over the whole of creation. Even after our falleness, when we chose other than God, and became entrapped in the state of sin (estranged from the eternal and ourselves), the Biblical story calls us to be in relationship to God and each other.

We are made for one another, without respect to our differences. We are all of equal value, with the same eternal stamp upon our souls. At the heart of the gospel is the matter of overcoming our estrangement and alienation from each other and God.

A theology of affirmation is more than a call for rugged individual self-love. Rather we love ourselves in order that we might understand what it means to love others. The affirmation of ourselves and others is the opposite of the sin of racism, which by denying the Godliness of the other also denies our own Godliness. A theology of liberation permits the celebration of uniqueness while at the same time affirming the goodness of all creation.

— *Rev. Mac Charles Jones.*

The pastor of St. Stephens Baptist Church in Kansas City, Missouri, Rev. Jones is the Chairman of the Social Justice Commission of the National Baptist Convention of America, Inc. Rev. Jones also serves as the U.S. moderator of the Urban Rural Missions Contact Group of the World Council of Churches (WCC) and serves on the Central Committee of the WCC.

Center for Democratic Renewal • P.O. Box 50469, Atlanta, GA 30302-0469 • 404/221-0025

side body can actually direct a local congregation in what to do, and local churches and ministers can differ radically from the national body without being disciplined. In this way, Martin Luther King was able to build SCLC and a national movement even though the President of the National Baptist Convention opposed him.

African American churches reflect the unique role of the Black minister in the community — often the only prophetic voice, the minister's relative independence is derived from his/her spiritual and financial relationship to the congregation rather than to white power structures. The African American minister's relationship with the local congregation, therefore, is crucial; and it is a relationship that turns on the power of preaching to determine the direction the local church should go.

The Jewish community is organized on both a religious and a secular level, and as in the African American church, there is much autonomy at the local level. The four main bodies of Jewish faith are Orthodox, Conservative, Reform, and Reconstructionist, and most synagogues will generally belong to one of these. Synagogues have a great deal of autonomy at the local level. Each of the four movements has a national office and some, like the Reform Movement's Union of American Hebrew Congregations, has a Washington office as well. Secular local Jewish organizations in larger cities include both Jewish social service agencies, such as retirement homes or Jewish Family Services, and the Jewish Community Relations Council. The JCRC is responsible for Jewish-Christian relations, fighting anti-Semitism, Holocaust education, and so forth. The social service agencies, synagogues, and the JCRC all make up the local Jewish Federation, which is the umbrella organization of the local Jewish community.

At the national level, in addition to national offices of the various religious bodies, there are a variety of secular organizations — the American Jewish Committee, the American Jewish Congress, the Anti-Defamation League, and Women's American ORT, as well as others. The Hillel network on college campuses provide Jewish student centers and worship services.

When working in coalition with the Jewish community efforts should be made to contact the JCRC, individual rabbis, or the Federation, if the community is too small for a CRC. At the national level, both religious and secular organizations are actively engaged in work against bigotry and hate violence.

Dos and Don'ts for Clergy

1. Do provide leadership from the pulpit. Do preach about the role of religion and theology in bringing justice in society, as well as about particular incidents in your home town or city.

2. Don't wait for a crisis. Do establish lines of communication among white clergy and the clergy of churches of color, as well as synagogues or mosques or other religious institutions that may be in your community.

3. Do seek support from officials in your denominations.

4. Do use your position to encourage leadership and practical assistance from local and state officials, including the state Human Relations Council, the police, the governor, and other officials.

5. Don't neglect victims of hate violence. Be sure that they have pastoral care. Offer your services directly and, if the victim is a member of a congregation, to the leader of that congregation.

6. If a church or synagogue is defaced in your community, do respond with public offers of assistance and condemnation of the attack.

7. Don't assume that the Klan or other hate group represents only a tiny segment of the white community and thus can be ignored. Klan numbers might be small, but they often speak for a much broader spectrum of whites. The assumption that members of hate groups are sometimes down-and-out and thus are insignificant is a form of class prejudice.

8. Do address the frustrations, fears and alienations that cause people to join far right groups.

Role Plays for Clergy Trainings

This is one of the role plays that CDR has used in its trainings for religious leaders.

Scenario: You live in a medium-sized town that has some industry, some farmers who live on the edge of town, and services for the surrounding farm community. In the last year, an integrated couple that recently moved into town had their home vandalized and "Nigger Go Home" painted on their garage; a Jewish clothing merchant on Main Street had a swastika painted on his store; and a sixth grade Black child was beaten by three white classmates who shouted racial epithets during the fight (all four children were suspended for three days). Finally, an Identity minister is scheduled to speak in ten days on a Thursday evening in the basement of a local white Baptist church. "Rev. Fred Smith," a local white minister who had attended his denomination's training on the far right, calls a community meeting to discuss a response. He calls the meeting to order and tries to facilitate a response to recent events. The following people are present at the meeting:

(1) Fred, the white minister of a middle-sized Protestant congregation that contains both working class congregants as well as a handful of the town's power brokers. The minister has been in the community for four years and is known for bringing up "controversial" issues. He is the person who called the community meeting.

(2) Anita, a white woman who is mayor of the town. A member of Rev. Smith's congregation, she is concerned about anything that might give the town a bad

Christian leaders have been compelled to react to Anti-Semitic, Klan, or paramilitary demonstrations.

Christian Anti-Semitism

Even the term "anti-Semitism" is ominous. It assumes that there are some precepts called "Semitism" that one can legitimately oppose, even as one can be anti-labor or anti-capital, anti-liberal or anti-conservative.

In fact, there is no such thing as "Semitism"…no dogma, ritual, creed, body of thought or philosophy. "Semitism" is really a euphemism for Jews and Judaism.

The term "anti-Semitism" was first used in Germany in the second half of the 19th century, and quickly became the codeword for hatred of Jews and Judaism.

But, of course, that hatred and malevolence existed for many centuries before the term "anti-Semitism" was invented. Some scholars point out that the Greco-Roman civilization which predated the rise of Christianity expressed hostility to a religion, Judaism, that linked moral behavior to a God who requires

justice from human beings. Better to offer material sacrifices to the quixotic and "visible" gods than to believe in an invisible God who has eternal and rigorous ethical standards.

But the coming of Christianity, with its Jewish roots, added a new factor because Jesus, his family, and early followers were all Jews.

Instead of affirming the theological legitimacy of Judaism, early Christian thinkers chose to incite hatred against the Jews. According to Stanford University history professor Gavin I. Langmuir, early Christian leaders sought to validate Christianity by refuting Jewish scripture.

Nearly 60 years ago, James Parkes contended that this early Christian teaching "prepared the soil" for modern anti-Semitism.

If Parkes is correct, then there is something inherently anti-Jewish in Christianity beginning with Paul's dislike of Jewish religious law, the Gospel of

John's harshly negative references to "the Jews," and the teachings of some church fathers during the first three centuries of Christianity.

Other scholars have attempted to make a distinction between "theological" anti-Judaism on the part of Christians and modern "scientific" and racial anti-Semitism as practiced by the Nazis, which some Christian leaders assert is actually anti-Christian.

For most Jews such arguments are finely wrought distinctions without real differences. Whether it was ancient anti-Judaism or modern anti-Semitism, the Jew was always the victim. Both forms of hatred have resulted in terror, brutality and murder. In medieval Europe there were many cases of Jews being forced to convert to Christianity or face death. In the later Middle Ages, faithful Jews — even those who formally converted to Catholicism — were burned alive in many Spanish cities .

Jews were linked to sorcerers, witches and heretics as root causes of societal evil. The bubonic plague of the 14th century was blamed on Jews, and in Eastern Europe priests used their Holy Week sermons to foment murderous attacks upon their Jewish neighbors. The Russian word for these bloody attacks, "pogrom," has entered the world's vocabulary.

Because Jews were often physically indistinguishable from their Christian and Muslim neighbors, distinctive clothing was sometimes imposed. Dunce caps and the yellow Star of David were often required garb. In Venice, Italy, Jews were compelled to live in a segregated area. The Italian name for such an area, "ghetto," has also entered the vernacular.

The anti-Semitic campaigns of the past culminated in the Nazi Holocaust from 1933 to 1945. The government policy of the Nazi state was to murder every Jew it could find. Gypsies, the disabled, "mental defectives," and homosexuals were also targeted for liquidation.

After the Holocaust, many Christian leaders were compelled to examine their religion in a new light. These leaders were shaken and appalled by the tragic record of what has been called the Christian "teaching of contempt" against Jews and Judaism.

In 1948, the World Council of Churches, representing Protestant and Orthodox churches, officially condemned anti-Semitism, and the second Vatican Council in its famous NOSTRA AETATE Declaration of 1965 began the Roman Catholic Church's effort to eradicate anti-Semitism from all aspects of Church life.

These efforts by Christians since 1945 represent one of the great success stories of the 20th century. In a century that has seen two global wars, countless regional conflicts, the Holocaust, the use of nuclear and chemical weapons of mass destruction, intense ethnic and racial violence, and a host of other ills, the efforts by Christians to build human bridges of mutual respect and understanding with the Jewish people is truly remarkable.

But near the end of this century, anti-Semitism is once again emerging in central and eastern Europe, the traditional home of this acute human pathology of the soul.

The removal of Communism has brought with it the poisonous weeds of extreme nationalism, xenophobia and anti-Semitism.

Because of this concern, in March 1990 an American Jewish Committee Leadership Delegation met with Pope John Paul II in the Vatican library to discuss resurgent anti-Semitism.

At that meeting, the Pope strongly endorsed safeguarding human rights and religious freedom and promoting cooperation between Christians and Jews.

In January of this year, the Roman Catholic Bishops of Poland issued a Pastoral Letter that repudiated anti-Semitism and asked the Jewish people for forgiveness for all acts of anti-Semitism that took place on Polish soil.

What is needed now is the will and the systematic effort to change Christian teachings and preaching about Jews and Judaism. With the exception, perhaps, of the bloody crusades, why is it that hundreds of millions of Muslims, Buddhists, Hindus, Shintoists and members of other religions have never evoked the anger and hatred that the existence of a far smaller number of Jews has drawn?

The answer lies in the origin and early development of Christian beliefs, rituals, preachings and teachings regarding Jews and Judaism. What did and did not happen in those formative centuries of Christianity is critical to any real understanding of anti-Semitism.

What is needed is a comprehensive campaign to eradicate anti-Semitism from church life ranging from baptisms to funerals, from nursery schools to seminaries. Ultimately it will mean a sea change in Christian theological understanding of Jews and Judaism.

The road of mutual acceptance, the road of Christianity providing theological space for Judaism, its parent religion; the road that sees in the Jew not a theological rival or a sinister threat, the road that sees Jews as part of the eternal human quest for God; it is that road that must now be taken and reclaimed by Christians if there is ever to be an end to hatred of Jews and Judaism.

There is an urgent need for us to be about the vital work at hand. As one of Judaism's greatest teachers, Rabbi Hillel, said "And if not now, when?"

— *Rabbi A. James Rudin*

Center for Democratic Renewal • P.O. Box 50469, Atlanta, GA 30302-0469 • 404/221-0025

name.

(3) Joyce, an African American woman who is mother of the child who was beaten. She is outraged by the treatment her child received but has remained quiet. She only vaguely knows the African American woman in the couple of the home that was vandalized.

(4) Louis, the Jewish merchant whose store was vandalized. He is concerned about his business, but he had family die in the Holocaust and is also concerned about the recent upsurge in hate violence.

(5) Ivan, a white sheriff who is strongly opposed to anything that disrupts the public order. For that reason, he has not closed the books on the two vandalism cases, even though he has no suspects. He is also quietly opposed to African Americans moving into town, because it "lowers property values."

(6) Bill, a politically active farmer who plays poker every Friday evening with the husband of the PTA President.

(7) Meg, a white woman who sings in the choir for the church where the Identity minister is going to speak. She is politically conservative but believes in "fair play" and is against racism and anti-Semitism. She also believes that all Christians should have access to the church.

Instructions: Set the scene and get each "character" in place. Feel free to add or modify the character descriptions to fit your locale. Then take about twenty minutes to have the meeting, seeing if you can get a majority decision to take some action. After the role play, have the audience discuss what they saw happen. Then get the characters to comment on what they learned doing their roles. Was the group able to come up with an agreed-on action? Why or why not? What might have been done more effectively?

Discussion Questions for Clergy

1. Have each person in your study group write down their own personal definition of racism, anti-Semitism and/or homophobia. List them on newsprint and discuss how they are similar or different.

2. Talk about one or two occasions when the subject of racism or bigotry became a topic of discussion in your congregation. How did you and others react.

3. Have you or anybody you know - or someone in your community or neighborhood - been the victim of a hate crime? Describe what you or others did to respond. Discuss what was positive or negative about the experience. Did you wish that you had done more? If so, why do you think you did not and what would you do differently if the incident happened today?

4. Imagine you discover a friend or family member is becoming involved in a hate group. How you would approach them. Select a partner and conduct a short role-play session. What would you say? How might they

respond?

5. Have you ever received or been given copies of hate group literature such as the *Spotlight*, Christian Identity publications or anti-Semitic pamphlets? What did you do? Would it make a difference if you knew the person who gave you the material? Choose a partner in your group and conduct a short role play while others observe.

6. Racial, religious and ethnic minorities are not the only persons targeted by hate groups. Increasingly, gay men and lesbians are the victims of hate crimes. What would you do if a close friend, family member or co-worker was assaulted because of their sexual orientation. How would you respond?

7. Have each person in your group describe how they have been involved in an effort or organization to challenge bigotry. Have them describe how they became involved and explain why they are (or are not) involved today.

8. Describe what you think the appropriate role is for religious institutions in fighting racism and bigotry. Brainstorm a few ideas about the kinds of programs your congregation or denomination could institute.

9. List what you think causes people to join hate groups. Then list what kinds of programs, policies, interventions and activities might prevent people from becoming involved. ■

Center for Democratic Renewal • P.O. Box 50469, Atlanta, GA 30302-0469 • 404/221-0025

CAMPUS AND YOUTH ISSUES

Introduction

This section examines the upsurge of campus hate violence, ultra-conservative organizing on campuses, the progressive student response, and administrative strategies to deal with issues of institutional racism and hate violence. It also examines the Skinhead youth culture and free speech issues involved in student codes.

By the late 1980s, evidence indicated a new epidemic of hate violence on college campuses. The crisis was partly a legacy of resegregation in the nation's primary and secondary schools. White students from sheltered suburbs were exposed for the first time to multicultural environments, with little preparation and few resources. Fraternity racism, sexism, anti-Semitism, and homophobia, fueled by heavy drinking, exacerbated these situations. White students, many of them male, began to reach for the most blatant expressions of their disquiet, symbols from other eras where violence was explicit and condoned — black face, swastikas, Confederate flags. Larger communal tensions between African Americans and Jews also played themselves out in the campus arena, often painfully.

An '80s Epidemic of Hate Violence on Campus

Adding to the tensions was a decade of well-funded ultra-conservative organizing on college campuses, as campus newspapers like *The Dartmouth Review* provided white students with justifications for backlash. The racist incidents also set off a wave of protests at universities across the country, which challenged the institutional racism that lay behind individual expressions of bigotry. Some administrators were genuinely alarmed and helped bring about a series of changes in administrative policy and curricula.

Backlash to those changes emerged full-force by the 1990-91 school year, labeling the progressive movements on campus as "politically correct." The latest version of "reverse discrimination" ideology, these arguments (many of them emerging from ultra-conservative think tanks) portrayed the "real victims" on campus as the defenders of "Western values" who were being "silenced" by the challenges to their insulting behavior. Many of these arguments fixed on "free speech" issues raised by new campus codes regulating biased behavior and "hate speech," but severed the link between these administrative responses and the original racist, homophobic, sexist, and anti-Semitic actions that necessitated them.

Late 1980s Upsurge in Campus Hate Violence

The academic year 1986-1987 was "the most turbulent year on the American college campus since the anti-war demonstrations of the 1960s," according to a lead story in the newsletter of the National Institute Against Prejudice and Violence. The fire this time, however, was ignited by a series of racist incidents on some of the most prestigious campuses in the country. Here is a sample from the late 1980s:

Incidents Occurred on Prestigious Campuses

University of Massachusetts/Amherst: Hundreds of drunk white students pouring out of their dorms after the Mets beat the Red Sox began shoving, then chasing and beating anyone they saw who was black. According to press reports, the mob numbered up to 3,000 before it was over, and ten students were injured.

Dartmouth College: Writers on *The Dartmouth Review* harassed a black music professor in their publication as a "cross between a welfare queen and a bathroom attendant," then tried to pick a fight with him after class, in front of his students. Other

Center for Democratic Renewal • P.O. Box 50469, Atlanta, GA 30302-0469 • 404/221-0025

articles in *The Dartmouth Review* were titled "Genocide Means Never Having to Say You're Sorry," "Dis Sho Ain't No Jive, Bro'," "The Only Good Indian is a Dead Indian," and "Feminism Causes Warts." The *Review* subsequently attracted national attention when it ran a quote from Hitler's *Mein Kampf* across its masthead during the Jewish holiday of Yom Kippur in 1991.

University of Wisconsin/Madison: The Zeta Beta Tau, a Jewish fraternity, held a "slave auction," with pledges in black face and Afro wigs complete with skits that imitated the Jackson Five and Oprah Winfrey. Another white fraternity on campus in 1986 had a "Harlem Room" theme party, complete with garbage on the floor, watermelon punch, and students in black face, according to press reports.

University of Chicago: Gay and lesbian students, their neighbors and families, received a barrage of homophobic mail, including Christmas cards wishing them dead.

University of Alabama/Tuscaloosa: Students burned a cross on the lawn of a house into which a black sorority planned to move.

University of Texas at Austin: Two armed men wearing masks tried to throw a black student activist out of the window of his dorm room.

On many campuses, Jewish women students were the targets of vicious sexist and anti-Semitic incidents with the theme, "Slap a JAP (Jewish American Princess)."

The rapid upsurge sent out alarms. It was one thing for white youths to chase down Yusef Hawkins in the working-class neighborhood of Bensonhurst, New York, but it was quite another for middle- and upper-class students in some of the nation's most prestigious universities to so readily flaunt racism and bigotry. In one year alone, the number of campuses given an "alert" status by the Justice Department rose from 48 to 77. By 1988, the number of campus anti-Semitic incidents reported to the Anti-Defamation League was 38, up from just six in 1984. A survey of black students at 16 predominantly white colleges revealed that four out of five had experienced some form of racial discrimination, according to the *New York Times*. Between 1986 and 1989, reports of campus racial incidents to the Justice Department had tripled.

A 1987 study of the University of Maryland/Baltimore campus by the National Institute Against Prejudice and Violence revealed that 20 percent of Asian, African American and Jewish students had been harassed in some way during the year, with one-quarter of those experiencing more than one incident. The Institute's

Baltimore study also showed that, while 84 percent of the black and 74 percent of the Jewish students knew about the incidents, 65 percent of white students did not. Although 80 to 90 percent of white students did not perceive any prejudice toward racial or ethnic minorities, eight out of ten black students felt that they could be targets for discrimination.

White supremacists attempted to exploit this growing tension to gain new recruits.

At Bradley University in Peoria, Illinois, the American White Supremacist Party began recruiting. In Gainesville at the University of Florida, the White Student Union won official university recognition. At the University of Texas in Austin, Klan literature was mailed to four fraternities and three Jewish fraternities received the racist tabloid, *Racial Loyalty*. In Hammond, Louisiana, at Southeastern University, Kappa Delta Theta awarded David Duke honorary membership. Duke was also endorsed by the Louisiana Northwestern University Young Republicans.

With the budget cuts of the 1980s and intensified competition for scholarships, and far fewer student loans, admission to top colleges had become increasingly competitive. In 1987, Berkeley accepted only 3,700 of 21,200 applicants to its freshman class — just 14 percent. As Jon Wiener pointed out in *The Nation*, "At the same time, some college campuses are beginning to reflect the diversity of the American population: Berkeley's incoming class in 1987 was 12 percent black, 17 percent Latino, 26 percent Asian and only 40 percent white." The perceived favorable treatment of minority students in an increasingly competitive economic environment has generated a college-based backlash against affirmative action among young people. Most were born after the civil rights movement and tend to minimize the effects and extent of racism. Many of these white students, shocked at this new diversity, blame African Americans and Latinos for taking up the places of "more qualified whites," while they blame Asians for being "over competitive." The endemic racism of the fraternity culture also feeds these sentiments, especially given the amount of heavy drinking in these settings.

> **African Americans and Latinos are blamed for taking the places of 'more qualified whites' while Asians are blamed for being 'over competitive.'**

The upsurge of campus violence in the late 1980s took its toll. In 1960, 75 percent of all black United States college students were in traditionally black institutions. By 1984, only 14 percent were. But by 1988, the percentage was back up to 20 percent.

Recent studies show that retention, graduation and success rates for African American students at historically black institutions are much higher than for the historically-white universities. Black students seeking refuge from student and administrative racism are increasingly turning back to historically black schools. In 1988, black colleges accounted for 34 percent of all blacks graduating from undergraduate institutions, although they had only 20 percent. The success rate seems to continue beyond graduation (a counter to the argument that black institutions have lower standards). Among all black Ph.D graduates over a recent five-year period, 55 percent had undergraduate degrees from black colleges.

Nor do most students of color on majority-white university campuses have adequate role models, given the small pool of teaching Ph.Ds who make it through the United States educational system. The national high school completion rate was 83 percent for whites, 75 percent for blacks, and 62 percent for Hispanics, according to a report by the University of Wisconsin. In the national "senior class of 1980," one out of five white students went directly to college and remained for four years, one out of seven blacks, one of ten Hispanics, one of three Asians, and one of 12 American Indians. In 1984-85, out of 32,307 Ph.Ds awarded in the United States, 1,154, or 3.6 percent, went to blacks (who made up 13 percent of the college age population) , 677, or 2.1 percent, went to Hispanics (who made up seven percent of the college age population), and 119, or .4 percent, went to Native Americans (who made up one percent of the college age population). The National Congress of Black Faculty has reported that blacks without tenure end up moving from college to college as lecturers or assistant professors, many of them ending up in small towns with little support system for blacks.

Many minority students come from low-income families that lack the economic base to borrow confidently for increasingly expensive higher education. Between 1968 and 1985, the percentage of black graduates of high schools with family incomes of $10,000 or lower increased from 27 to 35 percent (compared to a shift of from nine to ten percent for whites), according to the Wisconsin report. Under such economic pressure, excellent students of color do not go on to graduate programs that lead to university teaching because they see the tenure process as too fraught with "old-boy" networking to risk, or seek the immediate economic benefits of other professions. On the other end, under the pressure to diversify, universities compete heavily for a handful of academics of color they consider "qualified."

Increased tension on campuses took their toll on inter-ethnic relations as well. At UCLA, a speaker at a Black Student Alliance forum on Zionism drew great applause when he declared: "The best Zionist is a dead Zionist." Tensions also rose between Asians on the one hand, and African Americans and Latinos on the other.

Ultra-Conservatives Fund Campus Backlash

A variety of factors create the nasty new mood on university campuses. Perhaps the one that has received the least public exposure, however, is the ultra-conservative funding that has targeted college youth for the past decade. Writes Pamela Wilson in the AFL-CIO *Interface:*

"Conservative organizers have said that the goal of their organizing is a fundamental change at all levels of the public policy-making process, from the campus, where opinions are most easily shaped, to the media and the Administration. As part of this effort, right-wing organizations have invested substantial resources in shaping the view of America's youth, both on and off the campus. Clearly, the Right conceptualizes youth as both a key target and an important resource."

In 1978, the Institute for Educational Activities was founded to implement a plan for large-scale corporate and private philanthropy to conservative causes. It established the Philanthropic Roundtable, a conservative alternative to the Council on Foundations. Since 1980 IEA has funded approximately 70 conservative campus publications with grant amounts ranging from $1,000 to $15,000. Wilson points out that 31 percent of the organization's $835,000 expenditures for 1987 supported these campus publications, offering not only money but also technical advice and ideological training through newsletters, conferences, on-site visits, an alumni program, a hot line, and free conservative reading material.

In addition to campus publications, other ultra-conservative organizations on campus include the USA Foundation, Young Americans for Freedom, Students for America, and Accuracy in Academia. "The financial support provided by such philanthropies has fueled the development of a conservative elite, whose emergence has been called one of the most dramatic developments in recent American political life," Wilson comments.

The Dartmouth Review was one of the first and continues to be one of the most abrasive conservative student publications. The *Review* is perceived as an "escalator to the top in the increasingly conservative country outside the liberal campus zoo," in the words of a former editor. One former editor is now an editorial writer for the *Wall Street Journal;* another was a speech writer at the 1984 Reagan-Bush headquarters; another Director of Special Projects at the Heritage Foundation. The writer of the "Dis Sho Aint' No Jive Bro" column that "quoted" a black student at Dartmouth ("Dese boys be sayin' that we be comin' here to Dartmut an not takin' the classics. You know, Homa...") became a speech writer for William Bennett, Secretary of Education. Denish D'Souza, the editor who published the "Jive"

column, became a policy analyst in the Reagan White House. D'Souza's book, *Illiberal Education,* helped launch the "political correctness" debate.

The arrival of Dr. Charles Murray at the American Enterprise Institute signaled an intensification of academic racism among ultra-conservatives. Murray's *Losing Ground* argued for the abolition of social programs in the United States because they did their recipients more harm than good. The detail with which Murray developed his argument bolstered the position of officials within the Reagan administration, many of whom brandished his book as they set about slashing the federal budget. Murray was, however, careful to remain race-neutral in his argument.

Now he and Harvard Professor Richard Hernstein are working on a new study focusing, according to the *New York Times,* on "whether there are differences in intelligence between blacks and whites that help explain differences in their economic and social standing." (In 1971, Hernstein predicted that in an increasingly "meritocratic" society, people with lower IQs would intermarry at the bottom of the social scale.) When Murray revealed his newest research interests, Manhattan Institute no longer wanted his association. The American Enterprise Institute, however, was willing to take him in.

In the past, research on race and intelligence was done by eugenics supporters such as the Pioneer Fund. Eugenicists advocate "selective breeding" for "superior" characteristics, qualities that are often understood as racial. Nazi Germany favored the practice of eugenics — not only breeding selectively, but also killing selectively

to create a "master race." Founded in 1937 with money from a textile millionaire, the Pioneer Fund was incorporated by two American scientists with explicit ties to Nazi eugenicists to promote the "propagation" of white descendants of the original thirteen colonists and to support academic research on the "problem of heredity and eugenics" and the "problems of race betterment." Its first project was distributing Nazi eugenics propaganda to United States high schools, colleges and churches. In the 1950s and 1960s, the Fund supported the House Un-American Activities Committee and the fight against desegregation. Today, the Pioneer Fund has an endowment of $7.2 million and has funded researchers at the University of Delaware, the University of Minnesota, Stanford, and the University of Northern Iowa/Cedar Falls.

Hate Incidents Spur Student Organizing

The upsurge of hate incidents on campus spurred a new generation of campus activists, who began to respond to these attacks with broader strategies that also challenged institutionalized racism within the academy. Feminist and gay and lesbian students also organized, often joining progressive campus coalitions against hate and institutional inequities.

When Wisconsin students learned of the "slave auction" on the Madison campus, a first-year student went on a hunger strike and chained himself to a bench outside the ZBT House, and was soon joined by seven other students. The Wisconsin Black Student Union demonstrated outside the fraternity. The Minority Coalition, which had organized earlier in response to previous racist incidents, presented a ten-point action plan at a rally, demanding a range of reforms.

On campuses across the country, students responded to racist attacks and institutional racism with similar confrontational and militant tactics — building takeovers, rallies, petition drives, meetings and negotiations. They demanded both changes in the curriculum and greater inclusion of people of color. At the University of Massachusetts, 200 students held a five-day sit-in. At Penn State, campus police arrested 89 students at a sit-in. After massive student mobilizations, Stanford expanded its core "Western culture" requirement to include gender and third world issues. And there are many more examples.

Campus bigotry and hate violence prompted coalitions between African American, Latino, Asian, Jewish and gay and lesbian students. For example, at Brown University in 1989, fliers and graffiti appeared reading "Keep White Supremacy Alive" and "Kill homos." Minority students there sent an open letter to the university community explaining that the episodes were part of a pervasive societal bigotry and formed a coalition to continue organizing.

The coalition demanded that the university strongly condemn homophobic and racist violence, expel perpetrators, improve security and investigative procedures, and develop a long-term agenda for combatting racism and homophobia. Brown's president responded by sending a letter of concern to every Brown student and to every member of the Brown community, condemning the incident and outlining measures to be taken to improve conditions on campus.

Administrative Responses

When student-based initiatives forced many university administrators to acknowledge patterns of institutional racism within their schools, some began to institute reforms in hiring and retention, campus security, training of residence hall staff, and revised codes of conduct (many of which came under sharp criticism on First Amendment grounds). In some schools students were supported by a new generation of progressive professors and administrators, who began to advocate for far-reaching curriculum reforms spurred in part by the challenge of Black Studies and Women's Studies programs instituted in the late 1960s and the 1970s.

One of the most far-reaching programs emerged from the University of Wisconsin at Madison. Chancellor Donna Shalala announced "The Madison plan" in February of 1988, budgeting $4.7 million over three years to implement the program.

The core of The Madison Plan was an ambitious program for hiring and retaining minority students and faculty. It called for a doubling of minority undergraduates in five years by beefing up financial support to low income students regardless of ethnic background, adding 150 new financial aid packages a year (with a goal of $4 million in additional scholarships through the school's capital campaign), as well as restructuring the university's scholarship programs to allow for more flexibility of student choices.

The plan also committed to establishing 25 new minority graduate and professional fellowships and hiring 70 new minority faculty members and promoting 125 academic staff members over a three-year period.

Campus security is another important aspect of an administrative response to bigotry on campus. The American Jewish Committee's publication "Bigotry on Campus: A Planned Response," states that, "The campus police forces are frequently a source of tension on campus. Sometimes they instigate incidents. Frequently, they exacerbate them. In many universities male minority students complain that campus police officials are more likely to stop and question them than whites or women." Policies for campus police and other "frontline" staff are therefore an important component of a university-wide, administrative strategy.

The AJC recommended that administrators should weed out bigots before they are hired, and establish clear guidelines for detaining students. Larger universities should train a campus security team, on duty or on call at all times, to respond to every type of bias incident, aiding victims and preventing riots, and that they be higher-paid than the regular security staff, giving security guards an option for advancement that requires sensitivity to all students.

Top administrators have an obligation to speak out against hate violence. "Presidents must make themselves as public as possible," explains the American Jewish Committee, "and say — in the most powerful words — that bigotry has no place on campus. Period. Failure to act quickly with a clear statement will create an escalating crisis."

Adding sexual orientation to university anti-discrimination policies for students, faculty and employees helps to protect gay and lesbian people in the university community and sends a strong message that harassment against them will not be condoned. For example, after the Georgia Attorney General fired an Emory's Law School graduate in 1991 after learning she was a lesbian, the Dean of Emory Law School barred the AG's office from recruiting any more law students on campus — a bold move for a prestigious and image-conscious campus.

Revised campus codes of conduct proved to be the most controversial of the changes brought in response to hate violence and harassment. The broadest codes banned speech that created an "intimidating, hostile or demeaning environment" on the basis of a broad range of issues. The University of Michigan and Wisconsin

Center for Democratic Renewal • P.O. Box 50469, Atlanta, GA 30302-0469 • 404/221-0025

Racist Skinheads attend a rally in Pulaski, Tenn.

used this broadest model, and both codes were ruled unconstitutional violations of student's First Amendment rights. Other codes sought to sanction students for "extreme or outrageous acts of communications that are intended to harass, intimidate or humiliate a student ... and reasonably cause them to suffer severe emotional distress" on account of race, color, or national origin. The narrowest codes prohibit "fighting words," banning only that speech that is "likely to provoke the average person to retaliation and thereby cause a breach of the peace," as a 1942 Supreme Court decision explained.

Both civil libertarians and conservatives responded strongly to these codes. "The problem is content discrimination," said Nadine Strossen of the ACLU. "These policies are saying it's OK to convey an anti-conservative opinion but not OK to convey an anti-feminist opinion." The ACLU's board in 1990 passed a policy opposing "all campus regulations which interfere with the freedom of professors, students and administrators to teach, learn, discuss and debate."

The constitutional issues for these codes of conduct are complex. "The truth is that the precise scope of the First Amendment and its applicability to offensive and demeaning speech on campus is unsettled....In the end, we may not know the answer until the Supreme Court addresses these difficult questions," explained attorney David Tatel, former director of the Department of Health, Education and Welfare's Office for Civil Rights.

The American Association of State Colleges and Universities' pamphlet, "How the First Amendment Applies to Offensive Expression on the Campuses of Public Colleges and Universities," reviews this unsettled terrain. The due process clause of the Fourteenth Amendment subjects public institutions such as state universities to First Amendment guarantees of free speech. However, the First Amendment does not generally cover private institutions, although they may be subject to state and federal regulation or university charters. There are few and limited exceptions to the general tendency against government regulation of the content of speech — "incitement to a lawlessness that is imminent," "fighting words," certain kinds of defamatory speech, and obscenity. In general, the Supreme Court has cited academic freedom as even more protected than other forms of speech, guarding especially against laws that "cast a pall of orthodoxy over the classroom."

On the other hand, the Court has recognized "special characteristics of a school environment," such as private residence areas where offensive speech intrudes on privacy rights, or the captive nature of the audience for classrooms and libraries. Public universities may "exclude even First Amendment activities that violate reasonable campus rules or substantially interfere with the opportunity of other students to obtain an education."

The Supreme Court has recognized a limited exception to the First Amendment for "that small class of 'fighting words' that 'are likely to provoke the average person to retaliation, and thereby cause a breach of the peace." This principle hasn't been upheld since 1942, however, though recent cases upholding the constitutionality of flag burning mentioned that similar protection could be extended to "virulent ethnic and religious epithets." The New York state court has said that "words which, by themselves, inflict substantial personal injury" may be limited, even without conditions of imminent danger. Several states' courts permit civil penalties for expression that is racially abusive. In general, narrowly tailored limits on "time, place, and manner" of speech can be constitutionally restricted; and rules that are content-neutral are subjected to less scrutiny.

Given this uneven mosaic of law and opinion, Tatel's advice, published by the National Institute Against Prejudice and Violence in a special report is to:

(1) Avoid or minimize First Amendment considerations in approaching hate violence on campus.

(2) Investigate federal — and many state — laws that protect citizens from interference with constitutional rights such as attending universities that receive public funds. These laws often provide both civil and criminal remedies. "I cannot think of a more effective way to signal to the university community that racial harassment is unacceptable than by treating it as a criminal offense," Tatel explained. Such statutes are narrow and prohibit only the worst offenses, however.

(2) Make university policy both narrow and clear — such as "time/place/manner" rules or prohibitions of "fighting words" (which he defines as "one-on-one racial epithets").

(3) Identify the types of speech the university wants to penalize before drafting its policies, to avoid over-broad language.

(4) Involve the entire campus community in making the policies.

(5) Have a program that is much more comprehensive than any policies prohibiting bigoted speech, programs that might include mediation, education, faculty recruitment and retention to ensure that policies only cover the most extreme types of harassment.

(For more information on legal developments concerning hate speech see the legislative and legal sections of this manual.)

Skinheads and Youth Subcultures

Across the country reports of escalating racial tension at high-schools, music clubs, parks and in neighborhoods have increased. Some of the most shocking incidents of bigoted violence involve white youth unaffiliated with white supremacist groups. The scope of the problem is evident: A survey of hate crimes committed in New York City during 1990 noted that 70 percent of those arrested were younger than 19 and 40 percent were under 16. Unfortunately, this is not an aberration, but rather the norm for cities and even small towns across the United States.

More impressive, however, is the creativity, effectiveness and varied forms of responses forged by anti-racist youth to such expressions of white supremacy.

- In San Francisco, California, frequent "Rock Against Racism" benefits were held and successful counterprotests stopped "White Workers Day" celebrations from being staged by neo-Nazi skinhead organizations.

- After a school newspaper comic strip promoting stereotypes of African American, Latino and Asian American students, sent racial tension soaring, North Carolinians Against Racist and Religious Violence (NCAARV) helped area youth produce a comic strip designed to deflate racial stereotypes. Soon thereafter a "teen summit" on bigotry was held that attracted young people from around the state.

- In Minneapolis, Minnesota, members of a multiracial youth group called Anti-Racist Action have worked with gay and lesbian organizations, progressive campus student groups and others, forging important alliances in their battle with neo-Nazi skinheads.

- Students in Gainesville, Florida, successfully exposed links between a campus "white student union" and a local Ku Klux Klan chapter, resulting in the resignation of that group's faculty sponsor and the denial of a school charter for the WSU by administrators.

- In Nevada, young people from Reno-area junior high and high schools came together to form "Teens Against Racial Prejudice" in response to the racist murder of African American Tony Montgomery by neo-Nazi skinheads in 1988.

These very different examples of confronting racism and bigotry all have in common a "peer-based" approach to organizing. Peer-based organizing simply means a strategy and practice for dealing with racist violence and other forms of bigotry that are formed and led by youth themselves. Divesting one's peers of bigoted beliefs and confronting organized white supremacists can be done by young people within their respective "scenes" or "youth subcultures," without the aid of established community organizations, churches or government.

Center for Democratic Renewal • P.O. Box 50469, Atlanta, GA 30302-0469 • 404/221-0025

Hate Groups and Popular Culture

Police and niggers, that's right get out of my way
Don't need to buy none of your gold chains today
No, don't need no bracelets, clamped in my front and back
Just need my ticket, children, won't you cut me some slack

Immigrants and faggots
They make no sense to me
They come to our country
And think they'll do what they please.

These lyrics are from an immensely popular band called "Guns and Roses." The open support of such racism, xenophobia and sexism "trickles down" and provides a certain amount of legitimacy for gay bashing and racist attacks on the streets. A similar scene existed in 1970s' England. According to Anderson:

"While [politicians] spoke of sending colored migrants back to their countries of origin in the name of nationalistic pride, and as a means of curbing unemployment, skinheads served warning as to what life might be like if they stayed..." The lyrics of the neo-Nazi band Skrewdriver echo the words of Guns and Roses:

Put up a fence,
Close down the borders,
They don't fit in
In our new order...

Nigger, nigger, get on that boat,
Nigger, nigger, row!
Nigger, nigger, get out of here,
Nigger, nigger, go, go, go!

Young People as Catalysts

Because youth are the perpetrators of much racist violence, they must also play an important role in ending that violence.

Sometimes it takes young people to even bring about a recognition of bigotry within a community. After the murder of African American Tony Montgomery by racist skinheads in Reno, one student commented, "At my school they [adults] never talked about (Montgomery's) death...They didn't seem to want to deal with it as an act of racism. They didn't want to face the fact that things like this do happen in Reno." This student went on to help found Teens Against Racial Prejudice.

Often, young people are mobilized precisely because other young people are doing the mobilizing. This is especially the case with young people who are alienated as a result of being politically and economically isolated. These conditions often cause young people to view authority with skepticism. Christina-Davis McCoy, executive director of NCAARV says, "It's sad that at times there has been a sort of vacuum where students haven't been given the opportunity to act responsibly. Teens can play a vital role in breaking the cycle of bigotry."

It is important to recognize that the experience of most young people contradicts assurances that the United States is a "color blind" society. Many young people have been told that equality of opportunity has been achieved and, as a result, many white students are led to believe that affirmative-action policies are an unfair special concession to people of color. Young anti-racists may be the first to point out that this understanding of affirmative action involves the denial of a historical legacy of racism and forces students of color to accept a burden of self-doubt and victimization. The expression of such an argument may not be found in the curriculum of a social studies class, and may not be accepted by white students when coming from a teacher. But it may very well be found in the lyrics of a rap band or in the pages of a music newsletter.

While the violent, anti-Semitic and misogynistic lyrics of some rap artists have commanded national attention, other popular rap musicians have played a positive, critical role in politicizing both African American and Latino youth. Their message is often in support of radical change for oppressed communities and, most importantly, for a rejection of the politics of despair associated with gang activity. For some young people a way to express this opposition is through alternative music, dress and behavior. And this is what a "youth subculture" is all about.

Youth Subcultures

According to Dick Hebdige, author of *Subculture: The Meaning of Style*, youth subculture involves,

"the expressive forms and rituals of those subordinate groups...who are alternately dismissed, denounced and canonized; treated at different times as threats to public order and as harmless buffoons. Punk rockers, hippies, crips, bloods, and skinheads all challenge power relations within our society through their distortion, alteration, and ironic use of common everyday symbols and

Center for Democratic Renewal • P.O. Box 50469, Atlanta, GA 30302-0469 • 404/221-0025

An anti-racist skinhead speaks during a session on youth activities in the Chicago area.

explored downward mobility, expressed through their shift in style from fastidious dress and polished mannerisms to the boots, suspenders, and aggressiveness that foreshadowed the skinheads.

The music of ska was the source of their influences from young blacks in England. Anti-racist skinheads today continue to insist that this is the true origin of the "skinhead style": an exchange between "Rude Boys"— young West Indian blacks and white working class youth. As one anti-racist skinhead group puts it, "The true skinhead spirit lives on today, from the movement that started in the late 1960s. A movement based on people who loved a style of black music called ska. The skinhead spirit stood for unity between all races. It was a movement where racism had no place."

As the economy of England faltered, however, a large number of white skinheads became increasingly bigoted and chauvinistic. The early aspect of "British nationalism" associated with skinheads became increasingly associated with racialism. Their appearance was also a reaction to the presence of "hippies" who posed a challenge to the traditional male gender role so heavily reinforced by skinheads.

By the early 1970s, many white skinheads were joining the ranks of established neo-fascist organizations, swelling their numbers. The Thatcher government facilitated this by encouraging a racist climate towards immigrants which legitimized violent attacks upon newly-arrived Pakistani and North African immigrants. As their transformation into neo-fascists progressed, white

styles. They question and disrupt, demanding to know why some groups have more say, more opportunity to make the rules, to organize meaning, while others are less favorably placed, have less power to produce and impose their definitions of the world on the world."

When these groups intersect with political movements, they actively work to change these power relations. In the case of racist skinheads, this change in power relations is undeniably for the worse.

The Skinhead Subculture

Skinheads are a cultural import from England. Teddy Boys and Hard Mods were their cultural predecessors in the late 1950s and early 1960s.

Teddy Boys were young, primarily white working class men; England's first generation of white working class youth to experience a decline in industrial employment opportunity. According to Hebdidge, Teddy Boys were "uncompromisingly proletarian and xenophobic," and were implicated in numerous unprovoked attacks upon the newly expanding immigrant community of West Indians. The Mods, on the other hand, were white working class youth who, coming some ten years later than the Teddy Boys, responded positively to their exposure to West Indian youth, who by this later date (mid-60s) had been firmly established in England. Mods paid close attention to neatness of dress, expressed a desire for upward social mobility, and listened to ska, a form of music that was a precursor to reggae.

"Hard" Mods appeared sometime later and rather than explore avenues of upward social mobility, they

Advice from Anti-Racist Skinheads

- Don't allow (racist) skinheads into shows.
- Inform people and friends that it isn't cool to hang out with racist skinheads, even if it seems harmless.
- With a group, confront skinheads who are alone and let him/her know that they're not wanted in the neighborhood
- Set up a phone tree. If someone is in need of assistance, it can be activated.
- Take photos of especially menacing skinheads, enlarge them, and poster them around town with some information.
- Expose racist skinheads by holding demonstrations in front of their homes. Being exposed takes away some of their power.
- Collect information on them and keep it in files. If they move to another city, you can exchange this information.

skinheads rejected ska and championed "Oi," a new brand of rock music that English skinheads viewed as a tougher "British" sound.

Skinheads in the United States

Skinheads first appeared in the United States during the early 1980s. By 1986, the CDR had counted 300 neo-Nazi skinheads. By 1991 their numbers had risen to nearly 3,500.

Skinheads consciously adopted the style, dress and behavior of their English counterparts but without the actual working class origins. Instead of being rooted in a declining industrial working class, it seems that early United States skinheads, at least in San Francisco, originated from primarily middle class suburbs where they began to express similar attitudes of chauvinism as their European counterparts. Also, similar to their European counterpart's opposition to hippies, these skinheads defined themselves in opposition to another sub-culture prevalent in San Francisco — punks, according to anthropologist Eric Anderson.

Being a (racist) skinhead "involves the power to invent your own subculture — one that has a deep meaning as a street soldier cleaning up America of unwanted elements. These kids honestly believe white culture is on the decline," said Anderson in an interview with the *Los Angeles Times*.

The political and social climate within which these developments occur should be noted. While skinhead group identity is formed in opposition to other youth subcultures, it can also be seen as a reflection of broader societal trends, especially those within popular culture.

Direct Action and Education

The peer-based organizing approach has been best exemplified — both in its downfalls and unique advantages through two youth networks: Skinheads Against Racial Prejudice (SHARP) and Anti-Racist Action (ARA).

Made up primarily of anti-racist skinheads and punk rockers, these young people organized themselves on the one hand to "preserve the true heritage of skinheads" and on the other to rid their neighborhoods, music clubs and schools of bigotry. To achieve this, various Anti-Racist Action chapters around the country have adopted the mutually reinforcing tactics of education and direct action.

One anti-racist skinhead from Chicago describes the formation of ARA as "an anti-racist caucus within the alternative music scene to deal with the infiltration of neo-Nazi youth." Education takes place through distributing flyers, holding conferences and regular meetings.

As described in "Turning the Tide," the newsletter of the youth-oriented group, People Against Racist Terror (PART):

"ARA believes that racism, in whatever form it takes (white supremacy, anti-semitism, national chauvinism, etc.) is an evil that not only must be opposed, but also vigorously combatted whenever and wherever it appears. ARA understands that the punk scene has many who are proud to be called nazi punks and skinheads, and as members of the local punk scene we consider it our responsibility to fight this type of racism."

The direct action component of ARA chapters involves the pledge to physically confront neo-Nazis if they attempt to attack anti-racists, people of color and other minorities. As one SHARP member in Los Angeles puts it, "We can't just walk away from everything that happens to us. We have to take a stand someplace. If I'm approached by two Nazis...they're going to try and beat me up. So I'm going to have to fight them."

Christina Davis-McCoy of NCAARV comments that, "We've certainly had an organized presence of racists here. But we've also had youth who are anti-racist activist skinheads and there have been challenges in working with that group. The skinheads were really talking about the need to have themselves identified as anti-racist youth and have people recognize them as allies."

A recurring problem for young activists is that the police and media on occasion describe them as "just as violent" as their racist counterparts. Such situations have occurred in Minneapolis, San Francisco and Portland, Oregon, with the outcome being strained relations between anti-bigotry groups and a criminalization of ARA or SHARP members.

ARA chapters and SHARP had a brief national coordinating body during 1988-1990 through what was known as "The Syndicate," a network through which numerous anti-racist groups maintained contact.

The Syndicate evolved through two national conferences of ARA and SHARP chapters that took place in Portland, Oregon, in April, and again in October 1990. The latter was set to correspond with the trial of white supremacists Tom and John Metzger. Both conferences were well attended, and the growing sophistication of the movement was evidenced through issues the young people addressed, such as Heterosexism and Homophobia, AIDS and Youth, Native American Treaty Rights, Women and Sexism, Multicultural Education, Immigration and Labor, and Anti-Apartheid Activism. The second conference also focused on racism, sexism

> **The importance of autonomy for youth-based anti-bigotry efforts is a recurring issue for young activists.**

and homophobia, with separate workshops on each topic.

Anatomy of a Conflict

Much of the activity described above takes place in and around music clubs. As with skinheads in San Francisco, Portland skinheads emerged from the punk subculture around 1986. In 1987 clashes between punk rockers, increasingly drawn towards anarchist political tendencies, and skinheads, overwhelmingly patriotic and chauvinistic, produced a split. Unlike Minneapolis, where anti-racist skinheads predated the racist variety, Portland took three years to form a unified anti-racist opposition. During this interim white racist youth were responsible for numerous bigoted incidents and the city's reputation as a place where racists could organize was established.

As in other cities, the problem in Portland was that membership in racist skinhead groups carried status within the alternative music subculture, and a number of prominent musicians were members. It wasn't until mid-1989 that the first of two "Rock Against Racism" concerts were held that targeted bands and fans who had previously tolerated racists organizing within their scenes.

By mid-1989 Portland's Metropolitan Human Relations Commission had documented 84 hate crimes in the Portland area alone. From May 1989, to May 1990, that number jumped to 146 hate crimes. A significant portion of these incidents were being carried out by members or associates of neo-Nazi skinhead groups, which by early 1990 were going by names such as "Youth of Hitler," "North West Separatists," "American Front," and "Southern Justice."

As tensions escalated in and around the alternative music scene, a chapter of both Anti-Racist Action and Skinheads Against Racial Prejudice formed. In response, racist skinheads in the Portland area began to get acquainted with more professional neo-Nazis, like Richard Butler's Aryan Nations compound in Idaho, where they received ideological instruction and training in street tactics:

On April 27, 1990, just five days after an "Aryan Youth Conference" in Idaho attended by some 30 neo-Nazi skinheads from the Portland area, an apartment where Anti-Racist Action members were staying was attacked by approximately 12 neo-Nazi youth. Peace activists, neighborhood church members and students provided food, medical supplies, computer time (for press releases and posters) and technical support to the beleaguered anti-racists.

Two nights later, a group of six anti-bigotry youth activists in the same apartment were attacked by approximately two dozen fascist youths who attempted to kick-in the door of the apartment. Less than one week later an associate of the young anti-racists was run down, beaten with a cane and stabbed in the lung. Instead of characterizing the attacks as violent assaults on anti-racists, however, some Portland law enforcement officers and media observers described the events as a "gang war."

Allies or Isolation?

The power of initiatives such as ARA and SHARP has in large part rested in their development of leadership, commitment, value systems and organizing within the sub-culture that nourishes them. However, by maintaining these styles, symbols and activities, these organizations are often isolated from progressive and/or institutional support. The need for stable employment for young activists, technical support, leadership training and the like goes unfulfilled. Rock Against Racism concerts, the publication of anti-racist newsletters, and the development of greater political awareness are excellent examples of actions that larger, more mainstream groups can launch to curb the appeal of young racists.

On occasion the violence associated with punk and skinhead subcultures, or rap and hip-hop bands, deters mainstream groups from supporting young anti-bigotry efforts. The need to constantly recruit a new generation of activists to replace those graduating, starting families, or moving on to other political work is an additional burden. The presence of more established, community-based and/or institutionally supported groups that could help these organizations may provide them with the longevity they need to transfer their abilities and resources to a succeeding generation.

However, the importance of autonomy for youth-based anti-bigotry efforts is a recurring issue with young activists. It is imperative for older activists to provide support to youth groups in a way that acknowledges this need for autonomy. □

Center for Democratic Renewal • P.O. Box 50469, Atlanta, GA 30302-0469 • 404/221-0025

Responding to the Rural Radical Right

Introduction

The late 1970s and early 1980s brought to the Midwest the worst agricultural economy since the Great Depression. Using this opportunity, the nation's far right racists and anti-Semites launched a widespread recruitment and propaganda campaign. Their fundamentally anti-democratic message was dressed in the clothes of concern for family farmers and, unfortunately, this strategy met with some success.

A Far-Right, Anti-Semitic Message Was Concealed

Progressive farm organizations that responded to the agricultural economic crisis also faced this "anti-establishment" neo-Nazi movement among farmers. While farm groups acknowledged that the radical right's efforts should be opposed, they vigorously debated how to counteract this trend.

Farm, rural and religious leaders eventually countered the radical right's campaign, and their success merits study by communities experiencing economic or policy initiatives by hate groups today.

Farm Crisis brought economic distress

Low farm prices and the United States agricultural depression of the 1980s that followed caused wrenching economic and demographic changes for the 27 percent of the nation's population that lives in rural America. The crisis was fueled by the loss of approximately 625,000 family farm operations from 1981 through 1988. The agricultural economic crisis particularly affected producers of wheat, feed grains, beef and pork. For example:

- Almost one-third of all farm households fell below the poverty level in 1986. The average United States net farm income in 1984 was just over $6,000 with several major farm states averaging net farm income losses, according to United States Department of Agriculture statistics.
- Of the 2400 non-metropolitan counties in the United States only 300 had unemployment rates higher than nine percent in 1979. By 1985, 1100 had unemployment greater than nine percent Meanwhile, the poverty rate for rural counties was 18.3 percent compared to 12.7 percent for metropolitan counties.
- The United States lost 2,000 farm equipment dealers in 1983 and 1984. Also, 80,000 jobs in farm implement manufacturing were lost between 1980 and 1985.

Young Farmers Were Often Hardest Hit

- The market value of United States farm land fell $142 billion between 1982 and 1985. That lost land value was equal to the combined assets of IBM, General Electric, Eastman Kodak, Proctor and Gamble, Dow Chemical, McDonalds, RCA, Upjohn, Weyerhauser and CBS.
- The agricultural crisis of the 1980s disproportionately burdened young farmers – threatening the future of family farm agriculture. In 1985, over 60 percent of farm operators under the age of 45 were reported in serious financial trouble in the Midwest; the figure was over 40 percent for all the other regions of the country.
- Black farmers had been experiencing land loss at a rate 2.5 times greater than white farmers for 25 years. In addition to the general decline of the farm economy, black farmers also experienced racial discrimination, neglect and economic exploitation. Black landowners traditionally received separate and unequal treatment through the South's land tax, partition sale and foreclosure

system.

- Black farmers also suffered discrimination at the hands of the Farmers Home Administration (FmHA), established by Congress in 1921 to be the "lender of last resort" for farmers unable to obtain loans elsewhere. As a proportion of the total dollar amounts loaned in 1982, blacks received only one percent of the Ownership Loans and 2.5 percent of the Operating Loans offered by FmHA.

The unraveling of the farm economy in the 1980s created disbelief after the optimistic agricultural climate of the 1970s. Even the experts missed the warning signs of the impending crisis. Merrill Oster, President of Professional Farmer said in 1981, "the 1980s will create new wealth for well-informed farmers...

The Federation of Southern Cooperatives and the Center for Democratic Renewal sponsored a farmers' training session at Epes, Alabama, on countering right-wing intervention.

before 1990 you will see $5-a-bushel corn, $15-a-bushel soybeans, and $8-a-bushel wheat..." From 1983 on, grain prices hovered at half or less of these projections. The Kipplinger Agricultural Letter of February 20, 1981, predicted that land prices would "triple by 1990...average United States farmland costing $1,000 an acre now will sell for $3,000 in nine years."

Many farmers going bankrupt in the early 1980s had followed all of the experts' advice in the 1970s. Yet, the news media called the early victims of the economic dislocation "bad managers" and "greedy expansionists."

Farmers who were losing their farms became isolated and alienated from their communities. In a study of farm families forced out of agriculture between 1980 and 1985, respondents were asked to identify help that they received from churches, other organizations or governments agencies in facing their farm financial crisis. Out of 42 responding families, only five reported receiving assistance from any community institution.

The rural far right stepped in to fill this void. In most cases, Posse adherents actively offered the support fellow community friends were unwilling or unable to give. Beginning in 1978, far right activists enjoyed five years of relatively unhampered access to failing farmers.

How the radical right grew

The rural radical right of the late 1970s and 1980s grew out of pre-existing organizing efforts of the Posse Comitatus, the most successful of the early rural far right groups, which was formed by Henry Beech, a Portland, Oregon, dry cleaner operator and former member of the pro-Nazi, anti-Semitic Silver Shirts of the 1930s.

The philosophy of the Posse eventually pervaded

the spectrum of rural far right organizations. "Posse Comitatus" literally means "power of the county," and Beech and his followers convinced themselves that all laws passed by any governmental body higher than the county level were unconstitutional. The Posse held that "Christian common law" should be the basis for all 'lawful' authority. Posse organizers told their followers that the United States was a "Christian Republic," and not a democracy at all. Ironically, farmers who were losing their farms in record numbers came to embrace an ideology that proposed that only property owners have the right to vote. The Posse asserted that the Federal Reserve System was part of an international Jewish conspiracy and issued unconstitutional money — only gold and silver were "constitutional" to Posse followers. Income taxes were also considered unconstitutional, and "tax protestors" became the media name for the followers of this movement.

The Posse Comitatus of the early 1980s was explicitly racist and anti-Semitic. James Wickstrom, the Posse's self-proclaimed national director, was a reverend in the openly racist "Christian Identity" movement. Wickstrom and William Potter Gale, who had an "Identity ministry" in Mariposa, California, were regular speakers on a daily Posse broadcast on KTTL radio in Dodge City, Kansas, in 1982 and 1983. Excerpts from the broadcasts include: "All Jews should be shot, they're not fit to live"....."all the disco bongo congo from the bongo is gonna be gone."...."You're not gonna vote them out; Thus with violence shall that great city Babylon, that International Communist system – be thrown down."

Posse Comitatus followers usually also believed in the racist theology known as Christian Identity, which by the 1980s had become an important bridge between various groups within the far right, from the Ku Klux Klan and Aryan Nations to the Posse and the Christian Patriots. David Duke, when he headed the Knights of the Ku Klux Klan, said, "we work with the Posse Comitatus whenever we can...we get their material and funnel it to our groups." The religious beliefs of Christian Identity also provided a racist undergirding of the economic, legal and political theories of the more widely-peddled message of the rural radical right.

Anti-Semitism figured prominently in the bogus tax-protest and legal theories promoted by the Posse. The Federal Reserve System of the late 1970s instituted high interest rates to curb inflation, and the rural far right sharpened that issue. After linking the rural crisis to the Federal Reserve, the far right would make the leap to an "international conspiracy of Jewish bankers." This theory gained such wide-spread acceptance that many farmers could quote the far right's made-up list of supposed owners of the Federal Reserve — "the Rothschilds, Israel Schiff, Lazar Brothers," etc.

The results of a 1986 Louis Harris poll of farm and rural residents in Iowa and Nebraska gives some indication of both the far right's success in popularizing anti-Semitism, as well as bringing into the open existing latent anti-Semitism. The poll found that 42 percent of the respondents agreed with the statement that "Jews should stop complaining about what happened to them in Nazi Germany." Forty-three percent believed that, "when it comes to choosing between people and money, Jews will choose money." And, particular to the farm crisis, 27 percent agreed with the statement, "farmers have always been exploited by international Jewish Bankers." In an analysis of the poll data, Harris said:

"Any phenomenon which affects over one in four respondents must be viewed as a mass phenomenon, even if it is not massive. One does not have to venture far into either Iowa or Nebraska to find an abundant number of people who are prepared to lay some of the blame for the plight of farmers on international bankers, and many of these are clearly thought to be Jewish.

As a distinct organization, the Posse Comitatus was discredited and fragmented by 1984, largely because of lawsuits and the ultimate failure of its bogus strategies. Also, its leaders James Wickstrom and Gordon Kahl were, to say the least, subjected to bad publicity.

The Posse left a myriad of groups in its wake that continued to promote its ideas. The far right groups that met with the most success were those whose strategies offered distressed farmers hope and a course of action — however false. From Conrad LeBeau and his "Patriots Information Network" to George Gordon's, "Barristers Inn," farmers were sold bogus legal briefs, based upon "Christian Common Law." Other groups, like Rick Elliot's National Agricultural Press Association, paraded the

false hope of phony loan scams. Even after Elliot was indicted for stealing approximately a quarter of a million dollars from NAPA members, he drew large crowds of credit-desperate farmers during the fall and winter of 1984-85. He was convicted of the theft in 1986 and served four years of an eight-year sentence.

The Populist Party also made a strong effort to recruit distressed farmers. Formed in 1984 as a joint effort of former Klan, neo-Nazis, Posse Comitatus members and former John Birchers, the Populist Party met with some success. The borrowed name from 19th Century populism initially attracted farmers from legitimate farmers' organizations. Posse-like 'Christian Patriots' remained active in the Populist Party's electoral expression of the rural far right.

Farm organizations were infiltrated

Far right organizers began to infiltrate mainstream farmers' organizations during the late 1970s. The Posse Comitatus and Lyndon LaRouche's organizations both actively campaigned for recruits among the newly formed American Agricultural Movement (AAM), that was founded in 1977 and best known for its "tractorcades" to Washington, D.C. Despite a vigorous stand against LaRouche by AAM leadership, LaRouche and his organizers would still attend annual meetings and rent a room at the same hotel to deliver workshops. LaRouche's "Parity Foundation" used contacts within the Teamsters Union in an attempt to portray the "foundation" as a legitimate farm-labor coalition.

Prominent AAM leaders publicly linked themselves with Posse-style activists and activities. Eugene Schroder, an AAM founder, Jerry Wright, a Springfield, Colorado, AAM activist, and Alvin Jenkins, the national spokesman for AAM Grassroots, attended paramilitary trainings conducted by James Wickstrom and William Potter Gale in Colorado and Kansas in 1982. Jenkins was quoted in the *AAM News* saying "you cannot go too far to save your farm — bloodshed, tearshed — whatever it takes." However, he later sued the Denver *Post* for publicizing his presence at the so-called "bomb-making session." The libel suit never came to trial and was dropped.

In 1982, the once 20,000 member-strong AAM split into factions, AAM, Inc., and AAM Grassroots.

Far right organizers played a critical role in the break-up. Former AAM activists talked about leaving because of the "blatant anti-Semitism and racism." AAM, Inc., as well as some leaders of AAM Grassroots, both opposed the rural radical right's attempts to recruit farmers. On the other hand, a number of AAM Grassroots chapters continued to entertain the spectrum of ideas introduced by the far right.

The far right's disruption of AAM is an unfortunate chapter in farm organization history. Farmers were just beginning to lose farms in record numbers at the time of AAM's break-up. AAM's inception was the newest

Larry Humphreys of Velma, Oklahoma (right) and Tommy Kersey (center) of the "National Farm Products Minimum Pricing Union" (N.F.P.M.P.U) gather with weapons to protest the foreclosure of Georgia farmer Oscar Lorick.

expression of farmers' protest at the policies that created the agricultural crisis of the 1980s. The far right succeeded in discrediting social protest at a critical time when farmers needed to build community support and a democratic social movement for economic justice.

The rural radical right continued to make overtures and inroads into legitimate farm and rural organizations throughout the 1980s. Fred Huenfield, who served as president of the National Organization of Raw Materials (N.O.R.M.), was an ardent Lyndon LaRouche supporter at the time. LaRouche's farmer recruits included Lannie Dickson of Missouri and Don Scott of Ohio — both National Farmers Organization (NFO) members. Dickson ran as a LaRouche candidate in the 1986 Missouri Democratic Party primary. One of Rick Elliott's principal organizers was Leon Silkman, a past president of the Colorado Association of Soil Conservation Districts. And *Acres U.S.A,* a monthly tabloid on sustainable, nonchemical farming methods, sold a variety of far right publications through its own library and defended the promoters of anti-Semitism as "persecuted farmers."

In 1983 and 1984, farm leaders began developing a strategy of response to the rural far right. Many had noticed manifestations of the rural far right before, but assumed it was a marginalized phenomenon without access to the mainstream of rural communities. The deepening agricultural crisis changed that perception. Progressive farm movement leaders realized the far right's organizing affected their own ability to build a positive democratic farm movement.

On the one hand the radical right was offering conspiracy theories, bogus legal schemes, phony loan scams and the religious and racial bigotry of the Christian Identity movement.

On the other hand activist farm groups were encouraging farmers to lobby in Washington for higher farm prices, offering hotline counseling to distressed farm families, providing legal advice on how to fight foreclosures, and engaging in non-violent direct action protests to dramatize the plight of rural America. Some rallies drew tens of thousands. Still other more established conservative farm groups like the National Farm Bureau

Center for Democratic Renewal • P.O. Box 50469, Atlanta, GA 30302-0469 • 404/221-0025

supported Reagan Administration farm policy and criticized the critics for "crying wolf" about the farm crisis.

Farm movement leaders agreed that the rural far right was a problem. Disagreement came over how to oppose the far right. Two strategies came out of this early period:

Some thought public opposition to the far right would paint farmers as bigots and undermine the legitimacy of the farm movement. Their strategy was to "out-organize" the far right by more effectively building a legitimate farmers protest movement.

Others thought that the far right had already made too many inroads into the farm protest movement. Their strategy was to draw a bold line between democratic, nonviolent protest and the bigotry of the far right.

In 1984, the North American Farm Alliance (NAFA) initiated one of the first and most successful "out-organize 'em" counteraction strategies. NAFA invited Jesse Jackson to the foreclosure sale of a black farmer in Nicodemus, Kansas. Jackson and African American representatives from Kansas City heard Posse rhetoric that day. More importantly, the protesting farmers saw African Americans concerned about their way of life who joined their social protest against economic injustice.

Jackson's visit to Nicodemus was the first of his many efforts on behalf of farmers. Jackson, over the years, caused many white farmers to question their prejudices towards blacks. On the other hand, the far right's ideology around the Constitution, Federal Reserve System and anti-Semitism were left relatively unchallenged by this strategy. Jackson never denounced or even challenged the Posse's ideology. Consequently, those individuals influenced by the far right to believe in "a Jewish conspiracy to control the Federal Reserve System" often retained that part of the far right's message.

PrairieFire Rural Action, formerly Rural America, in Des Moines, Iowa, was the first farm advocacy organization to launch a public counteraction campaign to the rural far right. PrairieFire met with CDR in January 1984 following LaRouche's disruption of a presidential candidates debate in Iowa. The PrairieFire and CDR meeting resulted in two counteraction tools that were used by countless rural leaders over the next few years.

First, CDR and PrairieFire co-published a pamphlet entitled, "Who Is Behind the Farm Crisis?" The pamphlet was designed as a grassroots education tool to counter rural anti-semitism. Its four pages debunked the "international Jewish conspiracy" theory and other stereotypical myths about Jews. Over 30,000 printed copies and countless photocopies were eventually distributed by farm and rural organizations.

Secondly, PrairieFire introduced at CDR's suggestion, a resolution condemning the "exploitation of the rural crisis by extremist organizations" at the Iowa Farm Unity Coalition's annual meeting on April 13, 1985. The resolution was adopted and became a tool used by many rural organizations to visibly express community opposition to the far right's bigotry.

1985 – A Pivotal Year

The summer of 1985 marked a turning point in building the movement to counter the rural radical right; two events played a decisive role. On August 15, 1985, ABC News' *20/20* program played a 20-minute segment called "Seeds of Hate." Television viewers were shown distressed farmers who believed that the farm crisis was "caused by an International Jewish conspiracy to take Christian land."

"Seeds of Hate" was greeted with criticism and disbelief from all quarters. Farm groups criticized *20/20* for covering a symptom — "the far right fringe" — and not the cause of the problem — "the agricultural economic crisis." The New York *Daily News* declared, "We suspect that those groups are a sideshow."

Two days later, on August 17, law enforcement officials dug up two bodies on a Posse Comitatus encampment near Rulo, Nebraska. One five-year-old boy was murdered because the group considered him a "race mongrel." A 25-year-old man was tortured to death because he had questioned the group's beliefs and considered leaving. Just two months before, officials had found stolen farm machinery, automatic weapons,

A training session on countering the rural radical right.

Center for Democratic Renewal • P.O. Box 50469, Atlanta, GA 30302-0469 • 404/221-0025

and 100,000 rounds of ammunition in a raid on the same encampment.

This was no "sideshow." The events at the Rulo encampment came to symbolize the real danger posed by the rural far right. While some still denied its existence, for many others, *20/20* and the murders at Rulo made visible a problem that could no longer be ignored. Countering the rural radical right took its place on the agenda of rural crisis problems that had to be solved.

PrairieFire, NAFA and CDR began plans in 1984 for a jointly sponsored workshop on countering the rural radical right. The events of the summer of 1985 demonstrated its necessity. Workshops were conducted in Minneapolis, Minnesota and Council Bluffs, Iowa, in November 1985. A new level of counteraction was underway.

How the Church responded

In the early 1980s, local churches and their pastors experienced the recruiting of their congregations by the rural radical right. Key church leaders, just as certain farm movement leaders, recognized the problem posed by the rural far right. Others did not. One Lutheran pastor in Oakley, Kansas, went to his local ministerial alliance in 1982 to ask them to denounce a proposed visit by Christian Identity leader, James Wickstrom. Fellow pastors told him that "at least these groups get people to read the Bible." Other pastors found Sunday school classes on non-traditional subjects such as the United States Constitution or "Christian Common Law" being held in church basements.

Churches and church leaders were key players in stopping the rural far right because they recognized that counteraction was a moral issue. The predominately white denominations of the rural Midwest knew they had a responsibility to take a lead in defeating the anti-Semitism and racism of Posse-type groups.

Local pastors and lay church leaders became essential to challenging and educating their neighbors on the dangers of the rural far right. Effective pastors did not wait for distressed farmers to call, but instead, sought out farmers at the local coffee shop and grain elevator. "These far right groups are working hard, but we must work harder," said the Rev. Gene Mengarelli.

Other pastors sought to bring alienated farmers back to their congregations by "enabling people to care for each other as a church community" that included both bankers and failing farmers. "Farmers will respond positively when there is an alternative to being left

isolated to die," said the Rev. Charlotte Reif. Many church leaders actively met the far right toe-to-toe.

Religious bodies at both a regional and national level increased their counteraction efforts after the critical year of 1985, which marked national recognition of the deepening rural crisis which set out to train local pastors and others on farm crisis issues. Regional and national church bodies effectively placed education and counteraction of the rural far right on the agenda of rural pastor's workshops on the rural crisis.

The trainings encouraged pastors to use the tools of counteraction. Local pastors distributed thousands of the pamphlets, "Who Is Behind the Farm Crisis" between 1985 and 1988. Other pastors used the information on the far right to educate from the pulpit. Resolutions passed by state and regional religious bodies' condemning the far right were also disseminated by local pastors.

> **Far right organizations did not walk into rural America in the white sheets of the Klan or the brown shirts of the neo-nazis.**

Other efforts to encourage church leaders to respond to the rural far right were not successful. Just as with other rural community leaders, some wanted to ignore the problem. The tradition of standing by people in pain, no matter who they are, created problems. The adoption of this liberal philosophy without discrimination prevented some pastors from drawing distinctions about who to stand by. In one dramatic instance, a so-called "radical progressive" priest stood by and was arrested at the foreclosure sale of the son of one of the most anti-Semitic farm organizers. Other pastors recognized that they must support farmers in a way that did not endorse bigotry.

The bogus teachings of so-called Christian Identity were particularly troubling to rural church leaders. One pastor noted that he knew when his members were participating in Identity Bible study groups because they would say to him, "I don't agree with the way you read the Bible any more." When James Thimm was murdered by fellow Identity followers in 1985 at Rulo, Nebraska, it became clear that the danger implicit in the teachings of Christian Identity had gone undetected and unopposed for too long.

Thimm's story inspired Leonard Zeskind of CDR to write *The Christian Identity Movement: The Theological Justification for Racist and Anti-Semitic Violence*, a publication of The National Council of Churches. Zeskind initiated the monograph when he learned that Thimm had approached his pastor with theological questions. This pastor did not recognize Identity's racial interpretation of scripture and dismissed Thimm's questions.

In 1988, rural Kansas church leaders tried to urge their urban counterparts in Wichita to publicly respond to a three-day conference by national leaders of Identity. Unable to see the broader context, the urban church leaders thought that "the local Wichita organizer was insignificant and exposing these people will only aid their efforts."

The primarily white rural churches of the Midwest also found ways to challenge racist assumptions and create alternatives to bigotry. Rural Midwesterners had little or no contact with Jews, African Americans, or Latinos.

The First United Methodist Church of Sabetha, Kansas, hosted members of the African American, Latino and Jewish communities for a convocation on racism. The audience heard about the horrors caused by pogroms against the Jews, the anguish of black mothers who must teach their children how to deal with intolerance and the dismay of Latino families in neighborhoods tyrannized by drugs and crime. After a morning worship service, potluck dinner and speeches, the visitors were paired with farm couples to learn something about farm life through afternoon farm chores. Rev. Buurman, the pastor, reflected on the day by noting "how few occasions this town has to think about racism. But, it is just such places that by their silence, permitted the Holocaust."

Jewish community responses

Jewish community organizations responded to the rise in rural anti-Semitism with calls for "vigorous counteraction" as well as with concern for the "economic conditions fostering anti-Semitism." The National Council of Jewish Federations and National Jewish Community Relations Advisory Council passed a program plan that stated: "The Jewish community should call attention to the economic and social problems affecting a large segment of America's farm belt population and should explore participation in coalitions and study appropriate legislation to alleviate the plight of farmers and their families."

The national resolution was carried out by a variety of regional and national Jewish organizations. The American Jewish Committee (AJC) sought coalition partners among concerned Christians and initiated an interfaith conference on the rural crisis held in Chicago in March 1987. The Union of American Hebrew Congregations testified before the United States House Agriculture Committee, co-sponsored a petition drive on behalf of farm crisis relief legislation, and coordinated a conference on the rural crisis in New York City in February 1988.

The most innovative Jewish program to address the twin concerns of the farm crisis and rural bigotry was a joint effort by Women's American ORT and the Jewish Community Relations Bureau of Kansas City, Missouri.

The Liberty Lobby's *Spotlight* newspaper.

ORT, a national Jewish women's organization, provided the funding for the JCRB's action-orientated Farm Crisis Project. The project joined with farm and rural groups and mobilized members of the Jewish community to respond to the rural crisis.

One strength of the JCRB/Women's American ORT Farm Crisis Project was its emphasis on grassroots community-based activities. Rural people met Jews demonstrating their concern about the rural crisis.

The JCRB/ORT's first program was a forum on "rural anti-Semitism and the farm crisis" The forum attracted over 600 urban Jews who were encouraged to participate in a variety of action oriented projects including a farm tour, letters to Congress, and a petition drive. The farm tour took an estimated 60 Jews to the site of a 142-day protest vigil at the Farmers Home Administration office in Chillicothe, Missouri.

The initial forum also spawned other Kansas City area Jewish community actions on behalf of farmers. The local Women's American ORT chapter sponsored a clothing drive. Another synagogue collected canning jars at the request of a rural relief organization. Temple youth made friendship bracelets that were given to the fourth and fifth grades of a rural Missouri school district.

Another strength of the JCRB/ORT's Farm Crisis Project was its recognition of farmers' need to organize for rural economic justice. David Goldstein, Executive Director of the JCRB, addressed the national convention of the American Agriculture Movement in January 1988.

Goldstein said, "When legislators are callous and indifferent to improving farm policy while corn prices are still only 33 percent of parity, it helps to band together with other farmers in organizations like AAM. Just as it helps me, when I overhear remarks like 'the Holocaust never happened,' to be a part of an agency doing something about anti-Semitism."

The JCRB/ORT's sensitivity to farm crisis issues inspired farm organizations to respond to rural anti-Semitism in new ways. Farm leaders in Kansas extended a reciprocal hand of friendship to the Jewish community by adopting Soviet Jewish families.

Counteraction steps 1985-1988

Farm, rural and religious leaders actively and vigorously discredited the rural radical right from 1985-1988.

Not every counteraction attempt was successful. Sometimes concerned rural leaders were told that raising the issue of the rural radical right was "only discrediting farmers" and that "paying attention to the rural radical right only diverts resources and energy from the real problem – the farm crisis."

One person wanted their farm advocate organization to co-sponsor a CDR/PrairieFire training on the rural radical right. The group's board voted not to co-sponsor the training, but did agree to a presentation on the far right at a board meeting. One religious leader on the board asked, "does it mean you are anti-Semitic if you are critical of the Federal Reserve Board?" Later, one board member questioned the presenter's criticism of the *Spotlight* by noting that he was a member of the far right Liberty Lobby's Board of Policy.

Farm and rural leaders learned two lessons about the failure to build effective counteraction: First, precious resources — both human and financial — can be lost. For example, the 100,000 rounds of ammunition at Rulo's Posse encampment or the $500 dues to purchase Rick Elliot's chapter charter or the $40-plus annual dues paid to the Liberty Lobby's Board of Policy would each have made a critical difference to the financially struggling farm advocacy movement. Secondly, by not counteracting the false notions perpetuated by the far right on such complex issues as the Federal Reserve System, anti-Semitism might actually be condoned. The summary below includes just a few of the examples of the creative activities that took place.

1. Identify and Acknowledge the Problem

Far right organizations did not walk into rural America in the white sheets or brown shirts of the Klan and neo-Nazis. A speech critical of the Posse Comitatus was on the agenda of the annual meeting of the Kansas Cult Awareness Network. A Network member reacted angrily to the program by saying, "the Posse is a positive organization in my community."

The first step to counteraction was to recognize the problem. To do that, rural leaders had to look for the facts behind the patriotic appeal of Constitutional fundamentalism or the false hope of phony legal scams to the real message of intolerance.

2. Monitor Local Far Right Activity

The next step after identifying the problem of rural far right organizing was to monitor which groups or strategies were in operation in each local area. Who were the local and national leaders? What were the publications that they read? Were free stacks of these turning up at the local library or corner cafe? The Liberty Lobby's *Spotlight* newspaper became the far right's movement newspaper for a number of years. Stacks of the *Spotlight* could be found at local grain elevators and other community locations.

The trainings on the rural radical right proved to be one of the best tools to get the facts to those who could put them to use. PrairieFire and the CDR conducted workshops in 20 states including Minnesota, Iowa, Kansas, Missouri, Illinois, Nebraska, Alabama, Montana, North Dakota, Wyoming, Colorado and Texas. Over 1,500 community leaders from more than 25 states and Canada were trained. People from all sectors of rural America – farmers, religious leaders, mental health professionals and others – were given information to identify which far right strategies were in operation in their communities. For example, farm crisis hotline advocates could recognize the context for bogus legal theories they were hearing over the phone. Pastors understood why church members wanted "study groups on the United States Constitution."

3. Make Joining Hate Groups Unpopular

To keep the radical right from gaining new recruits among distressed farmers, 'aware' individuals educated fellow citizens and community groups to the true agenda of far right groups. Rural communities demonstrated that bigotry was not embraced as a shared community value. In Kansas, a Posse Comitatus group met weekly at a local restaurant. The local United Methodist pastor spoke to the restaurant owner about the real message being disseminated. The owner decided not to allow this group to meet in public at his restaurant.

Many farm advocacy organizations and religious bodies adopted resolutions condemning the activities of the rural radical right. It was especially important for farm organizations to take a clear position, since the far right had so successfully tainted the early farm protest movement with its brush of bigotry and violence. These resolutions were often published in organizational newsletters or accompanied by a press release. Once again, community opposition to hate groups was made visible. One of the common arguments against counteraction is that the far right should be ignored – that publicity only helps them grow. Rural communities found out the hard way that this is bad advice. In the July 1986 Kansas City trial of one of Rick Elliott's former followers, a farmer was accused of selling hogs and hiding a tractor that were pledged as security to his local lender. This farmer genuinely believed the "Christian common law" theories of the rural radical right; he believed that he could sell the hogs without penalty. He was wrong and spent time at Leavenworth Federal penitentiary.

Hate groups suffer from effective exposure. The far right credit scheme called Common Title Bond and Trust (CTB&T) was met at the outset with vigorous counter-action and public education. CB&T purported to sell an instrument that could be presented to banks for payment of loans. Within weeks of its first use at a bank, every major paper in the Midwest carried stories that educated the public about CB&T, including its link to hate group organizing. Grassroots meetings in far right circles continued, but there were few purchasers of the bogus hope held out by Common Title.

4. Reach Out to Victims of Far Right Strategies

The rural radical right created a unique situation: the potential recruits of far right organizing were also one set of its victims.

On November 15, 1985, over 50 protestors, many of them armed with rifles and pistols, prevented the foreclosure of a black farmer in Bleckley County, Georgia. Identity Church adherent Larry Humphreys

Prairiefire

550 Eleventh Street, Des Moines, Iowa 50309, Telephone: 515/244-5671

C O N F I D E N T I A L   M E M O R A N D U M

TO: Key Farm & Rural Contacts

FROM: Daniel Levitas, Research Director; Rev. David L. Ostendorf, Director

RE: Lyndon LaRouche "Food for Peace" Campaign

DATE: November 1, 1988

LAROUCHE PROMOTES FARMBELT DISINFORMATION CAMPAIGN

"Food for Peace" is the captivating title of Lyndon LaRouche's latest effort to dupe unsuspecting farm and rural people into believing that his far-right political movement has a solution to the farm crisis. Despite the slogan, this effort has nothing to do with the official U.S. government Food for Peace (PL 480) overseas food aid program.

The campaign was launched Sept. 3-4 with an international meeting in Chicago that reportedly attracted as many as 400 people from 30 states and 10 nations. Many of those in attendance were farmers.

While organizers and candidates associated with LaRouche have been present in rural America since the late 1970s, the recent "Food For Peace" campaign represents a strategic departure from more recent LaRouche activities in the farmbelt which have primarily involved smear campaigns and electoral forays.

An Ambitious Effort:

In short, "Food for Peace" is an ambitious organizing drive designed to develop a new group of organizers drawn from a constituency of financially distressed and politically vulnerable farm and rural people.

In the past several weeks, LaRouche operatives promoting "Food for Peace" have attempted to reach beyond their existing followers by approaching farm, rural and religous organizations - as well as individual farmers - with phone calls, mailings and personal visits. A series of approximately 20 meetings - which have routinely drawn 20 to 30 participants, most of them farmers - have been held in more than 15 states from Oct. 15 - Nov. 6. A second international gathering, which LaRouche organizers claim will attract upwards of 1,000 participants, is planned for Dec. 10-11 in Chicago.

Because LaRouche and his organizations have received considerable negative publicity about criminal indictments they face in Boston, Mass., and Alexandria, Va., rural and religious activists may be tempted to ignore this latest round of recruitment activities. However, as discussed below, the "Food for Peace" campaign requires our attention and response.

Example of research materials produced by PrairieFire.

from the Heritage Library in Velma, Oklahoma, and Tommy Kersey, a LaRouche supporter and AAM activist from Unadilla, Georgia, organized the armed action.

After the guns were put away and Humphreys had left town, the Federation of Southern Cooperatives, a black farmers' advocacy organization, did the real work of helping the Bleckley County farmer work through the financial and legal options that could salvage his farming operation.

5. Create Real Alternatives to Bigotry

Rural communities found positive ways to demonstrate and build positive alternatives to the far right's scapegoating of Jews, African Americans, and others. Dialogue between the people that hate groups seek to divide can be very creative.

The Farm Issues Coordinators for the Mennonite Central Committee in Kansas invited members of the Jewish community in Kansas City to participate in a "Mennonite/Jewish Conversation." More than 50 Jews from preschool age to grandparents spent two different weekends together with 20 Mennonite farm families, first in south central Kansas and then in Kansas City. In addition to traditional foods and religious services the urban Jews learned about how each of the farm families was affected by the farm crisis. The Mennonites shared Shabbot dinner in their Jewish hosts' homes and took a tour of Jewish history in Kansas City.

Farm and rural leaders also knew that they had to create alternatives to the far right's bogus claim to save family farms. This meant they had to search for answers to the frustrations facing farmers. Farm crisis hotlines offered credible legal and financial advice to aid distressed farmers. Support groups and public meetings allow farmers to overcome isolation from community concern.

"The collective efforts of the progressive farm movement saved countless farms across this nation. In the process, policies were changed, political power was gained, and progressive political work was furthered for the future," said PrairieFire executive director Rev. Dave Ostendorf.

PrairieFire – A Model Response

Based in Des Moines, Iowa, PrairieFire Rural Action is a farm and rural advocacy organization which became a leader in creative, effective responses to the agricultural economic crisis of the 1980s. On the national scene, PrairieFire served as an information source on rural issues to cities and the media. On a regional level, PrairieFire provided training to both new and established rural organizations, as well as to the religious community on agricultural legislative policy, rural women's leadership, corporate control of agriculture and rural poverty. At a grassroots level in Iowa, PrairieFire operated a farm crisis hotline and lobbied for the passage of state credit policies which became models for other Midwestern states.

PrairieFire played a decisive role among progressive farm organizations in counteracting the rural radical right. Throughout the 1980s, PrairieFire took the definitive lead in establishing that the far right's agenda had to be publicly named and visibly fought.

In the early 1980s, PrairieFire faced the dilemma of being a farm advocacy organization when farmers were recruited by far right organizations who also characterized themselves as advocates for farmers. In 1983 and 1984, PrairieFire was actively organizing in rural communities for new federal farm policy, and at the state level for the declaration of a state of economic emergency that would reinstate a 1930s statute on foreclosure moratorium. PrairieFire was deeply engaged in on-farm protest of farm sales. "But, we made it clear in the press and at public meetings that PrairieFire was committed to non-violent protest. In spite of all we did, we would hear that 'PrairieFire was a far right organization.' The confusion in people's minds became another reason to fight the far right publicly," Ostendorf said.

"In the beginning, we did not realize that counteraction of the rural radical right would emerge as an important part of PrairieFire's agenda, primarily because we did not understand that the far right's movement was so geographically widespread and deep into communities. We began in 1983-84 to warn farmers over the hot line and at credit rights' meetings to beware of 'snake-oil salesmen.' When the 'snake-oil' was linked to the mythical 'international Jewish conspiracy,' we also started

addressing anti-Semitism publicly. But, we didn't realize yet that we needed whole meetings to address the far right."

PrairieFire did realize that the far right had to be taken on. It was PrairieFire's position "from the beginning that we couldn't just let the far right espouse racist and anti-Semitic reasons for economic problems without counteraction," explained Ostendorf. In addition, the far right had already had an ominous impact upon the progressive farm movement. "Within our own constituency and across the spectrum of the progressive farm movement, we had a number of people who believed parts of the Posse ideology."

> "We couldn't just let the far right espouse racist and anti-Semitic reasons for economic problems without counteraction."

Parts of the progressive farm movement criticized PrairieFire for publicly countering the far right. "Although a lot of people knew the Posse-type groups were out there, they didn't want PrairieFire to put farmers' dirty laundry out on the line by talking about it," said Ostendorf.

In August 1985, ABC's "Seeds of Hate" segment, threw the gauntlet down on the debate. Farm movement groups began to call PrairieFire for suggestions on how to deal with the far right in their own back yards. Farm organizations saw their own membership being raided by the far right. The far right also attacked progressive farm movement leaders in an attempt to enhance their organizing efforts. As progressive farm movement leaders saw farmers going bankrupt using 'Posse advice' who could have otherwise been aided by programs run by their own advocacy groups, their commitment to respond intensified. □

Farm Crisis Counteraction Tools—
An Interview with the Rev. Dave Ostendorf

By the end of 1985, PrairieFire had already implemented a number of the counteraction tools that would become mainstays of the rural counteraction movement. According to an interview with Rev. Dave Ostendorf, these early counteraction tools included:

• The "Who's Behind the Farm Crisis?" brochure that debunked anti-Semitic myths. *"With that conspiratorial title, we attempted to use their own rhetoric to get the far right to open the brochure. The brochure didn't dance around the issue of anti-Semitism, but, instead, directly took it on. People of good will seemed relieved to have a piece that put the Posse's anti-Semitism openly on the table. We had lots of calls requesting more of those brochures."*

• Resolution on Extremism by Iowa Farm Unity Coalition in April, 1985. *"We never had complete consensus within the Coalition to vigorously counteract the far right, but a solid majority agreed with the approach. It was disconcerting that people took such progressive positions who on other issues, still decided to go along with the old adage, 'if you don't mess with it, it will just go away.' We simply convinced a critical mass of people that the radical right was a moral issue that they had to respond to."*

• Training Workshops on the Rural Radical Right. PrairieFire co-sponsored approximately 14 trainings with CDR between November 1985 and 1989. *"The trainings were especially important for the big picture analysis they provided. Everyone had their own 'local Posse guy' and tended to dismiss him as unimportant. The trainings let people see that their little 'local Posse group' was part of a whole broader national movement. Also, the training manuals that my staff and CDR kept pasting and patching together were a critical counteraction tool."* The far right's movement among farmers was so new that the legal and financial scams were not covered by any other text. It was exciting to see the counteraction section of the manual grow from one or two examples to twenty pages – and, we had to leave counteraction events out of the manual in the last couple of years of trainings."*

• KWWL-TV, Waterloo, Iowa, produced a half hour segment entitled "Harvesting Fear" in the fall of 1985. The show was a factual, comprehensive treatment of the rural radical right that served as an effective education tool for public meetings throughout the 1980s. (It is still available from the CDR for a $5 rental fee.) *"Our staff worked closely with KWWL's production team and was integral to the completed piece. "Effective media exposure was critical to linking the far right's* legal and financial theories with its racist and anti-Semitic roots. Many farmers joined the far right because they thought it was something 'anti-establishment.'"*

By late 1985, PrairieFire realized that considerable organizational time was going into the effort to counter the rural radical right and the work needed financial support. PrairieFire created the "Rural Radical Right Monitoring and Action Project" — called the MAP Project for short. *"Even though never fully funded and only a piece of our total work, the MAP Project declared to funders that PrairieFire was intentionally committed to monitoring and counteracting the rural far right."*

PrairieFire's MAP Project made the organization the central clearinghouse among farm advocacy organizations on the far right's rural organizing. PrairieFire published regular memos on the far right's activities and sent them to rural leaders who had participated in counteraction trainings and to other farm crisis organizations. The memorandum became an additional critical tool to help people see the whole bolt of cloth — *"many people saw one little thread out of the fabric of the rural radical right and thought it wasn't significant."*

The creation of the MAP Project stimulated internal discussion at the PrairieFire office. *"None of us, as staff people, had ever been confronted by a grassroots, anti-establishment neo-Nazi political movement before. There was no debate about whether or not to do the work, just lots of healthy debate about how much to do and what to do."*

In spite of its tremendous record, PrairieFire recognized the limitations of counteraction. *"For the farmers already recruited by the far right, information about its neo-Nazi nature was not a deterrent to participation. The success of our efforts was not based upon a war of conversion, but rather, broadening the coalition of people who were willing to be anti-racist."* Other communities experiencing economic or policy organizing initiatives by the far right could learn from rural America's experience. PrairieFire staff tried to persuade a particular northeast Iowa organic farmer not to attend a far right public meeting. The farmer said, "I don't care if Rick Elliot is a Nazi, I'm going to this meeting."

"Counteraction was crucial to isolating the rural radical right. Farmers already committed to the far right were prevented from recruiting their friends and neighbors. Even people in the gray areas of the Posse fringe were moved out of far right circles. More importantly, PrairieFire's counteraction helped democractic people of good will to stand firm and draw the line that bigotry in any form is intolerable."

Center for Democratic Renewal • P.O. Box 50469, Atlanta, GA 30302-0469 • 404/221-0025

Workplace Responses

Introduction

This section explores hate violence in the work place and far right attempts to exploit economic issues, and the responses of both unionized and nonunionized workers to these phenomena. It also traces the history of Klan opposition to trade unions and the new third position of neo-Nazi leaders such as Tom Metzger. This section also addresses the need for white working people to address the root causes of economic problems, rather than scapegoat others. It looks at violence against immigrants and how some organizations are responding.

When far-right organizing and hate violence target the work place, they have a particularly brutal edge, blaming, punishing and further limiting access for the people already the most closed out of the economic system. At some times, this can mean trying to keep individuals out of a job or a union; at others, it means keeping migrants from ever arriving in the United States, legally or otherwise.

Competition for Jobs Fuels Far Right Activity

The work place embodies the paradox of black-white relations in American society, wrote Howard J. Ehrlich of the National Institute Against Prejudice and Violence in his report, *Studying Workplace Ethnoviolence.* "While intergroup contacts have increased, there is evidence to suggest that new styles of discrimination and conflict are emerging.... [Meanwhile] institutional discrimination [remains] a pervasive feature of work in America."

Competition for American jobs and demographic predictions that white people will be in a minority in the United States by the year 2050 have made both ultra-conservatives and far right organizers especially vehement about immigration. An influx of immigrants from Central and South America and Asia has stirred sometimes violent anti-immigrant sentiment among ordinary citizens. At the same time, predictions that the work place will be made up mainly of women and people of color by the year 2000 have made others attend more carefully to issues of diversity.

Hate groups have always blamed people of color and Jews for the economic

difficulties faced by white working people. In the 1970s, both the Invisible Empire Klan and David Duke's Knights of the Ku Klux Klan attacked affirmative action in order to win new recruits. Other sections of the Far Right have lobbied for years against the income tax and the Federal Reserve System. But in the 1990s, the white supremacist movement has developed a more sophisticated approach to the bread-and-butter needs of white working people.

Historically, Klan groups have also targeted labor organizers (especially those working for interracial unions), and in some periods Klansmen have acted as vigilantes for employers. More recently, neo-Nazi leaders have developed more pro-labor, anti-immigrant positions that put them in competition for the hearts and minds of white workers. Because hate groups traditionally use economic hard times to build up mass support, this trend deserves serious attention.

Klan vs. Labor

The antagonism between the Ku Klux Klan and organized labor is almost as old as both movements. Paul McLennan and Trisha McLennan traced this antagonism in "Solidarity or Division: The True Story of the Ku Klux Klan vs. Organized Labor," a CDR publication. The labor movement has also been a counterforce to Klan organizing.

During the 1870s, sharecropper organizers and members of the Knights of Labor unionists clashed with Klansmen, who along with other employer-hired vigilantes in the late nineteenth century attacked and killed union members.

During the Klan resurgence of the 1920s, Klansmen targeted the thirteen million foreign-born immigrant workers (many of them Catholic and Jewish) who formed a core part of the industrial work force. Management pitted native-born workers against immigrants and kept wages down. Standard Oil, for example, maintained nationality quotas at its New Jersey refineries. During this period, the Klan had allies in sectors of the labor movement. Robed Klansmen marched in Atlanta's Labor Day parade, and the American Federation of Labor failed to organize unskilled black workers or to challenge color bars in its unions.

During the 1930s, the Klan opposed both the New Deal and the Congress of Industrial Organizations. The CIO organized millions of workers; growing from one million members in 1935 to nearly four million by 1940. The CIO's first constitutional convention pledged its uncompromising opposition to any form of discrimination, whether political or economic, based on race, color, creed, or nationality.

The Klan declared the CIO a subversive, radical, Communist organization and vowed to "fight fire with

---

Statement by the AFL-CIO Executive Council on the Ku Klux Klan

Fear and anxiety stemming from economic insecurity and unbearably high unemployment are creating dangerous social strains among the American people. Hate organizations, like the Ku Klux Klan, are seizing this opportunity to sow dissension, bigotry, and racial conflict from coast to coast. In its long fight for human brotherhood, racial justice and social solidarity, the American trade union movement has battled such enemies of freedom whenever and wherever they appear.

There is no place in America, now or ever, for apostles of racial or religious bigotry. The AFL-CIO Executive Council calls on all affiliates to establish or reinforce educational programs to counter the propaganda of the Klan and other extremist organizations.

We urge union civil rights communities and departments at both the national and local levels to alert union members to the dangers these hate groups pose to the labor movement and to the nation.

February 28, 1983
Bal Harbour, Florida

fire." The southern industrial piedmont was the scene of Klan campaigns of cross burnings and beatings. The Klan and labor clashed in Florida's citrus industry. In Detroit and Pennsylvania, the Black Legion (dark hoods taking the place of white robes) murdered auto workers, financed by some of the largest corporate figures in the country.

In many places, labor fought back. In West Virginia and Kentucky, United Mine Workers leader John L. Lewis opposed the Klan, knowing that the UMW's survival depended on its organizing black coal miners. In Georgia, strong interracial unions existed despite Klan marches around CIO meeting halls.

During the 1950s, Klansmen and segregationists built company unions like the Southern Employees Associations (SEA)

The SEA tried to drive the AFL-CIO out of the South and supported right-to-work laws as well as proposals for sterilizing all advocates of integration. When labor supported the civil rights movement, it was attacked. Many unions spoke out against segregation, which caused them to temporarily lose some southern locals.

"Whenever unions were infiltrated by Klan-types or bowed to segregation, they became weak and ineffective," explain the McLennans. "But when unions joined hands with the civil rights movement or fought the Klan, they gained strength."

White Supremacists Court White Workers

If the "100 percent American" Klan during the 1920s opposed communism, far-right leaders such as Tom Metzger now reject both communism and capitalism, advocating a third position. If management once paid Klansmen to act as anti-labor vigilantes, today Metzger targets white bosses as the biggest enemy of white workers. For example, during the P-9 strike in Austin, Minnesota, he called on his followers to boycott Hormel products.

Many of these new populists are urging protective tariffs. *Spotlight* writer Martin Larson argued that unrestricted free trade is a conspiracy by international financiers to bring American life down. Thus the *Spotlight* sounds supportive of those trade unions, who also support higher tariffs to protect American jobs. These new "populists" are even more concerned with keeping out Third World workers. Beginning with a call to protect American jobs through tariffs, this populism ends with appeals to racial integrity and Jim Crow segregation.

If conservatives fear the political effects of severe economic crisis, white supremacists hope to turn any

---

Characteristics of Hate Violence in the Work Place

1. Incidence of serial ethnoviolence — a series of attacks on one individual — was unusually high.
2. Assailants often use the "tools of the trade" in work place ethnoviolence — i.e., a warehouse worker was threatened by someone driving a forklift.
3. Physical violence in the work place is less frequent than psychological violence.
5. Threats of force usually take the forms of threats of physical violence or of being fired.
6. Hate violence in the work place is often triggered either by the entry of the first "minority" into the work place or by a challenge to the institutional authority structures of the work place.

Howard Ehrlich, "Studying Work place Ethnoviolence," *International Journal of Intergroup Tensions*, 1989, Volume 19, Number 1.

---

crash or hard times to their own advantage. In fact, some far-right organizations believe that economic cataclysm is a pre-condition for the race war that they hope is imminent.

For example, a commentary in David Duke's National Association for the Advancement of White People publication, the *NAAWP News*, stated: "Don't look upon the stock market crash or a currency collapse as being a misfortune for this country; it may be that a disaster of this kind will bring with it the very opportunity White people need to have Majority views examined and permit the education and re-education of our kind."

Labor Fight-Back

Many strategies must be used to respond to hate violence and far-right activity in the workplace. But they all share some characteristics:

- Hate group activity and bigoted violence must not be tolerated in the workplace.
- Organizations which are respected by working people, such as trade unions, are among the most effective deterrents to the growth of hate group activity.
- The effort to stop white supremacists should be combined with the fight for economic and social justice.

It is important for unions to take strong stands nationally against hate activity both within the work place and in the general culture. For example, the Civil

Rights Division of the United Auto Workers [see box, page 124] conducts training on hate groups and hate violence at regional conferences, as well as at its national conference using CDR's "Solidarity and Division" and other educational material. Locals are encouraged to conduct similar programs once they get home. The UAW Civil Rights Department also responds to hate incidents in plants.

Union locals have also helped organize community responses to Klan rallies. In October 1980, the Civil Rights Committee of District 15 United Steelworkers of America spearheaded an anti-Klan rally in Uniontown, Pennsylvania. The district office set up a full-time rally organizer for a week, helping to foster a diverse response. The Steelworkers contacted mineworkers in UMWA District 5 and pulled together one of the broadest representations of organized labor from Southwestern Pennsylvania and Northern West Virginia in quite a few years, according to a memo by the District 15 Civil Rights Committee. International President McBride issued a public statement in opposition to Klan recruitment and labor unions from a dozen industries attended the rally.

In 1981, Ed Fields' New Order Knights of the Ku Klux Klan began recruiting in Cedartown, Georgia, when Zartic Foods, a local frozen meat packaging plant with bad working conditions and low pay, hired over 100 Mexican immigrants for third shift cleanup. When a white Zartic employee was fired, he went to the Klan for help. The New Order Knights began their own union, the American Workers Union. They asked that all illegal aliens be fired and deported and began a campaign of terror against Mexican workers. When there was no law enforcement response to early intimidation, the attacks escalated to a series of murders. One Mexican Zartic employee was killed in cold blood on the side of the road. The American Workers Union called a strike at Zartic, and robed Klansmen picketed the plant, intermixed with the company's white workers and even some African American employees, demanding better pay, humane working conditions "and the deportation of Mexicans."

At Zartic, the United Food and Commercial Workers Union entered the Cedartown strike the second week, on the condition that the Klan pull out. The Klan formally withdrew, but many members retained their connections. The UFCW petitioned for a NLRB election, and they won representation rights by one vote. The CDR (then known as the National Anti-Klan Network) worked to revitalize the local, and to rebuild a truly multiracial base that won over the Klan's labor constituency. A new organizing committee included whites, blacks, and Mexicans.

Unorganized Workers: How to Respond?

When there's no union in the work place, where can workers turn? That was the question Bobby Person asked in 1984, when he found members of the White Patriot Party in his front yard, pointing weapons at him and his family because he had applied to take the sergeants' test at the Moore County, North Carolina prison unit. A combination of formal complaints, legal action, and continuing public pressure brought a partial solution.

Person and his friend Jimmy Pratt worked as guards

at the prison unit where every day they were victims of some kind of racial harassment. According to "Betrayal of Trust: Stories of Working North Carolinians," a report published by the Durham-based Southerners for Economic Justice, (SEJ) the black correctional officers at the unit routinely were denied promotions, training opportunities, and desirable work assignments. According to the black guards, the captain at the unit routinely called blacks "niggers." Inmates of color, according to Pratt, were beaten and ignored when they were sick. Pratt filed formal complaints, brought media attention to the situation, and organized black prison guards to take the sergeants test.

> **The English-Only movement, another ultra-conservative campaign, also targets immigrants, both within and beyond the work place.**

Klan activity began at the prison. Officer Person had a cross burned at his home, and a white prison guard came in camouflage to his house to threaten him and his family at gunpoint. Pratt was fired in March 1983.

Pratt and Person got in touch with SEJ and the emerging anti-Klan network that would become NCARRV in North Carolina. They appeared at a press conference and on a television talk show. NAKN organizers visited the county. Klanwatch helped Person bring a suit against the White Patriot Party, on the basis of which a federal judge issued a restraining order that the organization was not to engage in illegal paramilitary activity.

Person and Pratt also sued the prison for discrimination. The state settled for monetary damages and promised Person the next sergeant's position. Person sued again and was finally appointed sergeant, although his family continued to get periodic threats. Pratt, on the other hand, was not rehired by the prison, and has had a hard time finding decent work in the state.

Economic Scapegoating and Anti-Asian Violence

It is important for unions and working people to oppose xenophobia — hatred of anything foreign.

In the 1980s the challenge to American goods and markets from international competition led to strong anti-Japanese sentiment in the United States. Part of a chronic trade imbalance, such imports were blamed for creating unemployment among American automobile workers. Congress passed a series of retaliatory bills aimed at Japan, and resentment at United States hard times was easily passed on to Japanese-Americans, and by extension to all people of Asian descent living in the United States.

According to a report on anti-Asian violence by the United States Civil Rights Commission, in Los Angeles County, anti-Japanese bumper stickers appeared reading: "Toyota-Datsun-Honda-Pearl Harbor" and "Unemployment Made in Japan." According to the United States Civil Rights Commission, a 1980 poll taken in nine cities that showed that 47 percent of respondents thought "Indochinese refugees take jobs away from others in my area." Not only whites, but also blacks and Latinos were identified as perpetrators of anti-Asian attacks on immigrants, with the targets often small businesses that open in black or Latino neighborhoods.

Despite these trends, far less attention has been given to the activities of those nations such as Germany, Great Britain, and the Netherlands. with a far more dominant stake in the United States economy in trade, real estate ownership, banking and investment

One alternative, to blanket bans on foreign imports is the Pease Amendment to the 1984 Trade Act, which stressed examining labor conditions and reducing corporate incentives for running up large profits by moving production to countries with substandard labor conditions.

English Only and Anti-immigrant Activity

The American Immigration Control Foundation has sent out inflammatory public polls warning that our borders have become a floodgate for millions who see America as nothing more than a vast welfare state. These aliens are portrayed as criminal and diseased, as both economic parasites and unfair competitors for jobs, and an easily manipulated voting bloc.

In actuality, undocumented workers from Central and South America are vulnerable to economic exploitation and racist violence.

The English-Only movement also targets immigrants. It seeks to pass local and federal laws to make English the official language and stirs fear that English is being displaced by Spanish or other languages. In 1986, California passed Proposition 63 making English the official language in California. It has had effects in the work place there that should serve as a warning. In Hungtingdon Park, municipal court employees were forbidden to speak to each other in Spanish, until a federal judge found the ban illegal. The head nurse at a Los Angeles hospital told workers they could not use any language but English and asked them to report violators. English-Only laws were passed in November 1989 in Colorado, Arizona and Florida.

The English-under-siege argument is simply wrong.

Center for Democratic Renewal • P.O. Box 50469, Atlanta, GA 30302-0469 • 404/221-0025

According to the 1980 census, 98 percent of American residents over four years old speak English well or very well. A 1985 Rand Corporation study found that among first-generation Americans whose mother tongue is Spanish, 90 percent are proficient in English and 50 percent of their children can't speak Spanish. In the aftermath of Proposition 63 and similar measures elsewhere, it is clear that English-Only policies only encourage hostility toward immigrants and increase intolerance toward citizens, especially Asians and Latinos, whose first language is not English.

Immigration and Hate Violence

The situation at the U.S.-Mexico border resembles an undeclared state of siege where the rights of migrants and Latinos, are concerned according to the National Network for Immigrant and Refugee Rights. Deadly force by government officials is often compounded by citizen vigilante action. Border Patrol agents killed or wounded at least ten people between April 1990 and April 1991. In more than 30 other incidents the Border Patrol fired weapons, according to the Network's April 1991 newsletter.

The Border Patrol harasses those who look like Mexicans and attempts to detain at any cost all who fit their profile of an illegal alien. The result is violence meted out with impunity. Such unrestrained abuse also fuels vigilante and racist hate groups who are propelled by the prevailing anti-immigrant climate to attack and rob migrants, according to the California Border Violence Delegation Project.

Roberto Martinez of the American Friends Service Committee (AFSC) has documented violence against migrant workers. Since 1980 there have been at least 14 killings, assaults or injuries in north San Diego County by self-proclaimed white supremacists or white gangs. In 1984, six Marines from Camp Pendleton went to trial for raiding workers caves and lean-tos. In one raid they had doused workers with kerosene and tried to set them on fire. In November 1988, self-proclaimed white supremacists who were "hunting" for Mexicans shot and killed two migrants.

The majority of undocumented workers are now women. In addition to racist violence, these women also face disturbing levels of domestic violence. The pressures of immigrating and finding employment add to fears of deportation and raise domestic tension, according to the Coalition for Immigrant and Refugee Rights Services.

In addition, an anti-immigrant group calling itself Light Up the Border brought more than 1,000 people to the U.S.-Mexican border to shine their headlights from more than 400 vehicles. At another Light Up the Border action, Roberto Martinez led counter-protesters, who held up mirrors to the headlights.

In September 1990, Martinez was the target of a death threat from a group calling itself the Holy Church of the White Fighting Machine of the Cross.

A few days before, someone had bombed the courthouse in San Diego, and the letter to Martinez explained their demands "that charges against Tom Metzger be dropped in Oregon, that the National Guard shut down the border, and that Martinez stop criticizing the border patrol."

In response to this crisis in anti-immigrant attacks, a delegation of 55 persons went to the San Diego-Tijuana area as part of the California Border Violence Delegation Project.

It included representatives from the San Francisco Black Firefighters, Break the Silence on Anti-Asian Violence Coalition, Service Employees International Union, and Human Rights Commissions from San Francisco, Sacramento, and Los Angeles. The delegation held three days of meetings with Mexican and U.S. officials, as well as municipal and private agencies and advocates for immigrants. They visited border crossings and migrant camps, and held a roundtable panel in addition to community hearings on border violence. The delegation called for greater accountability of the Border Patrol and the INS. □

Center for Democratic Renewal • P.O. Box 50469, Atlanta, GA 30302-0469 • 404/221-0025

UAW training, Black Lake, Michigan, Civil Rights Division

The UAW's Leadership Role in the Campaign Against Bias and Bigotry

In 1946 the United Automobile, Aerospace and Agricultural Implement Workers of America (UAW) created a Fair Practices and Anti-Discrimination Department. In 1983, it changed its name to the Civil Rights Department to deal with discrimination based on race, sex, religion, national origin and handicap. Each union local is expected to establish a civil rights committee.

The civil rights department and the local committees help process complaints of discrimination against management through the federal government's Equal Employment Opportunity Commission. It also handles complaints of discrimination by members against other union members or officers.

The UAW's Civil Rights Department has also assisted its membership in fighting all forms of discrimination. The department participated in the March 4, 1990, re-enactment of the 1965 Selma-to-Montgomery civil rights march and the August 26, 1989, protest against recent U.S. Supreme Court rulings involving affirmative action. In cooperation with the UAW CAP, the Civil Rights Department organized crucial voter registration and get out the vote efforts during the 1991 Louisiana Governor's race when David Duke was a candidate. The same drive was conducted during the Jesse Helms-Harvey Gantt U.S. Senate race in North Carolina.

The department and local committees also participated in anti-apartheid demonstrations against the Reagan and Bush administration's support for the apartheid regime in South Africa; it also participated in the Shell boycott.

In 1987, UAW members participated in the march against Klan and racist violence and intimidation in Forsyth County, Georgia. Joe Davis, the director of the Civil Rights Department, and others were pelted with rocks and verbal abuse during part of the march.

In a resolution against the racism and violence of the Klan, the UAW pledged to "set the record straight about the KKK its violent and murderous past, its current goals and objectives by placing more emphasis on education, the litigation of hate crimes and by exposing those in our midst who profit from engendering racial discrimination, violence, or hate."

For more information on establishing an active civil rights committee in your local union, contact:

UAW Civil Rights Department
8000 E. Jefferson Avenue
Detroit, MI 48214
or
Richard Womack
AFL-CIO Civil Rights Department
815 16th Street, NW
Washington, DC 20006
(202) 637-5000

RESOLUTION OF THE UNITED AUTO WORKERS ON THE KU KLUX KLAN

WHEREAS: The Ku Klux Klan was born of racial and religious hatred and remains a cult of violence whose cowardly rites include the bullet in the back and the torch in the night; and

WHEREAS: Neo-Nazi, Skinheads, and other domestic terrorist groups have but one goal — to enslave the ignorant amongst us and to imbue us with their hatred of Blacks, Hispanics, Native Americans, Jews, Southeast Asians, Catholics, labor unions, and women; and

WHEREAS: Thousands of Blacks, Whites, Native Americans and Hispanics have been brutally slain during 300 years of slavery and "Jim Crow" era.

WHEREAS: The KKK, during WWI, and WWII and immediately thereafter, killed hundreds of Black American soldiers; slain in our southern communities. Many were lynched still in the uniform of the United States Army in which they fought, in North Africa, Italy, France, Germany, and South Pacific.

WHEREAS: In 1965, the KKK shot and killed Viola Liuzzo and has a history of lynching both blacks and whites working in the civil rights movement of the 1950's and 1960's; and

WHEREAS: In 1981, the KKK lynched Michael Donald in Mobile, Alabama a 19 year old Black youth; and

WHEREAS: In 1988, the Skinheads of Portland Oregon killed Mulugeta Seraw, an Ethiopian, by beating him to death with baseball bats, simply because he was Black; and

WHEREAS: In 1984, another White supremacist group called the Order shot and killed radio talk show host, Alan Berg because he was a Jew; and

WHEREAS: The moral disease manifested by the Ku Klux Klan is again spreading its sickness to cities and towns across the land; and

WHEREAS: The Klan's primary victims are the unprotected and the helpless who are marked solely because of their race, their color, or their religious faith; and

WHEREAS: Racist forces in this nation are attempting to bring back the days of lynch law; the days when non-white Americans were treated as second-class citizens; the days when robbery and murder were acceptable — as long as the victim was black; and

WHEREAS: The drive is spearheaded by the re-born Ku Klux Klan — the group which headed up such activities in the past and is trying to spur a new upsurge of violence racism; and

WHEREAS: Racism is an insidious force which turns worker against worker and results in splintered working class — ripe for exploitation by bosses; and

WHEREAS: In the past few years we have seen an alarming increase in activities involving the Ku Klux Klan, the American Nazi Party, Skinheads, the Order, Identity Church, Posse Comitatus, and other White Supremacist organizations; and

WHEREAS: The News Media has given a wide and prominent coverage to cross-burnings; rallies and marches; secret camps for the purpose of training KKK members in the use of deadly force including automatic weapons and explosives; recruitment posters prominently displayed in public places and distributed at local junior and senior high schools, etc.; and

WHEREAS: Most right wing organizations in the U.S., including the so-called Moral Majority have been totally silent on the activities and the announced goals of the KKK (the elimination of Blacks, Jews, and the Catholic Church); and

WHEREAS: The KKK and its sympathizers, if allowed to proliferate, would destroy all human rights organizations, including the Labor Movement.

NOW THEREFORE BE IT RESOLVED THAT: The United Auto Workers will marshal its resources to expose and combat the right-wing organizations who would threaten individual freedom in the United States; and BE IT FURTHER RESOLVED THAT:

The United Auto Workers will urge the AFL-CIO, and all other Labor Organizations to unite with Women's Organization and Civil Rights Organizations and others, to combat and stamp out those reactionary forces which would push the Unites States back 50 years.

THEREFORE BE IT FURTHER RESOLVED: That the UAW International Union urge the local unions in every area to join our allies in a determined effort to crush the KKK and all racism, bias and bigotry; and

THEREFORE BE IT FURTHER RESOLVED: That the UAW urges the Congress and the state legislatures and the city government to enact stronger protections for the civil rights of this nation's citizens and residents, with felony penalties for the practice of terrorism or violence on the basis of race, heritage, or religious faith; and

BE IT FURTHER RESOLVED: That the UAW calls for a full-scale investigation and hearings by the appropriate committee of Congress on the activities of the Ku Klux Klan and its relationship to acts of terrorism and violence; and

BE IT FURTHER RESOLVED: That with fresh memory of our recent experience with foreign terrorism, the UAW and urges all Americans to increase their vigilance against those at home and abroad, who would pervert this nation's fundamental premise of respect and tolerance for the rights of all individuals, so that all may enjoy their freedom in dignity and peace.

THEREFORE BE IT FINALLY RESOLVED: That we all make the effort, and strengthen the determination and will to set the record straight about the KKK, its violent and murderous past, its current goals and objectives by placing more emphasis on education, the litigation of hate crimes and by exposing those in our midst who profit from engendering racial discrimination, violence, or hate.

Center for Democratic Renewal • P.O. Box 50469, Atlanta, GA 30302-0469 • 404/221-0025

Indian Issues and Anti-Indian Organizing

Introduction

This section examines the evolution of modern anti-Indian movements in North America, and the varied ways that Indian and Indian support movements have responded to them. It also contends that anti-Indian movements cannot be countered without an understanding of deeper economic, political, and cultural issues.

While the nature of relations between the first European settlers in North America and the Continent's indigenous people was at times ambiguous, it did not take long before the colonies and, later, the American state launched an all-out assault against the native population.

Native Americans have survived against tall odds

Native lands were also coveted by railroad, mineral, logging, and other interests, which widely advertised the promise of "free land." Settlers were sent to claim land within the sovereign territories of many Indian nations, often unaware of or ill-prepared for the hostile reception they would face. The inevitable clash 'justified' a rescue by federal armed forces, thus securing the land for business interests. Tribal leaders were convinced, coerced, or tricked into signing a total of 371 treaties up through the 1870s, ceding almost all their land to the government, save for some small reservations. By Supreme Court ruling, these remaining tracts of land constitute "dependent nations."

While some Indian resistance was crushed by dramatic massacres, for the most part Native Americans were subdued by a combination of disease, alcohol, food rationing, the cooperation of Indian collaborators, and the theft of children for boarding schools — a situation not radically unlike today. The Bureau of Indian Affairs (BIA), until its transfer to the Interior Department, was part of the War Department. White homesteaders were used to police Indian people — some taking the task more seriously and viciously than the Army would have them, while others came to see Indian neighbors as good trading partners. In 1936, federal authorities established tribal councils on the reservations, with some superseding traditional forms of government.

Nevertheless, even against these overwhelming odds, the traditional cultures and religions (and even some governments) survived. Technologies and practices adapted to Western society, but the core values of Native peoples remained, including their strong relationship to the land.

The Anti-Indian Movement

The modern anti-Indian movement was created out of a non-Indian "backlash" against gains made by Indians since the 1960s. At least three major factors motivate anti-Indian groups.

1) The call for "equal rights for whites." This concept is based on the assumption that increased political and jurisdictional power of the tribes infringes on the liberties of the individual American taxpayer. The use of civil rights imagery can reach such extremes that whites are described as an oppressed people victimized by "Red Apartheid." The legacy of Dr. Martin Luther King, Jr., is invoked to support an agenda to roll back Indian rights.

Gains of the '60s Led to an Anti-Indian Backlash

2) Access to natural resources. These resources can be fish or game, land or water, but the case is the same: no citizens should have "special rights" to use the resources. The case is made in anti-treaty pamphlets such as "Are We Giving

SPEAR...

...THIS!!!

This sign was found in a tavern in the Eagle River, Wisconsin area prior to the 1987 spearing season.

America Back to the Indians?," "200 Million Custers," and the ironically titled book *Don't Blame the Indians: Native Americans and the Mechanized Destruction of Fish and Wildlife* by Massachusetts writer Ted Williams.

3) Economic dependency. In a rural reflection of the "Welfare Cadillac" myths used against urban African Americans, all reservation Indians are said to wallow in welfare, food stamps, free housing and medical care, affirmative action programs, and gargantuan federal cash payments — all tax-free, of course. (No one has to pay state sales tax on reservations, but otherwise Indians have had virtually identical tax obligations as non-Indians.) While any quick drive through a reservation will show the Third World conditions Indian people have to live under, anti-Indian groups maintain that these conditions are caused by alcoholism and the breakdown of the Indian family, rather than the reverse. In the same breath, the groups denounce any tribal effort to establish economic self-sufficiency, through appropriate industries, small businesses, tourism campaigns, gaming, or the sale of natural resources.

Anti-Indian groups deny any trace of racism, and will even point to members whose great-grandmothers were Indian in order to prove their point. There are also some racists who will make an 'exception' for Indians, whom they romanticize as noble savages resisting big government. Even such figures as Posse Comitatus leader James Wickstrom has written of Indians as a "pre-Christian warrior race" (not unlike Hitler's images of ancient Teutonic warriors) that is being driven off the land by "Jewish bankers."

The Northwest

The modern anti-Indian movement was born in the Pacific Northwest, and moved from there to the Northern Great Plains, the Upper Midwest, the Southwest, East Coast, and Canada. Along the Pacific coast, where tribal fish harvests form the basis of the traditional tribal economies, the backlash to Indian rights was first felt in the 1960s. In Washington, Oregon, and Northern California, these harvests were seen as a threat to the commercial fishing industry (despite the real threat posed by pollution and huge fishing trawlers). Washington anti-Indian groups mushroomed in the 1970s, after federal judge George Boldt ruled that tribal members were entitled to 50 percent of the state salmon harvest.

The leading anti-Indian group, ICERR (Interstate Congress for Equal Rights and Responsibilities), and several property owners' associations on Indian reservations were joined by such groups as Steelhead/Salmon Protective Association and Wildlife Network (S/SPAWN). The groups formed a base in state legislatures, in local communities, and among violence-prone vigilantes who regularly shot at and beat up Indians. At one point in the early 1980s, the anti-treaty forces got a statewide referendum passed, but could not sustain their movement after the state finally began to negotiate with the tribes on a government-to-government basis.

Meanwhile, in the Northern Great Plains, land and water disputes erupted between the tribes and white ranchers. The result was the formation of Montana groups like the East Slope Taxpayers Association, All Citizens Equal (ACE), and the Citizens Rights Organization (CRO); groups in the Dakotas like the Cheyenne River Landowners Association, and the North Dakota Committee for Equality; and Nebraska groups like the Concerned Citizens Council. Some of these groups have members living on reservations, which have been heavily allotted (divided) since the 1920s. Resident whites voted for Bennett County to secede from South Dakota's Pine Ridge Reservation, and other whites have opposed many forms of tribal jurisdiction.

Connections between some of these groups and organized right-wing networks also exist. The Center for World Indigenous Studies, based in Washington state, has documented links between anti-Indian groups and

Christian Identity and neo-Nazi organizations such as the Idaho-based Aryan Nations. In its report "Competing Sovereignties in North America and the Right-Wing and Anti-Indian Movements," the Center states that "individuals associated with the anti-Indian movement now appear to have occasional, if not frequent association with right-wing extremist groups."

The Midwest

In 1983 the United States Supreme Court *Voigt* decision affirmed the treaty rights of the Anishinabe (Chippewa) to harvest off-reservation natural resources in northern Wisconsin, northeastern Minnesota, and Michigan's Upper Peninsula. The decision upheld the treaties of 1837, 1842, and 1854, which secured United States access to the Lake Superior region's timber and copper. Many local settlers maintained a respectful relationship with the Chippewa through the 1800s — even protecting the Wisconsin Chippewa from forced removal — until the beginnings of sport fishing. Traditional Chippewa spearfishing in Wisconsin-ceded territory was outlawed in 1908. At the same time as the 1983 court ruling, mining companies began moving back into ceded territory, potentially endangering the fish, deer, and wild rice that the treaties guarantee to the Chippewa.

Anti-Indian sentiment in Northern Wisconsin — seemingly dormant since white vigilantes attacked Menominee Indians in 1975 — reemerged in opposition to the Chippewa in the 1980s. Some whites decried what they saw as the "rape" of the fish resource, vital to the local tourist economy, even though the Chippewa never took more than three percent of the fish. Among the local groups were Equal Rights for Everyone (ERFE), and the Wisconsin Alliance for Rights and Resources (WARR). The groups merged in 1987 with Protect Americans' Rights and Resources (PARR), led by paper mill foreman Larry Peterson. PARR committed itself to lobbying Congress to limit the legal power of the treaties. PARR had some clout in the state's powerful paper industry, which at one time unsuccessfully urged the state AFL-CIO to take an anti-treaty stance.

At the same time, protesters began gathering at boat landings on spring nights during the two-week Chippewa spearfishing season. They chanted taunts such as "timber niggers," "welfare warriors," and "spearchuckers," and carried signs reading, "Save a Spawning Walleye, Spear a Pregnant Squaw," and "Too Bad Custer Ran Out of Bullets." The often-drunk crowds threw rocks, bottles, and full beer cans. The image-conscious PARR leader-

> **Some whites decried what they saw as the "rape" of the fish resource, vital to the local tourist economy, even though the Chippewa never took more than three percent of the fish.**

ship left it up to individual members whether to protest at the lakes. This initial timidity led to the formation of a more militant group, Stop Treaty Abuse (STA), led by pizza parlor owner Dean Crist.

Crist marketed an alcoholic beverage he dubbed "Treaty Beer," and organized mass rallies and civil disobedience, claiming to take his inspiration from Dr. King.

Starting in 1988, STA organized thousands of protesters to go to the boat landings, and the level of violence increased markedly. On the roads leading to and from the lakes, spearers' and other treaty supporters' tires were slashed, vehicles run into ditches, and elders nearly run down. On the landings, Chippewa were assaulted, threatened with death, harassed with whistles and mock drum chants, and pipe bombs were exploded. On the lakes, spearing boats were rammed, swamped, and blockaded by protest boats, youths fired metal ball bearings with high-powered wristrocket slingshots, and snipers fired rifles from the shoreline. Spearer Walt Bresette said in 1990, "Currently, the only Chippewa who are spearfishing are those willing to risk their lives. Everyone else, through violence or threat of violence, has already lost their rights."

While the anti-treaty groups seem home-grown in the depressed northeastern counties of the state, some links are evident. Central Wisconsin is the headquarters of some right-wing populist groups, such as the John Birch Society and the Posse Comitatus. Crist was quoted in the Wisconsin State Journal in 1990 as saying that "David Duke is saying the same stuff we have been saying, like he might have been reading it from STA literature." In 1989, the *Milwaukee Sentinel* reported the formation of a death squad, armed with land mines and

Protesters at Lake Nokomis

Center for Democratic Renewal • P.O. Box 50469, Atlanta, GA 30302-0469 • 404/221-0025

Dean Crist, STA founder and anti-treaty activist

offering money for the assassination of two Indian leaders. The same year, notes were found of a phone call from the "ANUnderground" (a possible reference to the Aryan Nations) urging anti-Indian snipers to open fire on spearing boats on their way to the lakes. PARR leaders Wayne Powers and Darlene Hangartner also spoke at meetings of the state's minuscule Populist Party chapter; and Milwaukee Skinheads of the White Patriots League have attended PARR rallies.

Elsewhere in the Midwest, the potential still exists for similar anti-Indian movements to grow. Opposition to the Chippewa fishing in Michigan has developed since the 1979 *Fox* decision upheld treaty rights, resulting in groups such as the Michigan United Conservation Clubs (MUCC) and Enough Is Enough. In northeast Minnesota, only the Fond du Lac Chippewa spearfish, with no protests yet apparent. In Northwest Minnesota, some non-Indian residents of the White Earth Chippewa Reservation have opposed Chippewa claims on lands illegally allotted (divided) earlier this century. White Earth Equal Rights Committee and Totally Equal Americans (TEA) have taken up the cause. (As with timber and water rights, the issue of land rights has serious economic implications.) Elsewhere throughout the United States, the anti-Indian backlash also centers on cultural/religious issues, such as Indian efforts to change demeaning team mascots, to preserve burial sites, or rebury their dead interred in museums and displayed as curiosities and tourist attractions.

National Groups

Anti-Indian groups throughout the continent are beginning to better coordinate their efforts. Both PARR and ICERR say they are national organizations representing thousands of members throughout the United States.

But they and other groups have united in a national coalition known as the Citizens Equal Rights Alliance (CERA). Its executive and advisory boards reflect participation from at least 13 states. CERA's national headquarters and president, Bill Covey, are based in Montana. CERA concentrates on pressuring Congress to modify or abrogate treaties. Perhaps the most insidious national groups are those that use legitimate sports or conservation images to cover for their anti-Indian activity. Among these groups are Trout Unlimited, the National Wildlife Association, and the International Association of Fish and Wildlife Agencies. The potential for local chapters of other environmental, sports, animal rights, or resort owners organizations to be manipulated into anti-Indian groups is significant.

The Pro-Indian Movement

The pro-Indian movement contains both Indian and Indian support groups. Many of the support groups were specifically founded in response to the formation of anti-Indian groups, but have since taken on a life of their own and tackled other issues. The movement supports treaty rights, and counters racism, as well as cultural and religious bias directed against Indian people. The support groups take it as their duty to counter racism in their own non-Indian communities. This is done through cultural events, media work, TV and radio programs, distribution of factual materials, and the development of school curricula on Indian history and culture.

Wisconsin Indian groups won the introduction of a mandatory public school curriculum in 1990, largely because legislators agreed that anti-Indian beliefs should not so easily be passed on to the next generation. PARR announced plans to picket schools in protest of the move. In a strange twist, such anti-Indian groups have focused more public attention on Indian values and traditions, resulting in the long term in a wider public understanding — precisely the opposite of their goals. Some Chippewa have publicly thanked PARR for agitating against them, since they have made more legal gains than they would have in its absence. Other Indian groups around the continent also see anti-Indian activity as an ironic opportunity for improving their situation beyond the status quo that existed before that activity began.

Many Indian activists are acutely aware of government policies of "divide-and-conquer" when it comes to their white neighbors. Even more so than most support groups, some Indian groups have developed a sophisticated analysis of non-Indian communities, tying declines in the economy such as unemployment and the closing of small businesses to the search for an Indian scapegoat. They tend to emphasize the outside "common enemy" — whether governments or corporations — that confronts their communities. Tied to this com-

Center for Democratic Renewal • P.O. Box 50469, Atlanta, GA 30302-0469 • 404/221-0025

mon enemy is often a threat to the environment facing Indians and non-Indians alike.

In South Dakota, Lakota (Sioux) Indians and white ranchers were at odds over water rights in the 1970s, until underground water supplies were threatened by mining and energy interests. Lakota leaders approached the ranchers with the news that, if corporate plans were allowed to proceed, there would be no water left in ten years to argue about. Together with environmentalists they formed the Black Hills Alliance, which successfully headed off major mining and coal slurry projects. This three-way alliance was repeated around the country, from the Western Shoshone fight to stop the M-X missile in Nevada, to the Cowboy and Indian Alliance (CIA) in Montana's coal country, to Wisconsin rural whites' support for using Chippewa treaties to stop metallic sulfide mines.

Legal Strategies

Pro-Indian groups use legal, educational, organizing and action strategies to lessen the appeal and impact of anti-Indian groups. Legal strategies center both on strengthening the treaties in federal court and on blocking harassment by anti-Indian groups. Any court victory for the tribes presents anti-Indian groups with a *fait accompli*, since few such decisions have been overturned on appeal. The risk is, of course, that decisions can go both ways, and Indian nations can find their sovereignty infringed by unsympathetic judges and courts.

In Washington state, the anti-Indian movement was largely marginalized by a court decision mandating that state and tribal governments co-manage natural resources in treaty-ceded territories. The decision gave the tribes legal standing to limit off-reservation projects that may endanger salmon. The interest of the resource was put ahead of either Indian or non-Indian interests, removing S/SPAWN's main arguments.

In Wisconsin, federal judge Barbara Crabb issued a mixed series of rulings on the treaties during the late 1980s and early 1990s. In 1991, the Lac du Flambeau Chippewa asked her to keep protesters away from the boat landings, to order three county sheriffs to enforce laws against pro-testers, and to stop protesters from physical harassing tribal members, especially on the lakes. She rejected the first two requests, but granted the third — issuing an injunction that strictly limited STA's direct action options. The order was backed by undercover observers from the FBI and United States Marshals (who ironically were the main culprits in violence against the American

Indian Movement on the Pine Ridge reservation and elsewhere). Anti-Indian leaders also knew that the state's Hate Crimes Law could be used to stiffen penalties against them if they assaulted Indians. That law has since been ruled unconstitutional, however (see Legislative section). On the one hand, federal and state intervention may strengthen the identification of Indians with "big government" in the eyes of some populist-minded whites. On the other hand, Crabb's court order effectively scared hundreds of potential protesters away from the lakes, severely embarrassing both STA and PARR.

Education and Organizing Strategies

The most important long-term strategy employs both education and organizing. This is especially true in the white "border towns" near reservations, where even a small anti-racist minority can dramatically lessen anti-Indian sentiment. The use of reservation radio stations — such as WOJB on Lac Courte Oreilles (Wisconsin), and KILI on Pine Ridge — has proved invaluable in this effort. Many educational strategies focus on building cultural understanding, fostering knowledge about the legal basis of treaties, and promoting the idea of living in peace with one's neighbors.

Another approach is to refute the false claims made by anti-Indian groups about resources, welfare, and other issues. In doing so, it is important to recognize the irrationality of many of these claims, and realize they are put forth for deeper economic, political, and psychological reasons. In other words, if one "fact" is effectively disproven, it will quickly be replaced by another fraudulent claim. The "facts" are there to fill more substantive needs; only by addressing those needs, and putting forth an entirely new framework for viewing the conflict, can we hope to erode the grassroots base of anti-Indian groups. It is also important not to let these groups set the agenda for debate, with irrelevant discussions about fish populations or blood quantum statistics, but to focus on issues to which *they* have to respond.

> **Anti-Indian movements cannot be countered without an understanding of deeper economic, political, and cultural issues.**

Indian activists are often very familiar with their adversaries in anti-Indian groups. They may have gone to school together, or have had business relationships. These activists often refrain from taking on hard-core racist groups directly, preferring to address their comments to the groups' followers, who may be genuinely affected by the groups' scare tactics, or are simply going along for the excitement. Native leaders go through pains to emphasize that their land claims are not made at the expense of local non-Indians. In a key 1980 speech,

American Indian Movement leader Bill Means said that the Lakota claim to the sacred Black Hills covered only state, federal, and corporate-owned lands, not private landowners. A subsequent claims suit by the Sioux Nation Council narrowed in on government lands.

In a 1987 article in the *Daybreak* newspaper, Native journalist Ismaelillo offered an original educational approach to land claims disputes. He wrote that many white settlers were, in fact, lied to when the federal government told them they had clear title to their new homesteads. By not telling them of the clouded title stemming from previous Indian ownership, the government committed an act of fraud. People or local communities whose lands may be covered by Indian land claims could, therefore, refrain from taking action against the tribe, and instead sue the federal government for compensation, with Indian support. In Wisconsin, the Chippewa have taken a similar approach, by trying to redirect sports groups' anger toward state government, which has tied its lowering of fish bag limits to spearfishing, even though it knew for years that the real damage to the fish population was caused by habitat destruction and mismanagement.

Two parallel networks were born out of the Wisconsin treaty crisis, which worked in different but complementary ways. Honor Our Neighbors Origins and Rights (HONOR) is primarily a church-based organization, involved in lobbying, and working closely with tribal governments. It has focused most of its educational work on racism, whether from PARR and STA, or from the anti-timber rights agenda of the Wisconsin Counties Association. The Midwest Treaty Network (MTN) is a looser alliance of grassroots pro-treaty groups, including reservation associations. Its base is mainly in the environmental and social justice movements, and it helped create the Witness for Nonviolence to actively monitor violations of Chippewa rights. Its educational work stresses positive economic and environmental uses of the treaties. HONOR and MTN have grown together in the realization that they need to confront both the racism emerging in the region, and provide alternative plans for change that can pre-empt such racism in the future.

Action Strategies

Ultimately, once people have been educated, they can be mobilized. A number of successful action strategies have been used by Indian and Indian support movements to directly counter anti-Indian groups.

For example, STA leader Crist marketed Treaty Beer nationwide as a fundraising and publicity gimmick, but didn't realize how his product would unite pro-Indian groups. Mass rallies at the Washington state capitol secured a denunciation of "hate in a can" by the governor. On the steps of the Wisconsin state capitol, community leaders poured the beer into a pink toilet bowl. A Chicago Indian group successfully petitioned

FIVE GOALS OF THE WITNESS PROGRAM

The MTN's Witness program had five purposes, not all easily coexisting in the same project:

1) To be a presence for all the Chippewa families at the boat landings, so they don't take 100 percent of the abuse;

2) To show by this presence that not all non-Indians oppose treaty rights, as is often conveyed in the media;

3) To prevent a high level of tension and violence, with a calming influence, and the deterrent use of cameras and recorders;

4) To actively use nonviolent tactics to defuse tense or violent situations;

5) To document harassment, intimidation, and violence that does occur, using detailed notes, photos, and audio/video tape.

local liquor stores not to carry the product. Three breweries that started canning the beer — in Wisconsin, Ohio, and Louisiana — were one-by-one threatened with boycotts by HONOR, and dropped the "true brew of the working man." Crist gave up after four frustrating years.

Some action strategies require more commitment and risk. At the height of some conflicts, activists have put themselves physically between Indian and anti-Indian forces in visible displays of support. During the 1973 Wounded Knee siege, and the 1986 Big Mountain crisis, non-Indians stood in front of government forces attempting to evict people from the land. A peace camp was also set up between Mohawk and government positions in 1990 by the Montreal-based Centre for Nonviolence Resources. All these efforts are a way to express that any assault on Indian people could also injure non-Indians.

This strategy developed in a highly organized and effective way in Wisconsin, with the Witness for Nonviolence. The Witness started informally during the 1987 spearfishing season when local women stood with Chippewa friends at the boat landings, in a gesture of moral support. Within two years, the multiracial Witness came to involve treaty supporters not only from all parts of Wisconsin, but from around the nation and world. By 1991, a total of about 2000 treaty supporters had documented anti-Indian harassment at the lakes.

Red Cliff spearer Andrew Gokee commented that "The more Witnesses on a given night, the more peaceful the lake will be." Even some protesters have been heard to say to each other, "Don't say that, the

Witnesses will hear you." Other protesters have said to Witnesses, "You white people are all traitors," and "We have red niggers, black niggers, and a few white niggers, too."

Witnesses are not pro-treaty protesters. At the Chippewa's request, they don't wear political buttons, carry signs, chant slogans, or carry on any unnecessary dialogue with the anti-treaty protesters. They are identified only by white armbands, and have signed a pledge of peace saying they will not participate in any conflict. Yet state and federal politicians tried to discredit Witnesses as merely the pro-treaty counterparts of PARR and STA, and as an obstacle to peace. This may be because one of the main targets of documentation has been the state-coordinated law enforcement effort, which has been spotty at best. While in some counties riot police helped protect the Chippewa, in counties with the largest PARR/STA memberships, many officers either looked the other way, or openly sympathized with the protests. The 1990 Witness report detailed incidents of racial intimidation, violence, and police response. The documentation was used not only for legal purposes, but for political purposes, such as responding to Gov. Thompson's contention that little racism was evident at the protests, and there were "no ugly incidents."

By 1991, the Chippewa and Witnesses regularly outnumbered the dwindling numbers of protesters during the spearing season. The media proclaimed 'Crist's Last Stand,' but it is abundantly clear that STA and PARR are down to a hard core that is far more racist and threatening.

Both a continuing Witness and police presence will be needed in the future. Some resort owners stopped supporting the groups because their racism and violence began to keep tourists away. And the fact that groups claiming to protect fish didn't lift a finger about threats from mercury and mining was not lost on environmentally conscious Wisconsinites. In a May 1991, *Wisconsin State Journal* poll, 59 percent of southern Wisconsinites supported treaty rights, and an amazing 42 percent of northerners agreed.

As each year passes, the Witness wrestles with various questions. Witness' obvious support for the Chippewa, such as standing between the protesters and the drum, can at times lessen the credibility of their documentation, unless it is collected by unimpeachable electronic means (such as camcorders). Also, protesters' attacks on Witnesses can become a media issue, detracting attention from attacks on Indians, unless it is made clear that Indians remain the primary target, and Witnesses are only present at their invitation.

Other potential pitfalls need to be addressed by Indian support groups. One is the stereotyping of working-class whites as "rednecks," without taking into account the similar economic forces working against both reservation and off-reservation communities. Local whites should be encouraged and supported to take a strong role in Indian support work. Another area to develop is a respectful relationship with grassroots Indian organizers, by keeping out of internal tribal politics. Non-Indians should limit their involvement in Indian issues to questions that revolve around non-Indian individuals and governments to limit Indian rights. Lastly, the cultural distinctiveness of Indian peoples needs to be protected not only from racists, but from romantic New Age consumerists of the "Wannabe" tribe, and from political activists who see Indian resistance as identical to other anti-racist struggles, lacking its unique national, cultural and spiritual dimensions.

Center for Democratic Renewal • P.O. Box 50469, Atlanta, GA 30302-0469 • 404/221-0025

GOVERNMENT AGENCY RESPONSE

Introduction

Government has a special responsibility to respond to hate violence and organized hate group activity. The 14th Amendment of the U.S. Constitution might guarantee "equal protection" and "due process" to racial, religious, and ethnic "minorities," but without the will to enforce laws at the local, state and national levels, the Constitution is meaningless.

This chapter deals with government agencies — mainly state and local human relations councils, governor-appointed task forces, and law enforcement agencies. It is designed for professionals in those areas, as well as citizens who desire to make their state and local government more accountable to issues of bigoted violence and hate activity.

Government's Response Must Be Accountable

The late 1980s brought an upsurge of response to neo-Nazi groups at the national level, whose revolutionary approach led groups such as the Order and the Posse Comitatus to target law enforcement officers and public officials for assassination because they were seen as agents of "ZOG," or the Zionist Occupational Government. When government officials were targeted, both personally and institutionally, it gave them a different stake in investigating, prosecuting, and countering far right groups. Federal action has sometimes helped to initiate stronger state and local action over the past five years.

Human Relations Commissions

Strong leadership at the state level can make a big difference in combatting hate activity. Usually this response comes from state and local Human Relations (or "Human Rights") Commissions and state-level task forces. Many HRCs were set up in the late 1960s in response to the demands of the African American freedom movement. Today these agencies have an important role to play in catalyzing responses to hate violence and organized far right activity.

The effectiveness of HRCs and Task Forces vary widely. State HRCs generally have both professional staff and a board of volunteer citizens appointed by the governor. HRCs in larger cities also have professional staff and a similar volunteer commission. In other counties and municipalities, there is often no staff, only volunteer commissioners. Other places, there is nothing at all. Some HRCs have subpoena powers for investigating incidents, some don't. Some have full staffs, others are sorely underfunded. In this age of budget cutting and with federal deficits passed on to state

Effectiveness of HRCs and Task Forces Varies Widely

legislatures, there are, unfortunately, likely to be fewer resources to deal with hate activity just as the economy may be breeding more of the kinds of pressures from which scapegoating grows.

Because both professionals and volunteers are political appointees, shifts in political climate and election turnovers can create problems for long-term programming. HRCs can also be hampered in their handling of politically sensitive cases.

Often after a highly visible incident or series of attacks, adverse publicity will create the political demand for politicians and government officials to shape an official response. For example, for years, Georgia had no state HRC, although Klan activity in Georgia led the nation. After the national notoriety of white supremacist attacks on a brotherhood march in Forsyth County, the Governor rapidly commissioned a state HRC. "Often they only want us when there's blood on the street," commented Adele

Terrell, Program Director for the National Institute Against Prejudice and Violence. Sustaining program and momentum after the spotlight turns away is part of the challenge to government human relations workers.

In spite of these political limits, even one or two dedicated people within a HRC can make a big difference. State agencies can help to legitimize and broaden coalitions opposing hate activity. HRCs and Task Forces can be especially effective leveraging responses from other government agencies, such as law enforcement, public schools, and legislators. Such agencies, however, can also play negative roles, trying to merely "keep the lid on" potentially explosive situations or to control activism. Government agencies that appear to be engaged in cover-ups lose legitimacy, especially with communities targeted by hate activity. It is ultimately up to citizens to make state and local governments accountable to their needs.

The Maryland Model

In the early 1980s, when people all over the country were beginning to realize the United States was in the midst of a resurgence of far right activity, Maryland provided one of the best models of proactive government response at the state and local level. A state coalition of business, religious, and civic leaders sparked a governor-appointed task force, and Montgomery County initiated highly effective local programming.

Incidents of racist and anti-Semitic violence were spiraling in Maryland in the early eighties. In one major metropolitan city alone in 1980, incidents doubled. About 100 African American and Jewish leaders met over several months in Baltimore in early 1980 to consider the disturbing upsurge in Klan activity and anti-Semitic and racist violence. Incident after incident of bigoted violence in the early months of 1981 sent additional signals of alarm. While each group represented at the meetings — the Baltimore Jewish Council, the Urban League, the NAACP, the National Conference of Christians and Jews, the Maryland Human Relations Commission, the Anti-Defamation League, and others — had worked individually toward lessening racial and religious bigotry, there had been no coordinated response. In fact, most of these groups had maintained a public silence of sorts, fearing that to speak out would aggravate the problem. Realizing that events required a shift in strategy, they decided to coordinate their efforts. The working group gave itself the name of Coalition Opposed to Violence and Extremism (COVE) and decided to hold a statewide conference.

Representatives of COVE began to fan out across the city and state to publicize the conference, but they met surprising ignorance and resistance. Despite their credentials, COVE members found they needed institutional credibility, so they sought and won the support of Governor Harry Hughes. Hughes created a Governor's

---

The Five Goals of COVE

1) To define and measure the extent of the problem;
2) To develop a reporting and recording system for racial, religious and ethnic incidents;
3) To meet the needs of victims in a systematic way;
4) To design effective public education, and;
5) To establish a speakers' bureau and statewide information service.

Task Force on Violence and Extremism, which coordinated public-sector efforts as COVE approached the private sector. Agency heads from law enforcement, secondary and higher education, juvenile programs, the attorney general's office, the legislature, the governor's office and more were assigned to the task force.

The task force worked with the Maryland Human Relations Council to carry out this agenda, activating local HRCs as well. When Governor Hughes asked the task force to come back with data and information on hate crimes and responses nationwide, the reply he got was: "There isn't any." He put his money where his mouth was, and under his leadership the state gave seed funding to start the National Institute Against Prejudice and Violence — $100,000 for the first year's budget.

Both COVE and the task force (renamed the Governor's Advisory Committee when Hughes left office) have maintained anti-hate programming for over a decade. Recently, COVE met with heads of the county school systems and the state superintendent of schools to try to get cooperation on data collection in public schools. COVE helped to sponsor police training programs as well, and recently lobbied for the inclusion of sexual orientation as a category in the state's hate crimes data collection law. In 1990, work by the Governor's Advisory Committee resulted in mandatory training on hate violence for all police officers in Maryland.

In Montgomery County, which borders Washington, D.C., the late 1970s had also brought an escalation of cross burnings, vandalism, and attacks, to which public officials had been slow to respond. Community leaders, like their state counterparts, first thought the best way to deal with racist and religious violence was quietly, behind the scenes. By June 1981, inspired by the Governor's actions, County Executive Charles Gilchrist called a meeting of 100 leaders from all segments of the community to bring the battle against hate violence into the open and to ask for support.

He announced the Montgomery County Coordinating Committee on Hate Violence, composed of religious, business, labor, community and education leaders, to coordinate public/private partnership. The Montgomery County HRC serves as the administrative arm, to carry out the Committee policy. The Committee immediately set about its work, encouraging the police department to sign a memorandum of cooperation with the HRC, encouraging the PTA to hold a human relations workshop for parents, urging the Chamber of Commerce to educate business and civic leaders. The Committee and the HRC also worked with the schools to create anti-hate materials, including training resources for teachers and administrators on handling hate/violence conflicts and adding a new unit to its secondary-level contemporary issues course on "Hate and Violence Groups in American Society." The HRC also created an innovative program of education and counseling to work with youthful bias crime offenders.

One of the HRC's most successful programs is the Network of Neighbors, put in place to give help to victims of racist or religious violence. The Network functions with help from the county police under an agreement formalized in a "memorandum of understanding." When a hate/violence incident occurs, the police department notifies the HRC. If the victim wants to talk to someone for support, the HRC puts her or him in contact with a network member. A Network of Teens was also established in 1982 to recruit youthful members who would reach out to offer support for peers who are victimized. There are two trainings yearly for both networks.

Recently, the HRC started a summer camp program, bringing diverse groups of teens together for human relations exercises and to share fun and life experiences. Trainings originally designed for police in hate violence, sexual harassment and cultural awareness are also now being conducted in work places. The county matches two to one private contributions to a Partnership Fund for victims of hate violence. The HRC also sponsors a Police/Language Minorities Dialogue Program to overcome immigrants' and refugees' fears of reporting crimes.

Over the years, the Montgomery County programs seem to pay off. The juvenile offender program — which now uses a network of teens and summer camp students to act as assistant facilitators

— has resulted in remarkably low rates of recidivism for teen offenders. Parents are required to attend as well, and an unexpected offshoot has been improved communications between teens and their parents, as well as greater parental awareness of how they might have passed on prejudices to their children.

Part of Montgomery County's success over the years comes from its tax base. As both a liberal and an affluent county, its leaders and citizens have had both the will and the tax dollars to devote to combatting hate crimes.

Documenting Hate Crimes

Documenting organized hate group activity and bigoted violence is one key role of HRCs. Government agencies often have more access to police reporting systems, and government-released information is often given more credibility by the media and the general public. For instance, after skinheads murdered Mulegata Seraw in Portland, Oregon in 1988, there was an upsurge in bigoted attacks in the city. Georgia Owens of the Metropolitan Human Relations Council staff was in charge of documentation. She established contacts with the five police jurisdictions in Portland and began to collect their reports on bias crimes. Each week the chief would send out a memo of "items of interest" highlighting the week's crimes. Owens would look closely at these lists to identify incidents that might be bias-related, then she would ask officers to check back into them. Half the cases were subsequently reclassified as bias crimes. In 1989 she compiled a report to establish

Ten Things HRCs Can Do

1. Help shape and lobby for legislation at the state and municipal level.
2. Organize victims' support, either directly using staff or through networks such as Network of Neighbors or Peace Patrols.
3. Encourage school officials to institute policies to deal with bigotry and hate incidents and use curricula on the history of the Klan and Nazis, the civil rights movement, African American history and the Holocaust.
4. Investigate incidents of bigoted violence with your staff or commissioners or through public hearings.
5. Organize responses to Klan marches or other types of recruitment activity.
6. Educate the community about hate activity through such events as forums or conferences.
7. Document hate activity — compile data on hate group organizing and bigoted violence and issue periodical reports to educate the public.
8. Educate the media on appropriate coverage of Klan-type activity.
9. Encourage public officials to speak out.
10. Organize liaison with police to establish protocols to deal with bias crimes as well as to facilitate police training.

Center for Democratic Renewal • P.O. Box 50469, Atlanta, GA 30302-0469 • 404/221-0025

Rising homophobia was discussed at a conference in Seattle, Washington.

"baseline data and a framework for annual reporting of hate crimes." On the basis of the report, the Metro HRC was also able to make a range of suggestions for community action.

Getting adequate documentation from immigrant groups takes special efforts, according to Eugene Mornell at the Los Angeles County Human Relations Council, which has been monitoring hate crime for eleven years. The Los Angeles HRC issues an annual report based on data from law enforcement and community groups. Many of their recommendations have been implemented, such as increased penalties for perpetrators and a county-wide task force.

In North Carolina, the state Human Relations Council began documenting hate crimes in the mid-1980s after national Klan-watching agencies reported that the state had some of the most active hate groups in the U.S. CDR and its affiliate, North Carolinians Against Racist and Religious Violence, had issued reports chronicling a wide range of activities. The HRC entered the picture, held hearings across the state, and issued its own report, calling on public officials to no longer ignore Klan activity and recommending that the Governor appoint a task force. In 1986, Governor James Martin responded and appointed the Task Force on Racial, Religious and Ethnic Violence and Intimidation, to be staffed by the state HRC. One of the first acts of the Task Force was to

establish an 800 number to report bigoted incidents. The Task Force is also working to encourage local law enforcement to add a check-off box for hate crimes on the state's uniform crime reporting form.

HRCs with subpoena power can go beyond compilation of data and conduct their own investigations. In Harrisburg, Pennsylvania, the local human relations council investigated charges that law enforcement officers had worn small KKK pins or tie clasps on their uniforms and that two of the officers had sold the pins while on duty and with the knowledge of their superiors. Using its subpoena power, the HRC substantiated the accusations and worked out an agreement with the mayor, public safety director, black police officers' association, and others calling for the officers to be disciplined. Although the mayor later reneged on the deal, the commission had exposed the truth and advocated for citizens whose rights were being abused.

Victim Advocacy

Victim advocacy is another important role that Human Relations Councils can play. Montgomery County's "Network of Neighbors" is one such model. In other cases, HRC staff can intervene directly, especially where local law enforcement fails to respond. In West Virginia, a black family who had moved into an all-white rural area was attacked repeatedly and the dispatcher at the sheriff's department refused to even send an officer to investigate. HRC staff went to the community and worked with a sympathetic doctor, who was also chair of the county commission. They formed a local task force, which was able to pressure the sheriff's department to investigate. The case was solved, and the harassment stopped.

In Portland after the Seraw murder, the Metropolitan HRC collected money throughout the Pacific Northwest to pay for the gravestone; and when Mr. Seraw came from Ethiopia to visit his son's grave, he asked Georgia Owens to accompany him. "It was one of the hardest things I had to do," she recalls.

Community Programming

Community programming by HRCs can help educate the public about hate activity and shape citizen responses. In Georgia, the state HRC appointed by Governor Harris after the Forsyth County incident proclaimed 1990 the "Year of the Multicultural Society." The HRC used the highly publicized event to bring people together and establish networks to continue effective work. An intercultural speakers bureau provided education in the schools. A five-weekend festival at Underground Atlanta highlighted a different geographical region of the world each weekend and got people to talking with each other. Cross-cultural communications training with law enforcement got the HRC's foot in the door with police. A statewide conference brought people together to discuss a range of issues. "In the session on religion," recalls Director Joy Berry, "it was the first time that many of the people representing a broad variety of religions had been in the same room together. They are continuing to come together in an Interfaith/Intercultural Coalition to figure out how to work together and within their own congregations."

In Kansas City, Missouri, when a local Klan group tried to run its own program on the local cable access station in 1988, there was an uproar, with deep and vocal splits in the community around First Amendment issues. As a result, Mayor Richard Berkeley appointed a Mayor's Commission on Hate Group Activities. After weeks of intensive study and a public hearing, the Commission submitted an extensive report to the city council. It recommended increased penalties and wider definitions for hate crimes (including sexual orientation); a local anti-bias ordinance; police systems for gathering hate crime statistics and training for law enforcement on bias crime; a monitoring review committee ("to record and analyze bias crimes and incidents on a metropolitan area-wide basis" and to develop an educational brochure on bias crimes for distribution to government and community agencies); a public education campaign involving neighborhood organizations, unions, mass media, schools, and religious organizations; and a community strategy team to handle unusual situations such as public demonstrations by hate groups.

The Kansas City Police Department voluntarily adopted guidelines to keep data on bias crime, then instituted trainings for law enforcement officers. The Commission's ordinance against bias crime, however, was derailed by vocal opposition to gay and lesbian rights. Other programming was affected by budgetary considerations.

The Los Angeles Human Relations Council has an active program to counter intra-racial tensions, heightened by rapidly shifting demographics and the presence of Korean-owned small-businesses in African American neighborhoods.

Tension often arises between the merchants and their clients over cultural differences, crime, and the antagonism toward economic "middle men" who are perceived as exploiting the community. In 1986, after four Korean merchants were murdered in a three week period, the Los Angeles HRC launched the Black-Korean Alliance to try to bridge the different cultural communities. It has met regularly since then, attempting proactive programming such as cultural and pulpit exchanges, as well as becoming involved in mediation when incidents occur, such as the shooting of a black female teenager by a Korean woman in March 1991. The HRC holds community meetings, eliciting lists of problems, and then follows-up with specific proposals in each area, enlisting committees from both communities to begin working on them.

Larry Aubry, HRC staffer in charge of these programs, assesses frankly, "We haven't yet engaged enough of the residents and the merchants themselves in these neighborhoods. We are working more through representatives of both communities. Also, in these sections of town, we are dealing with a worst-case scenario, in terms of poverty, education, employment, and housing. Government accountability and private sector involvement are crucial to help change the bottom-line conditions that generate these tensions."

The Black-Korean Alliance also worked to relieve tensions after the 1992 rebellion in south central Los Angeles.

In Portland, the HRC Director, under whose leadership much of the work had been done, left to take a job

> **HRCs can educate the community and shape citizen responses to hate group activity.**

with the Governor, pressured in part by Commission members who felt she was "doing too much." In North Carolina, the HRC efforts to put in place monitoring and victim advocacy networks have been hampered by an "on again-off again" Task Force and a weak commitment from the Governor. The Raleigh (North Carolina) Human Resources and Human Relations Task Force was threatened with defunding by the City Council when it backed African American youth against a local shopping mall trying to keep them out.

In Seattle, CDR affiliates chose not the Human Relations Council, but the city's Office of Neighborhoods through which to shape a citizen-based response to hate activity. Seattle prides itself on being a "city of neighborhoods" and had a strong neighborhood program in the 1970s, with active community councils. Organizers decided to work on reviving these neighborhood councils — a form of "democratic renewal" — encouraging them to hold neighborhood hearings to take testimony on hate violence. At first, police and the mayor were skeptical. But organizers went ahead in the Capitol Hill area, contacting civil rights organizations, schools, the Chamber of Commerce, and going door to door. At the hearing, fifty incidents of hate crime emerged — surprising most people, including the police (who had not sent an official representative). The Capitol Hill community followed-up with a meeting and sent their recommendations on to the mayor, who by then was ready to receive them enthusiastically. Capitol Hill residents also organized a neighborhood patrol, and several additional hearings were held in other neighborhoods.

"We wanted to work from the bottom up," commented Deni Yamauchi, former CDR Northwest staffer. "We didn't need government authorization to hold these hearings. We apprised them of our findings. We wanted to show that groups of citizens could get involved to truly change the city." ■

THE MEDIA AND HATE GROUPS

Introduction

This section is for journalists and media professionals, as well as others who are planning to cover news stories involving white supremacists. It discusses libel and "dirty tricks" operations, as well as the dilemmas news organizations face when deciding when and how to cover the Ku Klux Klan or neo-Nazis.

Mention white supremacy today, and most people still think of the KKK: potbellied rednecks in Mississippi in 1963. In reality, the white supremacist movement is very different in the 1990s, and so too is the challenge facing reporters, editors and producers who must cover the contemporary bigot beat.

Pitfalls Include Too Much Coverage...and Too Little

White supremacists want all the publicity they can get — preferably on their own terms — while others in the community may want newspapers and broadcast stations to ignore hate group activity altogether.

Both approaches are wrong. Ben Bagdikian, the author of several books on the media, told the *Kansas City Star*, "I think there are two pitfalls we face...one is doing too little and the other is doing too much."

Giving white supremacists unlimited coverage spreads and legitimizes their message of hate. Unfortunately this type of coverage has been all too common in white-owned newspapers and on radio and television stations.

Television and talk radio are especially vulnerable to articulate, unembarrassed white supremacists because these media thrive on controversy; a Klansman or neo-Nazi willing to debate his or her beliefs on camera or to a live call-in audience is a sure ratings booster, and far too many producers look no further.

On the other hand, it is real news when white supremacists are active. If the reporting is professional, editors and news directors have no reason to fear that they are boosting groups like the KKK, Skinheads or the Aryan Nations.

In the end, the journalists must decide how to cover hate-related events. Guidelines, however, can be helpful. The following suggestions are based on a study of news stories over the past few years and on the comments of a number of journalists.

1. *Do a thorough investigative job*

Few news organizations can afford to assign a Jerry Thompson (Nashville *Tennessean*) or a Dan Gearino (Flint, Michigan, *Journal*) to infiltrate a Klan or neo-Nazi group for months. However, the white supremacists are a news subject that demands extraordinary critical examination by reporters.

Reporters Are Often Slow to Dig Into KKK Claims

For example, when David Duke first ran as a Republican for the Louisiana state legislature, reporters rarely bothered to study his long career of neo-Nazi and Klan organizing, or to compare his radically racist speeches and writings of the past with his recent political statements. Not until late in Duke's 1991 Louisiana gubernatorial campaign — when it became clear that Duke was attracting a large vote from the white middle class and could possibly win — did reporters in his home state begin really digging into his background.

Similarly, many white supremacist leaders have criminal convictions that bear looking into, as a violent past may indicate a pattern of behavior by so-called

Center for Democratic Renewal • P.O. Box 50469, Atlanta, GA 30302-0469 • 404/221-0025

"reformed" leaders. The relationships between different hate groups may also be useful way for the thorough investigator to link these groups to violent activities.

2. Editors should assign the same reporters to the hate beat over an extended period of time.

This gives the reporters a chance to develop a real expertise on the subject, as well as a unique set of information sources. If at all possible, political, race relations or investigative reporters should be assigned, rather than general assignment or crime reporters.

Most reporters are assigned infrequently to cover stories involving white supremacists. When they are assigned, they rarely have time for background research. As a result, they are particularly vulnerable to manipulation.

Some white supremacist leaders, on the other hand, are frequent guests on radio and TV talk shows. They are interviewed dozens of times each month — particularly when a news story is breaking.

They are skilled at manipulating press conferences and interviews and staging media events which obscure the truth. Remember that for every one time a reporter interviews a white supremacist, that white supremacist has the experience of at least 100 interviews under his or her belt.

3. Reporters should attempt to pierce the mystique and deceptions that white supremacists try to affect.

"Because of its history of violence, there is still an ominous air of mystery surrounding the KKK," said William R. Moushey Jr., editor of *Pittsburger Magazine.* "To add to the drama, Klansmen usually display some high-powered weapons during interviews. The weaponry, meant to be intimidating, makes for a great bit of film for the evening news."

Faced with such "theater," ordinarily-skeptical reporters have taken at face value fictional statements by Klansmen or neo-Nazis, and have printed them without independent verification.

The Flint *Journal's* Gearino, who spent eight months on leave from his newspaper posing as a Klansman, wrote a series which illustrated this point. One article revealed that "a single interview by a weekly newspaper reporter resulted in a front-page story that announced to the small Michigan town of Fenton that its local Klan Klavern harbored 50 active members. In reality, there was only one Klansman. The other eight robed men at the interview were from out of town." Gearino concluded, "While recruiting efforts in that area had been largely futile, the newspaper report sparked dozens of membership inquiries."

The best preventive medicine is for reporters to

check with local, state and federal investigative agencies, and any of several private watchdog groups, like the Center for Democratic Renewal, Klanwatch, the American Jewish Committee or the Anti-Defamation League. These sources provide good estimates of hate group membership and activity and can help individual reporters with background information.

4. *Don't overplay news about white supremacists.*

The effects of reporting too often about the Klan could be seen in retrospect in Meriden, Connecticut, after almost a year of Klan and counter-Klan activity. In the fall of 1981, the news media began to appraise its role in covering the Klan, in response to criticisms of over-coverage and naive handling of a complex situation.

After the state's largest daily, the Hartford *Courant*, had run 17 page one stories on the Klan during a two-month span, one of the paper's editorial writers admitted that the paper had over-reacted and had failed to investigate stories adequately. The news director of a New Haven television station also admitted that his staffers had been manipulated by the Klan.

The Norfolk *Virginian-Pilot* ran an entire column of self-analysis and criticism following a Klan rally in early 1982 in Raleigh, North Carolina. Only 20 Klan members showed up for the rally which lasted only 20 minutes — hardly major news. Yet the *Pilot* treated it as an important news story.

5. *Let readers and viewers see the real Klan or neo-Nazis.*

Admittedly, white supremacists are a "sexy" news subject, but journalists must place responsibility ahead of ratings when doing such reporting. This task is made difficult by sophisticated racists whose public relations skills distort the truth of the continuing violence and anti-democratic philosophies.

Unfortunately, those subjects are sometimes too complex to be covered by reporters working on breaking news stories, so journalists resort to the cheap but easy tale of a dozen or so fanatics marching down Main Street and spewing out racial hatred. Dean Calbreath wrote in the *Columbia Journalism Review*, "We get good quotes that way, and a safe sexy story, but often wind up becoming nothing less than flacks for (Klan leaders)."

Journalists often believe that readers seeing straight-

Should Human Rights Advocates Do Television Programs With White Supremacists?

Television programs, particularly daytime talk shows, have increasingly used conflict between white supremacists and their opponents to stage confrontations and drive up ratings. This situation has created a dilemma for human rights advocates who wish to publicize their point of view. They don't want to "surrender the airwaves" to the white supremacists. At the same time, appearing on TV gives the appearance that racism and anti-racism are simply two different points of view, among which reasonable people can disagree. It dignifies the bigots and increases their legitimacy.

In 1988 and 1989 several television talk shows, including Oprah Winfrey and Geraldo Rivera, featured panels of young skinhead neo-Nazis, which were then a breaking news story.

Some talk show producers believe that by featuring white supremacists they shed light on an important topic and that the Klansmen and neo-Nazis were easily discredited. On several programs, conflict, even violent conflict, has erupted. When a White Aryan Resistance leader broke a chair over Geraldo Rivera's nose, the television program itself became a news item and the subject of controversy.

Instead of being discredited, however, the white supremacists received dozens — sometimes hundreds — of new inquiries for membership and literature. For many young white people, television appearances by skinhead neo-Nazis visually intertwine defiance of convention and authority with white supremacy. No amount of commentary about bigotry or racist violence can undo the powerful impact of young racists asserting themselves on TV. Verbiage is almost always a secondary element in television, which primarily depends on visual images to create lasting impressions.

CDR recommends that human rights advocates not appear on such conflict-driven formats.

When deciding whether or not to appear on television or radio programs, the following should be considered:

• Is the purpose of the program conflict and controversy or the straightforward presentation of news?

• Will the moderator or program host set the direction of the news segment, or will it be determined by the most forceful guest?

• Is there a news package which precedes the live interviews and sets the tone for the following discussion?

Under most non-news circumstances, appearing on television or radio with white supremacists only increases their stature and lends credibility to their cause.

How to Cover the Dukester

By Lanny Kellar

Most Louisiana newspapers tried the "less is more" strategy when David Duke ran for the U.S. Senate in 1990.

Duke nevertheless stunned the political establishment with 44 percent of the vote, and a runoff was avoided only because the official Republican Party nominee withdrew at the last minute. In 1991, Duke rolled into the gubernatorial runoff despite wide press endorsement of the incumbent. In the runoff, virtually every newspaper began editorial campaigns against Duke as the short-term economic interests of publishers (cancellations from Duke supporters) were overridden by the larger threat of boycotts of industry and conventions in Louisiana.

This lurching back and forth wasn't exactly "Profiles in Courage," but it produced some lessons about covering Duke.

1. He isn't a normal candidate. The National Press Club was filled with journalists in early 1992 when Duke announced his campaign for President, and it was virtually a C-SPAN advertisement for Duke.

He quipped his way past complex issues, and rarely were there follow-up questions that could have demonstrated his virtually complete ignorance of the facts. It was as if the Louisiana gubernatorial race had been totally ignored by a Washington press corps that showed up to poke at this new jellyfish washed up on the political beach.

Duke does not arrive at a position on, say, immigration, from a values-neutral context. He comes at the issue from a lifelong commitment to eugenics and the white supremacy movement. To cover Duke in a values-neutral fashion is to play into his hands.

2. He is a normal candidate. Duke is normal, at least in the very specific sense that he should be asked to explain his program, justify his numbers, show some specific knowledge of issues. Panelists on "Meet the Press" stumped Duke by asking him to name the three largest employers in Louisiana.

Such glib Duke campaign promises as a flat 10-percent income tax are not backed up by logic or reason. There is much news to mine

here, especially glaring inconsistencies between the Duke right-wing platform and the economic interests of his low-income supporters.

3. He must be taken seriously, because he is dangerous. This is not the two-headed baby of the political carnival. Duke's success is built on almost 20 years of experience at inflaming racial disputes, from burning crosses in Forsyth County, Georgia, to organizing vigilante squads against Mexicans on the Southwest border. His contributors are not only harmless suburban bigots. Various Duke staffers have graduated from notorious groups such as the Liberty Lobby. Further, covering Duke can be a harrowing experience; some reporters have been spat upon, some threatened physically.

Editors must assign reporters who can follow Duke at length. The Dukester suggests Joe McCarthy in the 1950s, with his ability to make outrageous and unsubstantiated allegations and then skip town before the facts can catch up.

"There is no silver bullet in covering this guy," said Jim Roberts, of KTBS-TV in Shreveport, who covered Duke in the 1991 race. Roberts said the one-shot question that will expose Duke as a phony does not exist. He requires journalistic follow-up.

4. Don't feel sorry for the guy. David Duke works himself up into a lather of indignant self-pity at the criticisms of "the liberal media." Duke told the Society of Professional Journalists that reporting about his iniquitous background represents a "double standard" compared to coverage of U.S. Sen. Robert Byrd of West Virginia, who in his youth was briefly a Klan member; comparatively, Duke is a 41-year-old senior citizen of hate groups.

Duke courts media attention, then whines about critics. "Sometimes I just get in the shower and let the hot water wipe away the tears," he said.

When I feel a glimmer of pity for this guy, I think about friends of mine in Shreveport who will carry to their graves the tattoo of Auschwitz. That was motivation enough to explain and editorialize about Mr. Duke.

Lanny Kellar writes for the Shreveport, La., Journal.

forward reports on hate groups can supply their own context, but this often is not the case. Journalists have the responsibility to put hate group rhetoric in the context of history and current activities. The sensationalism of the subject must take a back seat to the substance. Reporting on white supremacist activities is hard work, and requires research and a nose for smoke and lies.

6. *Don't be used*

Although this is more a problem in television and radio, print media is also often manipulated to the direct benefit of white supremacists, almost in lieu of actual paid advertising.

Allowing white supremacists to give out their addresses and telephone numbers on the air is, perhaps, the most obvious example of media manipulation. David Duke, Tom Metzger, and other hate group leaders report being inundated by literally hundreds, or even thousands, of letters and phone calls (not all of them positive, to be sure) after T.V. talk show appearances where they have given out their addresses over the air. Set ground rules ahead of time and simply don't let them do it.

7. *Don't overlook the victims of hate violence.*

Television and radio producers often try and stage "debates" between Klan leaders and their opponents. While the real reason for this is simply to boost ratings, some producers argue that they are just seeking to "balance" their coverage.

If a news outlet wanted to provide some in-depth coverage about the impact and activities of hate groups, it can be done easily *without* giving hate group leaders free publicity. In-depth interviews with hate violence victims, anti-Klan experts, law enforcement officials and others will give an audience as thorough an understanding as they need about the phenomenon without being subjected to the sensationalism of 20 minutes of racial slurs and other invective. "If you really feel compelled to let the hate group speak, put them on the air briefly and *alone*. Ask them the hard questions and have them leave the studio. Conclude the remaining 25 minutes of your show with the real-life stories of Klan-busters or hate violence survivors," suggests CDR executive director Daniel Levitas.

Potential Libel Suits

Reporters and editors should be careful not to take the representations of white supremacist and far right leaders at face value. But they should be equally careful about making potentially libelous charges without fact checking. Although most Klan and hard core neo-Nazi organizations do not routinely sue journalists, several organizations, such as those associated with Lyndon

Geraldo and the Klan

Dear KKK:
I have been looking for fellow brothers and sisters that believe the way I do.
After watching Geraldo, I know what I have been looking for — the KKK.
Please send information.
A.W./GA

Dear KKK:
I saw the Geraldo Rivera episode featuring your organization...I think you presented yourself well...even though he tried to make you look bad and silly over and over again...the only reason Rivera has groups like yours on his show is so he can make them look bad. I figure you know that and the only reason you went on was to reach a large audience, which you did...
D.C./FL

Dear White Patriot Staff:
...I am a student at Fort Lewis College in Durango, Colorado. I recently saturated my campus with Klan literature...the media attention the distribution received was overwhelming!...I alone made 4 newspapers, 2 radio stations and a Television station sit up and take notice!...
S./Colorado

The letters excerpted above are from Issue #88 of the White Patriot, the newspaper of the Knights of the Ku Klux Klan. The broadcast referred to had a half-dozen KKK members appearing on the Geraldo Rivera show. The Klan members were flown by CBS from Arkansas, Texas and Colorado to New York and put up at the Empire Hotel, where they were given a pre-broadcast briefing by head Klansman Thom Robb on what to expect and how to act.

Center for Democratic Renewal • P.O. Box 50469, Atlanta, GA 30302-0469 • 404/221-0025

dismissed. Use a tape recorder (with permission) and take careful notes while investigating the story.

Some libel suits are intended to stop investigative journalists. The aggressive use of the discovery process against a plaintiff in the initial stages of a lawsuit will sometimes lead to a quick settlement.

Journalists should be as specific as possible in their descriptions of far right organizations and individuals. For example, although they share some common ideas, the John Birch Society is not the same as the Ku Klux Klan. A funder of the Heritage Foundation should not be described as a "neo-Nazi" — unless, of course, there is distinct evidence of neo-Nazi beliefs or affiliations.

Lyndon LaRouche sued journalist Chip Berlet (who now works as an analyst for Political Research Associates), freelance writer Dennis King, the Anti-Defamation League and the NBC television network for a March 1984 news report. The judge eventually dropped Berlet and King from the lawsuit, but not before they had incurred substantial legal costs and lost time. NBC and ADL prevailed before a Virginia jury and the LaRouche organization was ordered to pay NBC $3 million in counterclaims.

For a highly critical TV news report in 1985, Black Hawk Broadcasting Company in Waterloo, Iowa, was sued by the Populist Party of Iowa for libel. The lawsuit was dismissed after Black Hawk submitted affidavits from the reporters and other material. Black Hawk's motion for dismissal read, in part:

"Characterization of an organization as neo-Nazi or of its views as anti-Semitic or racist is a constitutionally protected expression of opinion for which their can be no liability. *Holy Spirit Association v. Sequoia Elsevier Publishing Co., ...United States Labor Party v. Anti-Defamation League...Holy Spirit Association v. Harper & Row.*" The judge's ruling was based on a number of factors, including the absence of neglect on the part of the reporter.

LaRouche and the Liberty Lobby, have sued media outlets for libel. On occasion, some investigative reporters have been stymied by LaRouche or the Liberty Lobby's litigious reputation.

It is beyond the purpose of this handbook to fully examine libel law. In his book *Synopsis of the Law of Libel and the Right of Privacy*, Bruce Sanford briefly defines libel as a "false statement printed or broadcast about a person which tends to bring that person into public hatred, contempt or ridicule or to injure him in his business or occupation." The standards for finding fault in a libel case vary among the states and change with new U.S. Supreme Court decisions.

Proving libel of a public personality is more difficult than for a private individual. According to Sanford, a public person must prove the journalist made a statement "either knowing it was false or entertaining serious doubts as to its truth." A private person must only prove that the journalist "acted negligently in failing to ascertain that the statement was false." Because they are party to significant public controversy, Klan and neo-Nazi leaders have been reasonably deemed public figures.

Of course, truth is the ultimate defense in a libel case. But other safeguards are useful whether the journalist is working for a small circulation newsletter or a major metropolitan daily newspaper:

Since negligence is part of the standard for libel, careful documentation of the investigative process is sometimes all that is necessary to have a libel case

A lawsuit by Willis Carto and the Liberty Lobby against Jack Anderson had a more convoluted resolution. Liberty Lobby sued over articles in the October 1981 issue of *The Investigator*, written by Anderson and Paul Bermant, claiming 30 libelous statements. Anderson was publisher of the short-lived magazine. In 1983, U.S. District Court Judge Barrington Parker dismissed the libel suit. He ruled that Carto and Liberty Lobby were limited-purpose public figures and that the "reporter...thoroughly investigated and researched (the) article and relied upon numerous sources." The reporter, therefore, was not negligent.

On appeal, however, then-U.S. Circuit Judge Antonin Scalia ruled that the case should go to trial. Scalia's decision held that the "mere charge of journalistic inaccuracy was not actionable (and) mere opinions could not be basis of defamation," but that "alleged conscious, malicious libel was actionable even though preceded by earlier assertions of (the) same untruth." In other words, Liberty Lobby was not libel proof and that re-asserting untruths that were previously published is not necessarily a defense against the charge of negligence.

A May 1990 decision by U.S. District Court Judge Aubrey Robinson narrowed the number of issues for trial to two: whether an illustration which depicted Carto with a strong resemblance to Hitler would subject Carto to "scorn, hatred and ridicule;" and whether Carto delivered a speech in which he attempted to emulate Hitler.

Although the case had dragged on for ten years on appeal, Liberty Lobby dropped the suit shortly before the case was to go to trial. The Liberty Lobby failed to win a similar lawsuit against the Dow Jones and Company.

"Dirty Tricks" and the LaRouche Organizations

In addition to deceptive publicity stunts and exaggerations from Klan and neo-Nazi leaders, journalists should be aware of "dirty tricks" techniques pioneered by the LaRouche organizations. LaRouchians have attempted to short circuit interviews and have posed as reporters and editors in order to learn about a journalist's sources, according to an March 1985 article in *Columbia Journalism Review* by Pat Lynch.

Lynch produced a groundbreaking report for a NBC news magazine TV program. A LaRouche activist gained access to her interview schedule. Soon her sources received telephone calls by persons claiming to work for NBC, cancelling her appointments. A short time later, other Lynch sources received calls from a person calling themselves Rick Winslow, claiming to be Lynch's boss. "Winslow" pumped the sources for the names and phone numbers of other sources, including some that were sensitive.

He also attempted to find out just how much information Lynch had, under the guise of protecting the network from a potential libel threat.

Other reporters have been the target of other tricks, including a phony camera crew which taped an interview with a journalist who had written critically of LaRouche. According to Lynch, LaRouche activist Herb Quinde used an alias to find out if NBC correspondent Brian Ross was planning to report on LaRouche. According to Political Research Associate analyst Chip Berlet, Quinde has since attempted to float favorable news coverage of LaRouche by becoming a "source" for news on related intelligence topics.

Dennis King, whose book *Lyndon LaRouche and the New American Fascism* remains the definitive work on the topic, once uncovered a French LaRouchian who posed as a French defense ministry official for several years.

Such tactics have been borrowed by others, and journalists should exercise diligence when reporting on the far right. ∎

Community Access Cable Controversy

In the mid-1980s Klansmen and neo-Nazis discovered that community access cable television could be used to give themselves more public visibility, recruit new members and develop new forms of propaganda. By mid-1991, racist programming had aired in more than 30 U.S. cities. In most cases the community access programs have been ignored by the larger public. In several instances human rights groups have engaged in counter-programming — broadcasting community access cable shows which respond to the bigoted programs.

In Kansas City, Missouri, the local Klan's attempt to use the community access cable station provoked a serious controversy in the larger community which is instructive to others concerned about this problem.

In 1988 the Missouri White Knights applied to American Cablevision to broadcast on a weekly basis "Race and Reason," an openly white supremacist program produced by California far-right figure Tom Metzger. The station informed the Klan that only locally produced programs could be broadcast over the public access channel, and that in order to produce a program, Klan members were required to undergo training at American Cablevision's production facilities. There was a public outcry, particularly in the African American community, when the Klan agreed to undergo training and produce its own programs. The city council then changed the city's existing franchise agreement with American Cablevision, eliminating the community access cable channel altogether.

The American Civil Liberties Union filed a lawsuit on behalf of the Klan. When a federal judge refused to summarily reject the ACLU's lawsuit and ordered the case to trial, the city council changed direction and reached an agreement with the ACLU. A soap-box style community access channel was established and the ACLU's lawsuit was withdrawn.

> **Community access cable television has become a favorite tool of white supremacists seeking to spread their message.**

Background: the Cable Act of 1984

When cable television was first introduced in the 1960s, municipalities entered into franchise agreements with television companies similar to those under which public utilities are operated. In exchange for permitting the cable company to install cable across public thoroughfares, the municipalities often demanded that at least one of the company's stations be set aside for "community access." Community access became a euphemism for a designated free speech forum accessible to all without any form of censorship, excepting obscenity.

Since cable television was (and is) a relatively new venture, much of the commercial law governing its use has either not been written or tested in the courts. In 1984, Congress passed the Cable Act which clearly established a municipality's *right* to establish community access: "A franchising authority may establish requirements in a franchise with respect to the designation or use of channel capacity for public, educational or governmental use."

K.C. Council Eliminates Community Access Requirement

Before deciding whether to eliminate the community access channel, Kansas City's legal department argued in a May 12, 1988 memo, that the community access channel was indeed a public forum, "because it is designed to provide a general public right of access to its use....Only speech unprotected by the First Amendment could be eliminated." The city's legal department argued that as long as the community access channel existed as a public forum, then it could not prevent the Klan from using it. But, the memo argued: "The public does not have a constitutional right to the airwaves (and the federal regulatory scheme does not require public access channels."

In other words, American Cablevision — like other commercial ventures such as newspapers or radio stations — are not public forums. To the extent that

Kansas City required the cable station to engage in community access programming, a designated forum was established. The City reasoned that if it could establish a designated public forum, it could also eliminate it.

The American Civil Liberties Union brought a lawsuit on behalf of the Klan, an independent program producer and several viewers. They claimed that since the City had decided to eliminate the community access programming *because* the Klan planned to use it, they had abridged their First Amendment rights based on the content of their speech. Further the ACLU lawsuit claimed:

"The presence of a public access channel enables members of the general public to contribute to the marketplace of ideas. Public access channels are today what the speaker's soap box and the printed leaflet were yesterday; they have become the electronic equivalent of such traditional public forums as the public streets, sidewalks and parks."

The City Council voted to settle the lawsuit rather than await a full court hearing and a "soapbox" type program was established for the community access channel. Anyone who wanted was given a 15-minute program free from censorship.

When the Klan finally produced a program in June 1990, three Klansmen were arrested on various gun and drug possession charges as they began to harass an African American couple walking near the production facilities. The Klan has not taped or broadcast another show since.

Conclusion

The issues in Kansas City are similar to those elsewhere. But because American Cablevision's production facilities were located in the heart of the African American community, there was widespread concern about the potential impact of Klansmen in robes arriving at the station or driving through the area. In fact, American Cablevision stated that some of its concern about Klan programming was based on commercial considerations: fear that some cable subscribers would drop their subscriptions if the Klan used the airwaves; and concern about the safety of their facilities. But many local observers pointed out that the issue of cable programming probably would not have divided Kansas City as it did if other racial problems had not already existed in the community. A May 7, 1988 editorial in the *Kansas City Star* noted, "The sensitivity of the issue underscores the lack of continuing, cohesive, effort in this community to promote better race relations." □

The Police and Bias Crimes

This section is meant to help citizens and victims understand the role of law enforcement with respect to bias crimes. It should also serve as a useful aid for law enforcement officials involved in training their officers in this sometimes controversial arena.

Who to call?

Attempting to get help from a law enforcement agency can be bewildering. There are many jurisdictions: city or municipal police departments; county sheriff's departments; state highway patrols or state bureaus of investigation, and various federal agencies such as the FBI, the United States Justice Department Community Relations Service, the Bureau of Alcohol, Tobacco and Firearms, and others. Which agency or department you should contact depends both on where you live and the nature of the crime being reported.

Police Investigate Crimes, Not Discrimination Cases

Remember that police agencies are responsible for enforcing *criminal* law, not laws against discrimination in housing or employment, for example.

When in doubt about how to make a complaint to a law enforcement agency, consult an attorney, other agencies such as human relations commissions, the United States Justice Department Community Relations Service, or a community-based organization. In some cities, legal aid societies can help.

Uncertainty about reporting incidents

If you are reluctant to report a hate crime to police, consider telling the local Human Relations Commission or an advocacy group. Most experts on the subject of bias crimes believe that failing to report incidents leads to more serious trouble, either

Center for Democratic Renewal • P.O. Box 50469, Atlanta, GA 30302-0469 • 404/221-0025

for the specific victim or for the community at large.

When hate incidents are happening in a community, sweeping them under the rug usually leads to an escalation of violence. This is because hate crime perpetrators often are on the lookout for responses to their actions. When no public condemnation is made, or when local police don't announce that a vigorous effort will be made to investigate, perpetrators sense the isolation of their victims and often seek them, or others, out again and again.

However, hate crime victims, like sexual assault victims, are often reluctant to report and/or prosecute. Law enforcement officials correctly say they can't police a problem they don't know about. In Portland, Oregon, the police department's Bias Crimes Unit recognized the problems created by non-reporting. In a September 1991 interview with the Portland *Oregonian*, Capt. Roberta Webber discussed the relationship between the newly-created Bias Crimes Unit and the Metropolitan Human Relations Commission. "We're going to have to set up a formal mechanism with them and the neighborhood associations for people to report bias crimes if they don't want to call the police...at least we could get the information, give them support and talk to them about retaliation or other dangers."

Helping reluctant victims

Friends, relatives, ministers, social workers and community activists can be helpful to both police and victims. Victims of hate crimes often feel extremely isolated. A supportive listener can help reassure victims that the attacks are a matter of serious concern. When a victim is upset, a friend or supporter can serve as an intermediary to law enforcement, helping the victim recall details and give a thorough statement with which investigators and later prosecutors can work.

Many victims of hate crimes do not report incidents because they feel either the incident is too minor (to themselves or to the police) to report or that the police cannot do anything about it. Other victims keep the crime to themselves because they have a language barrier, fear retaliation by the offender, or wish to avoid public exposure. Fear of exposure of minority status,

> **When hate incidents are happening in a community, sweeping them under the rug usually leads to an escalation of violence.**

such as with a gay or lesbian victim, may also decrease reporting. The lack of basic civil rights employment protection laws cause underreporting because gay men and lesbians, can be fired from their jobs in many instances if their sexual orientation becomes known.

In the case of gay and lesbian hate crimes, victims may be concerned that reporting hate crimes in which they are the victim will result in their own arrest or harassment by police because a number of states still have laws which outlaw same-sex activity.

Handling of victims of bias crimes requires special attention. The training materials prepared by the Boston Police Department for its Community Disorders Unit noted that special consideration should be given to the needs of victims and witnesses during police interviews.

They suggest the following:
- calm the excited and emotionally upset witness; (if necessary, delay interview until witness had regained composure);
- create a favorable atmosphere for the witness to talk freely;
- conduct the interview in a quiet area;

> **Special order of the Sheriff of Kootenai County, Idaho, to his deputies:**
>
> "All too often such harassment is viewed as minor, isolated, a prank, a joke or outside the purview of law enforcement. It is none of these...To respond to such incidents with less than professionalism... can only degrade our profession and alienate the victims of such harassment."

- maintain privacy to the greatest degree possible;
- do not distract the witness or interrupt his story;
- only one officer should conduct the interview;
- display a sincere interest;
- be patient and tactful and respectful.

The Boston Community Disorders Unit realized that many of the victims of bias crimes, particularly immigrants, did not know their rights. The unit then began a series of education programs in the community. The unit noted that they had a significant problem among Southeast Asian immigrants who had a fear of the police and unfamiliarity with United States law. Therefore, the unit hired two Vietnamese interpreters and posted notices in Cambodian, Vietnamese and Laotian. The same procedures can be used by a department operating in a community with a significant Spanish-speaking population.

Feigned Facts or Hoaxes

As with any crime, a small number of incidents of

Victims who won't talk

A June 1991 "Report on Violence Against Gay Men and Lesbians in New York City" commissioned by Mayor David Dinkins found that 73 percent of the victims of bias incidents responding to the survey did not report the incident to the police. The reasons given by the survey's respondents varied:

- 25 percent reported that the act did not justify reporting;
- 25 percent reported that they believe the police would not act on the complaint;
- 17 percent reported that they fear police harassment;
- 15 percent reported that they mistrusted police;
- 4 percent reported that they didn't know their rights;
- 3 percent reported that they fear retaliation;
- 2 percent reported that the incidents were police perpetrated;
- 7 percent reported other miscellaneous reasons.

The data showed that the relationship between police and those victimized by hate crimes are critical to the proper prosecution of hate crimes against gay men and lesbians. It is likely that surveys of African American hate crimes victims and others would show similar results.

hate violence and harassment have been shown to be hoaxes, motivated not by bigotry and hatred but by the psychological or financial needs of the alleged hate crime victim. In one case, a suburban Atlanta couple set fire to their home, hoping to collect on the insurance. By painting racial slurs on the walls they hoped to distract police investigators from discovering the cause of the arson.

Other situations are less straightforward. For example, a Seattle man claimed he was the victim of a vicious, racially-motivated assault by a group of white youths. The incident was widely reported by the local media, but no evidence could be found to substantiate the charges and no perpetrators were identified. Instead, the publicity enabled police to identify and arrest the alleged hate crime victim as a major bank robbery suspect. He later pleaded guilty.

Even when a hoax is suspected, police must be especially careful not to announce this publicly. This is because hate crimes can attract intense community interest and sensational publicity. Stating that the incident may have been faked will often appear to be "blaming the victim." Vigorous criticism and a setback in police-community relations will quickly follow. On the other hand, if a solid investigation proves no bias was involved, police should rely on the strength of that evidence to convince a judge, jury and the general public.

The Role of Law Enforcement Agencies

Law enforcement agencies must develop an effective response to hate crimes at the same time they are faced with budgetary constraints and record levels of all types of crime. Resources for responding to bias crimes must compete with resources for drug enforcement or homicide investigations, for example. As a result, officials find it difficult to expend scarce resources investigating misdemeanor assaults or vandalism.

Hate crimes, however, often have a community impact disproportionate to the dollar amount of damage associated with such incidents as crossburnings or hateful graffiti. Law enforcement executives must therefore develop appropriate policy guidelines; agencies must enforce the policies; and all personnel must be adequately trained to carry out these policies. One great stumbling block in this area is negative police-community relations.

Local Bias Crimes Units

Law enforcement agencies must first state departmental policy and then enforce it.

In Baltimore, the Chief of Police issued a General Order setting up special procedures for handling bias incidents. However, the General Order was soon papered over and forgotten. Eventually, however, the

Baltimore department directly incorporated materials on bias crimes into the regular training program for new officers and in the main procedures manual.

In 1983 the Sheriff of Kootenai County, Idaho, issued a Special Order to personnel about the passage of a malicious harassment law by the state legislature.

In several large metropolitan areas the next step has been to establish a distinct unit within the police department to respond to hate crimes. The New York City Police Department established a Bias Incident Investigating Unit in 1980. Since then, the jurisdiction and operating procedures of the unit have changed and expanded.

In 1985 the New York Unit defined a bias incident as:

"Any offense or unlawful act that is motivated by bias or prejudice based on the victim's race, ethnicity, religion or sexual orientation."

According to the procedures manual the unit was responsible for:

1) Investigation of bias incidents.
2) Providing support and assistance to bias crime victims.
3) Preparing statistical reports on bias incidents.
4) Maintaining liaison with all district attorneys involved in the prosecution of bias crime.
5) Maintaining liaison with other city, state, and Federal enforcement and support agencies.
6) Maintaining contact with community and civic organizations.
7) Conducting follow-up interviews with victims two months after the case was closed in order to determine if there was a reoccurrence.
8) Providing staff assistance for precinct-level training.

Decoy Units

In New York City the Bias Crimes Unit has used decoys in areas with high levels of hate crimes or during particular periods of racial or ethnic tension. But the first decoy operation for crimes against gays and lesbians was established in August 1991 by the Houston Police Department.

The Houston decoy operation arose after an attack on three men that resulted in the brutal murder of a 27-year-old banker. For several years, the Houston Police Department did not consider crimes motivated by bias based on sexual orientation as hate crimes. Therefore the investigating officers did not at first consider the murder a hate crime. After a public outcry, the department

Assessing Bias Crimes

Because of the difficulty law enforcement officers encounter in ascertaining the offender's subjective motivation, bias is to be reported only if sufficient objective facts are present supporting the finding of bias such as:

1) The offender and victim were of different racial, religious, ethnic/national origin, or sexual orientation groups;
2) Bias-related comments, written statements, or gestures were made by the offender;
3) Bias-related drawings, markings, symbols or graffiti were left at the crime scene;
4) Certain objects indicating bias were used, such as white sheets with hoods or swastikas, or objects that were left behind, such as a burning cross;
5) The victim is a member of a racial, religious, ethnic/national origin or sexual orientation group which is overwhelmingly outnumbered by members of another group in the neighborhood where the victim lives and the incident took place;
6) The victim was visiting a neighborhood where previous hate crimes had been committed against other members of his/her racial, religious, ethnic/national origin, or sexual orientation group and where tensions remain high against his/her group;
7) Several incidents have occurred in the same locality, at or about the same time, and the victims are all of the same racial, religious, ethnic/national origin, or sexual orientation group;
8) A substantial portion of the community where the crime occurred perceives that the incident was motivated by bias;
9) The victim was engaged in promoting his/her racial, religious, ethnic/national origin, or sexual orientation group. For example, the victim is a member of the NAACP, or participated in a gay rights demonstration;
10) The incident coincided with a holiday relating to, or a date of particular significance to a racial, religious, or ethnic/national origin group (e.g., Martin Luther King Day, Rosh Hashanah);
11) The offender was previously involved in a similar hate crime or is a member of a hate group;
12) There were indications that a hate group was involved. For example, a hate group claimed responsibility for the crime or was active in the neighborhood;
13) A historically established animosity exists between the victim's group and the offender's group;
14) The victim, although not a member of the targeted racial, religious, ethnic/national origin, or sexual orientation group, is a member of an advocacy group supporting the precepts of the victim group.

changed its classification. It also changed the department's regulations about hate crimes to conform to federal standards established by the Hate Crimes Statistics Act.

Shortly thereafter the decoy operation began with teams of two officers posing as gay couples. In less than a week, three officers were attacked and 13 people were arrested.

Training

The FBI began a regional training program in 1991 to ensure that local law enforcement jurisdictions were prepared to supply reliable statistics on hate crimes to the Department of Justice as part of the Federal Hate Crimes Statistics Act. However, until all police departments train their personnel to identify and investigate hate crimes, the data they provide to state and federal reporting agencies will be of questionable value (see legislative chart for state-by-state reporting requirements). Comprehensive training is also necessary to ensure that police officers conduct themselves in a professional manner consistent with good community relations.

Investigating Hate Crimes

The types of bias covered under the Federal Hate Crime Statistics Act are limited to "race, religion, sexual orientation, and ethnicity." The object of the data collection is to determine whether an offender was motivated to commit the offense because of his/her bias against a member of the specified group.

FBI guidelines caution that even if the offender was mistaken in his/her perception that the victim was a member of the group he or she was acting against, the offense is still a bias crime because the offender was motivated by bias against the group.

It is important to note that only one of a number of factors may be necessary to conclude that the incident was a hate crime. In some cases a combination of factors might provide a stronger basis for this conclusion. Regardless of the specific factors involved, an incident involving bias can still be classified as a hate crime even if the motive of the perpetrator was mixed. For example, a mugger who singled out a gay victim, yelled epithets during the incident and then stole the victim's wallet would be reasonably classified as a hate crime perpetrator.

An effective criminal justice system requires that fairness and equal treatment be accorded to victim, alleged perpetrator and law enforcement personnel (from the beat cop to the prosecuting attorney to judge) alike. Bias is, by definition, the opposite of fairness and equal treatment.

Bias and the perception of bias on the part of police department personnel undermines good police-community relations, which are an important component of effective law enforcement.

Excessive Force

In the "Report of the Independent Commission on the Los Angeles Police Department," Hubert Williams, president of the Police Foundation and former Chief of Police for Newark, New Jersey, stated: "Police use of excessive force is a significant problem in this country, particularly in our inner cities."

The Commission's report also concluded that "the problem of excessive force is aggravated by racism and bias." Further it found that "racial bias (prejudice) on the part of officers toward minority citizens currently exists and contributes to a negative interaction between police and community...These attitudes ...are translated into unacceptable behavior in the field (as well as) conduct directed to fellow officers who are members of racial or ethnic minority groups." The Report also noted that a practice of discrimination towards women and gay and lesbian officers existed within the department which was at variance with the Los Angeles Police Department's stated policies.

Dealing With Law Enforcement

Because of the role played by some law enforcement officials and agencies in initiating, ignoring or covering-up acts of harassment and violence, it is often difficult for activists to agree on the most appropriate strategy for dealing with law enforcement. Some activists argue that there should be absolutely no contact with the authorities whatsoever; others believe that unconditional cooperation with law enforcement personnel is appropriate regardless of the circumstances. In reality, neither strategy is wise.

Activists need to be able to differentiate between the responsibilities of various police agencies and jurisdictions.

While some acts of violence and harassment have been carried out by and/or with the knowledge of people employed by law enforcement or police informants, the majority of incidents are not. And, while some law enforcement personnel will not be adequately receptive or responsive to reports about harassment — or even violent crimes — many are capable of doing their job.

One thing is certain: if hate crime victims and their advocates do not report incidents to the police, or are unwilling to cooperate with an investigation, then they will have little to say about the absence of an effective law enforcement response.

Center for Democratic Renewal • P.O. Box 50469, Atlanta, GA 30302-0469 • 404/221-0025

Police/Community Relations

The Durham-based organization, North Carolinians Against Racist and Religious Violence, monitors incidents of police-community conflicts in their state. NCARRV published a 1990 report, *No Reverence for Life? Police Use of Deadly Force in North Carolina.* Together with the Criminal Justice Department of North Carolina Central University, NCARRV established a Police/Community Relations Advisory Board. In their 1991 report on bigoted violence, NCARRV listed ten community "assumptions" which the Advisory Board found underlay tensions. They included:

- A lack of communication and trust between police and the community.
- Police officers lack multicultural training.
- African Americans perceive police as racist.
- Police fear minority citizens.
- Both police and citizens fail to understand the scope of the problems.

In New York, the Latino Rights Project was formed to respond to police violence and random racist attacks. According to the Project, on the night of the Howard Beach attack in 1986, another gang of white youths beat two Latino teenagers only a mile from where Michael Griffith was killed. The next year, Alberto Flores was beaten by policemen — an attack that was videotaped — yet the police were cleared, and Flores was indicted. In 1988, two Latino men were killed by police — one beaten to death by four police officers in his bedroom, another shot by a transit police officer. The Latino Rights Project grew out of the response to these attacks, as well as the realization that there were no institutions in New York City to provide medical support, counseling services, or legal assistance to Latinos. The Civilian Review Complaint Board and the Anti-Bias Unit of the NYPD did not provide bilingual services.

In a hearing before elected officials, Howard Jordan, Chairman of the Projects Board, explained: "[The pattern of racist violence against Latinos] is exacerbated where the victims do not speak English and the official cannot even establish a basic understanding of the facts

In the case of Latino immigrants, many do not even report these incidents for fear of discovery of their residency status." The Latino Rights Project advocated for a fairer civilian review process. According to Jordan, cases of police misconduct are heard by an infamous review board of members who are former police personnel, with 70 percent of its investigators paid by the police department.

Noting that the majority of officers within the Los Angeles police department carried out their responsibilities professionally and without bias or excessive force, the report was critical of supervisors who did not discipline racist or unprofessional conduct.

An April 16, 1991, meeting of police chiefs from 11 cities resolved that the United States Department of Justice should pay for research into the use of police force and develop a national system to gather information. The chiefs also called for a training center on "community policing."

New York City Police Chief Commissioner Lee Brown told the press after the meeting: "The problem of excessive force in American policing is real...Regardless of its cause, it cannot be condoned and must be actively countered by concerned police professionals."

Klan and neo-Nazi Recruitment of Law Enforcement

Like other sectors of society, law enforcement personnel have been targeted for recruitment by white supremacists. Membership in hate groups is particularly problematic for law enforcement officials, however, because they are sworn to provide equal protection under the law. On the one hand, Klan members swear loyalty to the white race and promise to lie about the Klan's activities if they think it is necessary. On the other, public servants are bound to the rule of law.

Almost immediately after a highly publicized incident of police brutality by the Los Angeles Police Department made national headlines, the White Knights of the Ku Klux Klan in Kansas City, Missouri, mailed application forms to ten different precinct stations of the LAPD. The White Knights also mailed application forms to Los Angeles area media in a successful bid for publicity. Department officials immediately denounced the recruitment stunt. But the *Los Angeles Times* later revealed the existence of an organized racist group in the department calling itself the Vikings.

Similar white supremacist groups, unaffiliated with well-known Klan and neo-Nazi organizations, have surfaced in other municipal police departments.

In Fort Worth, Texas, Police Chief Thomas Windham issued a memo that membership in organized white supremacist groups was "in direct conflict with the democratic principles we are sworn to protect."

In several instances officers have been fired for

membership in the Klan. Three members of the Tarrant County, Texas, sheriff's department were fired in February 1990, because of their membership in the Invisible Empire Knights of the Ku Klux Klan. Invisible Empire leader Thomas Herman was fired in December 1989, as a part-time officer in the Exeter, New Hampshire, police department.

Herman was able to keep his job as a dispatcher with the Rockingham County sheriff's department, however. Jefferson County, Kentucky, police officer Alex Young was fired in November 1985, after admitting that he used the National Crime Information Center computer for the Klan.

Young had organized a Klan-associated Confederate Officers Patriot Squad (COPS) in the Louisville area that had been responsible for terrorizing African American families with crossburnings and arson. The existence of COPS was exposed in a lawsuit by the Southern Poverty Law Center.

In a similar case, three members of the Blakely, Georgia, Fire Department, including the fire chief, resigned their posts after their membership in the Invisible Empire was disclosed in a lawsuit by the Center for Democratic Renewal. In settling the lawsuit the city also agreed not to hire any Klan members "in a public safety capacity."

Although some departments continue to allow Klansmen and neo-Nazis to be officers, there is significant legal precedent for greater restrictions on the activity of law enforcement personnel. In 1985, the 11th United States Circuit Court of Appeals held that law enforcement officials "are subject to greater First Amendment restraints than most citizens" because of the greater potential harm to the community at large.

Situations for Discussion

The Hate Crimes Data Collection Guidelines developed by the Justice Department include the following mock situations for use in training seminars:

SITUATION ONE

While driving through a predominantly white neighborhood a black male stopped his car to repair a flat tire. A group of whites leaving a bar across the street accosted the driver and then attacked him with bottles and clubs. During the attack, the offenders called the victim by a well-known and recognized epithet used

against blacks and told him that blacks were not welcome in the neighborhood.

Questions:

1. Should this incident be considered a hate crime? Why?

2. Assuming the assailants were arrested, with what should they be charged? (Be specific)

3. Would the incident be considered a hate crime if during the course of the investigation one of the assailants claimed that they attacked the driver because they thought he was selling drugs in their neighborhood? Why?

4. Would the incident be considered a hate crime if the assailants had been Mexican-American instead of white?

SITUATION TWO

Two white men walking arm-in-arm through a neighborhood known for its gay and lesbian residents are attacked by three young black men wielding baseball bats and knives. Two of the assailants call the victims a well-known epithet for gays. A beat police officer intervenes and arrests the assailants. Nothing has been stolen and the victims and the assailants do not know each other.

1. Should this incident be considered a hate crime? Why?

2. With what state law or municipal ordinance

should the assailants be charged? (Be specific)

3.   Would the incident be considered a hate crime if during the course of the investigation the victims both claimed that they were not gay and objected to being characterized as such during any subsequent criminal proceeding? Why?

4.   Would the incident be considered a hate crime if during the course of the investigation the assailants claimed that they were attempting to rob the victims, but were prevented from doing so because of the quick intervention of the officer?

SITUATION THREE

Police are called to a synagogue on a Friday morning. The walls of the building have been painted with graffiti, including anti-Semitic slogans and swastikas. Inside the building the silver candelabra and silver Torah ornaments have been stolen. The rabbi insists that the building walls be cleaned as quickly as possible, so that the vandalism is removed before the evening services. The crime lab informs you that they will be able to send over a team of technicians after they are finished at the scene of a drug-related murder, probably early afternoon.

Questions:

1. How should this incident be investigated?

2. What steps should be taken to respond to the rabbi's concerns about the impact of the vandalism on his congregation?

3. Should this incident be considered a hate crime?

4. With what municipal ordinance, state statute or federal violations should the perpetrator be charged?

5. At the end of the investigation you arrest a well-known silver thief who claims that his motive was pure larceny. Should the incident be considered a hate crime?

RESOURCES 4

Tools for Counter-Action

SOURCES AND RESOURCES

• Response Development/ Hate Crime Victim Referral

A number of organizations assist hate crime victims and help local communities develop appropriate responses. In addition to local police departments and human relations commissions, listed below are groups that may be of assistance if a problem with hate violence develops in your community.

Center for Democratic Renewal
CDR National Office
P. O. Box 50469
Atlanta, GA 30302
(404) 221-0025
CDR Midwest Office
P. O. Box 413767
Kansas City, MO 64141-3767
(816) 421-6614

American-Arab Anti-Discrimination Committee
4201 Connecticut Ave., N.W., #500
Washington, D.C. 20009
(202) 244-2990

American Jewish Committee
165 E. 56th Street
New York, NY 10022
(212) 751-4000
(Check local listing for a state or regional office.)

Anti-Defamation League of B'nai B'rith
823 United Nations Plaza, #1100
New York, NY 10017
(Check local listing for a state or regional office.)

Asian Law Caucus
468 Bush St., 3rd Floor
San Francisco, CA 94108
(415) 391-1655

Coalition for Human Dignity
P. O. Box 40344
Portland, OR 97240
(503) 227-5033

Center for Constitutional Rights
666 Broadway
New York, NY 10012
(212) 614-6464

Committee Against Anti-Asian Violence
121 6th Avenue, 6th Floor
New York, NY 10013
(212) 473-6485

Freedom of Information
Chief J. Kevin O'Brien
F.B.I. (Attn: FOI-PA Section)
9th and Pennsylvania Ave.
Washington, D.C. 20535

Klanwatch
Southern Poverty Law Center
400 Washington Avenue
Montgomery, AL 36104
(205) 264-0286

Lambda Legal Defense & Education Fund, Inc.
666 Broadway
New York, NY 10012
(212) 995-8585

Montana Human Rights Network
P. O. Box 9184
Helena, MT 59604
(406) 442-5506

NAACP
4805 Mt. Hope Drive
Baltimore, MD 21215
(410) 358-8900

National Gay and Lesbian Task Force Policy Institute Campus Project/Anti-Violence Project
1734 14th Street, N.W.
Washington, D.C. 20009-4309
(202) 332-6483

National Institute Against Prejudice and Violence
31 South Greene Street
Baltimore, MD 21201
(301) 328-5170

National Urban League
1111 14th Street, N.W. 6th Floor
Washington, D.C. 20005
(202) 898-1604

National Victim Center
309 West 7th Street, Suite 705
Fort Worth, TX 76102
(817) 877-3355

**North Carolinians Against
Racist and Religious Violence**
P. O. Box 240
Durham, NC 27702
(919) 688-5965

Northwest Coalition Against Malicious Harassment
P. O. 16776
Seattle, WA 98116
(206) 233-9136

People Against Racist Terror (P.A.R.T.)
P.O. Box 1990
Burbank, CA 91507
(213) 461-3127

Romani-Jewish Alliance
Box 325
Cashmere, WA 98815
509-782-4710

U.S. Department of Justice Hate Crime Hotline
1-800-347-HATE

The Women's Project
2224 Main Street
Little Rock, AR 72206
(501) 372-5113

• Human Relations Commissions

There are times when community activists need assistance from agencies which act as liaisons between private citizens and government. In addition to local or area human relations commissions, the following are a sampling of such agencies.

**Montgomery County Human
Relations Commission**
164 Rollins Avenue
Rockville, MD 20852
(301) 468-4260

**Metropolitan Human Relations
Commission for Multnomah County**
1120 S.W. Fifth Avenue Room 520
Portland, OR 97204-1989
(503) 796-5136

Georgia Human Relations Commission
100 Peachtree St., N.W., #350
Atlanta, GA 30303
(404) 651-9116

Los Angeles County Human Relations Commission
1184 Hall of Records, 320 W. Temple Street
Los Angeles, CA 90012
(213) 974-7611

• Resources for the Workplace

The growing presence of prejudice and violence in the workplace has caused many organizations to seek ways to respond. Listed below are some of those organizations.

AFL-CIO Civil Rights Department
Richard Womack
815 16th St., N.W.
Washington, D.C. 20006
(202) 637-5000

UAW Civil Rights Department
8000 East Jefferson Ave.
Detroit, MI 48214
(313) 926-5361

Federation for Industrial Retention and Renewal
3411 West Diversey, Suite 10
Chicago, IL 60647
(312) 252-7676

Southerners for Economic Justice
Box 240
Durham, NC 27702
(919) 683-1361

National Network for Immigrant and Refugee Rights
> 310 8th St. Suite 307
> Oakland, CA 94607
> (415) 465-1984

Latino Rights Project/Proyecto Pro-Derechos Latinos
> 666 Broadway, Suite 625
> New York, NY 10012
> (212) 722-1645

• Resources for College and Youth

To counter hate violence on campus and among youth there have been a number of useful books, reports, and videos produced to assist administrators and community leaders. Some are listed below.

Hebdige, Dick. *Subculture: The Meaning of Style.* New York. Methuen. 1979

Anderson, Eric. *Skinheads: From Britain to San Francisco via Punk Rock.* Unpublished anthropology masters thesis, Washington State University. December 1987.

Organizing for Equality Newsletter of the National Gay and Lesbian Task Force Campus Project, 1734 14th Street NW, Washington, DC 20009. (202) 332-6483.

"Still Burning," a two-part video examining "ethnoviolence" on college campuses. 20 minutes each. $60. per set, Marketing Coordinator, Instructional Technology, University of Maryland — Baltimore, MD 21228-5398. (410) 455-3686.

"Bigotry on Campus: A Planned Response." American Jewish Committee, Institute of Human Relations, 165 East 56 Street, New York, NY 10022-2746.

"Report on Racism and Discrimination in the College Environment." The Task Force on Racism of the Associated Students of the University of Washington, Seattle, WA

"When Free Speech Becomes Harassment: Developing Effective Campus Policies." A Special Report of the National Institute Against Prejudice and Violence (March 1990), 31 South Greene Street, Baltimore, MD 21201. (301) 328-5170.

"How the First Amendment Applies to Offensive Expression on the Campuses of Public Colleges and Universities." The American Association of State Colleges and Universities, One Dupont Circle, Suite 700, Washington, DC 20036.

University of Wisconsin-Madison Plan (February 1988), Office of the Chancellor, 158 Basom Hall, 500 Lincoln Drive, Madison, WI 53706.

Curriculum Resources

Teaching Tolerance
> 400 Washington Ave.,
> Montgomery, AL 36104

Facing History and Ourselves
> 16 Hurd Rd.
> Brookline, MA 02146
> 617-232-1595

• Resources for Monitoring and Research

The first step in countering hate activity is learning about hate groups. The following are some sources for learning about such groups and learning how to monitor their activities.

Anti-Defamation League of B'nai B'rith
> 823 United Nations Plaza
> New York, NY 10017
> (212) 490-2525
> (Check your local listing for a state or regional office.)

Coalition for Human Dignity
> P.O. Box 40344
> Portland, OR 97240

FAIR (Fairness & Advocacy in Reporting)
> 175 Fifth Avenue Suite 2245
> New York, NY 10010
> (212) 633-7600
> Publishers of *EXTRA!*, a bi-monthly magazine offering well documented criticism to correct media bias and imbalance. Inquire about rates.

Freedom of Information Office
> Executive Office of U.S. Attorneys
> U.S. Department of Justice
> Room 6410, PAT
> Washington, DC 20530
> (202) 501-7826

Freedom of Information
> Chief J. Kevin O'Brien
> FOI-PA Section, Room 6296, J. Edgar Hoover Bldg
> Washington, DC 20535
> (202) 324-5520

Freedom of Information
> Chief Nelson Hermilla
> Civil Rights Division, Department of Justice
> FOI-PA Branch, Room 7339
> Washington, DC 20530
> (202) 514-4209

Hotline for FOIA problems
> (202) 466-6312.

Klanwatch

Southern Poverty Law Center
400 Washington Avenue
Montgomery, AL 36104
(205) 264-0286

North Carolinians Against Racist and Religious Violence

PO Box 240
Durham, NC 27702
(919) 688-5965

PrairieFire Rural Action, Inc.

550 Eleventh Street
Des Moines, IA 50309
(515) 244-5671.

The Reporters' Committee on Freedom of the Press

Suite 300, 800 18th St NW
Washington, DC 2000

Searchlight Magazine

37 B New Cavendish
London W1M8JR England
This monthly, English-language magazine provides the most authoritative information on neo-Nazi activities throughout Europe. Overseas subscribers should pay by Eurocheque or International Money Order. Inquire by mail about rates.

The Women's Project

2224 South Main Street
Little Rock, AR 72206
(501) 372-5113.

For further reading:

Hate Crime Data Collection Guidelines, Uniform Crime Reporting, Federal Bureau of Investigation.

Reporter's Handbook: An Investigator's Guide to Documents and Techniques. New York, 1983.

• Resources for Lesbian, Gay and Women's Issues

Hate violence against gay men and lesbians has reached epidemic proportions. The following are resources to learn more about this issue and to report information regarding such incidents.

The National Gay and Lesbian Task Force

1734 14th Street NW
Washington, DC 2009-4309
(202) 332-6483.

The National Coalition Against Domestic Violence

P.O. Box 34103
Washington, DC 20047
(202) 638-6388.

The National Association Against Sexual Assault, c/o Rape Crisis Center of W. Contra Costa

2000 Vale Road
San Pablo, California 94806
(415) 236-7273.

For further reading:

"Female Victims of Violent Crime." A publication of the United States Department of Justice. Office of Justice Programs/Bureau of Justice Statistics.

Zeskind , Leonard and Segrest, Mab. *"Quarantines and Death: The Far Rights' Homophobic Agenda"* (CDR, 1989).

Katz, Jonathan. *Gay American History: Lesbians and Gay Men in the U.S.A.* New York, 1976.

Demilio, John and Freedman, Estelle B. *Intimate Matters: A History of Sexuality in America* New York, 1988.

Sample Resolutions

RESOLUTION OF THE UNITED METHODIST CHURCH ON KU KLUX KLAN AND OTHER HATE GROUPS IN THE U.S.

The Charter for Racial Justice Policies holds us accountable as United Methodists in the United States to be conscious that "we have sinned as our ancestors did; we have been wicked and evil" (Psalm 106:6, Today's English Bible). We are called to a renewed commitment to the elimination of institutional racism. We affirm the 1976 General Conference Statement *The United Methodist Church and Race*, which states unequivocally:

By biblical and theological precept, by the law of the Church, by General Conference pronouncement, and by episcopal expression, the matter is clear. With respect to race, the aim of The United Methodist Church is nothing less than an inclusive church in an inclusive society. The United Methodist Church therefore calls upon all its people to perform those faithful deeds of love and justice in both the church and community that will bring this aim into full reality.

The United Methodist Church has expressed its opposition to all forms of racism and anti-semitism in the past. Racism replaces faith in the God who made all people with a belief in the superiority of one race over another.

Nevertheless racism still exists in the United States congealed in its most violent, anti-democratic form — the white supremacist movement...

Therefore, be it resolved, that the General Conference, in solidarity with victims of recent outbreaks of racial violence:

A. Calls upon the appropriate boards and agencies of The United Methodist Church to:

1. Educate clergy and laity to the insidiousness of the "Christian Identity" movement, the Ku Klux Klan and other hate groups which claim their values and practices are based in Christianity. Education should include courses in seminaries as well as education for children, youth and adults in church programs.
2. Develop special programs to support churches and persons harassed by hate groups, particularly in rural areas where the social institutions that mediate conflict are weak and hate group activity is prevalent.
3. Support coalitions that oppose bigotry and hate groups.
4. Oppose the involvement of minors in paramilitary training sponsored the Ku Klux Klan and other racist groups.

B. Calls upon government and its agencies to:

1. Assure that law enforcement personnel take the necessary steps to maintain accurate records on racist violence and bring to justice the perpetrators of such violence and intimidation.
2. Hold hearings on racist violence, particularly in those states where statistics reveal an increase in the activity of the Ku Klux Klan and other hate groups. Congressional hearings should be held when there are allegations of government involvement or negligence exacerbating such violence.

Adopted 1988

RESOLUTION OF THE ATLANTA LABOR COUNCIL OPPOSING WORKPLACE DISCRIMINATION

Whereas, Organized Labor believes in equal employment opportunities for all workers regardless of age, race, creed, color, national origin, sexual preference, religion or gender; and

Whereas, Organized Labor feels we should reaffirm this belief at every opportunity; and

Whereas, It is essential that all Labor Organizations adopt Equal Employment Opportunity Guide Lines for the work place and the union hall; Now

Therefore be it resolved, The Atlanta Labor Council AFL-CIO reaffirms its commitment to Equal Economic Opportunity; and

Be it further resolved, The Atlanta Labor Council will work to eradicate discrimination in all work places, organized and unorganized; and

Be it further resolved, The Atlanta Labor Council will work to eradicate prejudice in all union halls and offices,

Be it further resolved, The Atlanta Labor Council and its affiliated organizations will promote educational programs to teach officers and members to recognize and prevent prejudicial or discriminatory behavior; and

Be it further resolved, This resolution be forwarded to all affiliated organizations for their consideration and adoption, and

Be it further resolved, any labor organization that knowingly engages in or permits its officers or members to engage in prejudicial actions or discriminatory behavior will be censured and disciplined to the fullest extent allowed by the AFL-CIO Constitution, and

Be it finally resolved, The Atlanta Labor Council and affiliated organizations will promote and support legislation to increase opportunities for women and minorities to participate in all facets of the American Economy.

Adopted April 1991

UNITED FURNITURE WORKERS OF AMERICA RESOLUTION OPPOSING RACISM AND THE KLAN

WHEREAS, Racist forces in this nation are attempting to bring back the days of lynch law; the days when non-white Americans were treated as second-class citizens; the days when robbery and murder were acceptable — as long as the victims was black; and

WHEREAS, This drive is spearheaded by the reborn Ku Klux Klan — the group which headed such activities in the past and is trying to spur a new upsurge of violent racism; and

WHEREAS, Racism is an insidious force which turns worker against worker and results in a splintered working class — ripe for exploitation by bosses;

THEREFORE BE IT RESOLVED: That UFWA delegates urge local unions in every area to join our allies in a determined effort to crush the KKK and all racism forever!

Adopted July 1980

RESOLUTION OF THE NATIONAL COUNCIL OF THE CHURCHES OF CHRIST IN THE U.S.A. OPPOSING BIGOTRY AND HATE CRIMES

The killing of Yusef Hawkins on August 23, 1989, in Bensonhurst, New York, highlights the continuing legacy of bigoted violence that has victimized the African American community. The violation of the civil and constitutional rights of African Americans that occurred in Virginia Beach, Virginia, over the Labor Day weekend, 1989, serves as another painful reminder that the majority culture can too readily deny racial/ethic people rights and opportunities freely enjoyed by European Americans.

The murder of Ming Hai Loo (Jimmy Loo) in Raleigh, North Carolina, on July 28, 1989, makes visible the reality that all racial/ethnic people are subject to stereotyping and prejudice and can too easily become the victims of racist attacks. Three gay men were murdered on January 17, 1987, by neo-Nazi assailants in an adult bookstore in Shelby, N.C. During 1988 there were more than 7000 incidents of bigoted violence and harassment against gay and lesbian persons. The incidences of anti-semitism have increased.

These hate crimes are disproportionately perpetrated by youth.

Therefore, the Governing Board of the National Council of Churches:

1. Urges its member communions to:

a. Initiate letter writing campaigns to ensure passage of the Federal Hate Crimes Statistics Act (S419/ HR1058), thus mandating for the first time federal data collection;

b. Educate their staff, clergy, and lay leaders about the problem of bigoted violence as well as the nature and scope and influence of organized far-right white-supremacist activity; provide literature, circulate articles, distribute audiovisual materials and disseminate factual information on this subject;

c. Develop and implement in-depth training and educational programs for the staff and clergy within their respective denominations and agencies to provide them with strategies, information and techniques for responding to bigoted violence and hate-group activity in their communities;

d. Formulate and distribute guidelines for local clergy that they should employ when confronted with evidence of bigoted violence and hate-group activity;

e. Work with local support groups to publicize the cause of the victims of such attacks, contribute financial, staff, and other resources to assist the victims of bigoted violence and the organizations that serve these victims;

f. Pledge themselves to the task of building a social justice movement that is actively anti-racist, multicultural and non-violent;

g. Acknowledge the importance of working with children and youth to educate, inform and activate them to resist and counteract bigotry and hate-group activity; and

h. initiate anti-racism and anti-bias education projects among children and youth associated with their respective denominations and agencies.

2. Calls upon its appropriate units

a. to reach out to children and young people so that they may find reasons for hope and discover there is a role for them to play in creating a world free from bigotry and fear, and

b. to support the activities of the communions in addressing this problem.

Adopted by the NCC Governing Board, November 16, 1989

AMALGAMATED CLOTHING AND TEXTILE WORKERS' UNION RESOLUTION ON IMMIGRATION

ACTWU has historically supported an immigration policy for our nation consistent with the immigrant tradition of our Union — a policy of compassion, a policy that safeguards the welfare of American workers. We understand that foreign-born workers who come to this country are seeking a better way of life free from political repression or economic hardship. Yet undocumented workers who come to the United States seeking jobs are vulnerable to exploitation by unscrupulous employers. Those who escape exploitation by becoming members of American labor unions are still victimized by the Immigration and Naturalization Service (INS) which frequently raids union shops while employers who resist unionization are left alone.

BE IT THEREFORE RESOLVED that the Third Constitutional Convention of the Amalgamated Clothing and Textile Workers Union, AFL-CIO, CLC:

1. There should be a comprehensive and generous amnesty for undocumented workers already established in this country;
2. Immigration policy must not encourage discrimination and harassment of Hispanics, Haitians, and other migrant groups, many of whom are here legally and in many cases are citizens;
3. There be an end to government raids of work places which often result in indiscriminate detention of union members and which deter workers from exercising their rights under the wage and hour laws and the National Labor Relations Act; and
4. That ACTWU pledges to continue to be a leader in guaranteeing that all workers, whether citizens, legal residents or undocumented workers, are accorded the full rights of union membership and full rights under the laws of this nation.

AMERICAN FEDERATION OF STATE, COUNTY AND MUNICIPAL EMPLOYEES RESOLUTION OPPOSING THE KKK

WHEREAS The Ku Klux Klan was born of racial and religious hatred and remains a cult of violence whose cowardly rites include the bullet in the back and the torch in the night and

WHEREAS The moral disease manifested by the Ku Klux Klan is again spreading its sickness to cities and towns across the land, and

WHEREAS, The Klan's primary victims are the unprotected and the helpless who are marked solely because of their race, their heritage, or their religious faith and

WHEREAS, An increasing number of the Klan's victims are members of the American Federation of State, County and Municipal Employees, whose more than one million members include substantial numbers of racial and ethnic minorities,

BE IT THEREFORE RESOLVED That AFSCME urges the Congress and the state legislatures to enact stronger protections for the civil rights of this nation's citizens and residents, with felony penalties for the practice of terrorism or violence on the basis of race, heritage, or religious faith; and

BE IT FURTHER RESOLVED That AFSCME calls for a full-scale investigation and hearings by the appropriate committee of Congress on the activities of the Ku Klux Klan and its relationship to acts of terrorism and violence; and

BE IT FURTHER RESOLVED: That with a fresh memory of our recent experience with foreign terrorism, AFSCME urges all Americans to increase their vigilance against those at home who would pervert this nation's fundamental premise of respect and tolerance for the rights of all individuals so that all many enjoy their freedom in dignity and peace.

Adopted January 1981

CENTER FOR DEMOCRATIC RENEWAL

P.O. Box 50469, Atlanta, GA 30302 • (404) 221-0025

Literature and Resources

LIST 013 JANUARY 1993

CENTER FOR DEMOCRATIC RENEWAL
MONOGRAPH SERIES

15% discount on orders of 10 or more of any one title from the Monograph Series

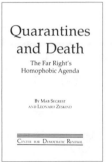

Quarantines and Death
The Far Right's
Homophobic Agenda

By MAB SEGREST
AND LEONARD ZESKIND

CENTER FOR DEMOCRATIC RENEWAL

Available
March
1993

They
Don't All
Wear
Sheets

A Chronology of Racist and Far Right
Violence — 1980-1986

Compiled by Chris Lutz
with an introduction by Leonard Zeskind

CENTER FOR DEMOCRATIC RENEWAL

PUBLISHED BY THE DIVISION OF CHURCH AND SOCIETY
OF THE NATIONAL COUNCIL OF THE
CHURCHES OF CHRIST IN THE U.S.A.

The
"Christian
Identity"
Movement

Analyzing Its Theological Rationalization
for Racist and Anti-Semitic
Violence

LEONARD ZESKIND
CENTER FOR DEMOCRATIC RENEWAL

PUBLISHED BY THE DIVISION OF CHURCH AND SOCIETY
OF THE NATIONAL COUNCIL OF THE
CHURCHES OF CHRIST IN THE U.S.A.

Quarantines and Death: The Far Right's Homophobic Agenda.

Did you know that neo-Nazis think AIDS is an African disease and that they plan to build an Aryan Republic on the ashes of this society? This 40-page booklet traces the homophobic violence and rhetoric of the far-right. It analyzes the differences between white supremacists who are also homophobic and homophobia on the New Right. By Mab Segrest and Leonard Zeskind.

Suggested donation $5.00

The Thin Edge.

This in-depth monograph highlights efforts by Lyndon LaRouche, Rev. Moon's Unification Church and other far-right elements to use deception, political action committees and finances to undermine African American support for progressive change in Africa and democratic movements in the U.S. Publication has been delayed by rapid change in southern Africa and other considerations. Projected publication is scheduled for March 1993.

Suggested donation $8.00.

"They Don't All Wear Sheets": A Chronology of Racist and Far Right Violence-1980-1986.

This 100-page book is the first to document bigoted violence on a national basis over an extended period of time. Indicates the nature of crimes against blacks and other people of color, Jews, gay people and others who have been targets of hate. By Chris Lutz. Published by The Division of Church and Society of the National Council of Churches.

Suggested donation $5.00

The "Christian Identity" Movement: Analyzing Its Theological Rationalization for Racist and Anti-Semitic Violence.

This 52-page booklet is the first in-depth treatment of the religious beliefs held by Klansmen, neo-Nazis and Christian patriots alike. Believing that racial equality is a sin, they are preparing for the final battle of Armageddon — a race war in the U.S. By Leonard Zeskind. Published by the Division of Church and Society of the National Council of Churches.

Suggested donation $4.00.

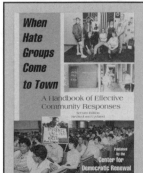

WHEN HATE GROUPS COME TO TOWN: SECOND EDITION!
A Handbook of Model Community Responses.

This new and expanded 192-page handbook has been completely revised. It includes sections on countering the rural radical right and anti-Indian activity; hate group activity in the workplace; responses by government agencies (including law enforcement); up-to-date information on law suits against white supremacists and hate crimes legislation and much more. For community activists, human relations professionals, religious leaders, journalists, and others. Includes state-by-state chart on hate crimes laws and a three-color wallposter-size chart of the far right and white supremacist movements

Suggested donation $18.95. 10% discount for 10-99 copies. For larger quantities call CDR.

Countering the Politics of Fear

CENTER FOR DEMOCRATIC RENEWAL
BACKGROUND REPORTS

Racist and Anti-Semitic Intervention in the Farm Protest Movement. BACKGROUND REPORT #2.

Initially released in September 1985 with a 1986 update, this document was the first to warn farm and rural advocacy organizations of the danger from the Far Right. Suggested donation $2.00

Racist and Far Right Organizing in the Pacific Northwest. BACKGROUND REPORT #6.

The Center for Democratic Renewal's 1988 overview of the manifestations of the white supremacist movement and bigotry practiced in the Northwest U.S. 11 pages. Suggested donation $4.00

Ballot Box Bigotry: David Duke and the Populist Party. BACKGROUND REPORT #7.

Released in March 1989, this 20-page report details the new far-right electoral strategy used by David Duke when he ran for President in the 1988 Democratic primaries, in the General Election as the candidate of the Populist Party and then won a Louisiana state seat as a Republican in 1989. Suggested donation $4.00

Peddling Racist Violence for A New Generation: A profile of Tom Metzger and the White Aryan Resistance. BACKGROUND REPORT #5.

Outlines the new "Third Position" strategy Metzger has borrowed from European neo-Nazis. Includes a new 1992 update since Tom and John Metzger's activities since their conviction in the beating death of Mulegeta Seraw by Portland skinheads. Suggested donation $4.00

It's Not Populism— America's New Populist Party: A Fraud by Racists and Anti-Semites. BACKGROUND REPORT #1.

Initially released by the Klanwatch Project and the National Anti-Klan Network, this report was the first to document the emergence of the Populist Party as a coalition-type effort by former Klansmen, neo-Nazis and others on the Far Right. Suggested donation $6.00

The Invisible Empire Knights of the Ku Klux Klan: A History of Violence. BACKGROUND REPORT #8.

Released in June 1990, this 25-page booklet details the history, ideology and structure of the IEKKK. Included is a special section on racist violence by IEKKK members and significant court cases involving the organization. Suggested donation $5.00

CENTER FOR DEMOCRATIC RENEWAL
INFORMATION PACKETS

Information packets include newspaper clippings, sample materials from the far right, and articles from the CDR's newsletter, *The Monitor*. Extremely useful for activists, students and others.

A) Thom Robb and the Knights of the Ku Klux Klan $5.00	B) Skinhead Neo-Nazis and Youth $5.00	C) Lyndon LaRouche and the NCLC $5.00	D) Women and the Far Right $5.00	E) International Connections of U.S. White Supremacists $7.50	F) David Irving and the Holocaust Deniers $5.00

Solidarity or Division: The True Story of the Ku Klux Klan vs. Organized Labor.

30-page history of Klan attacks on the labor movement. Section of anti-Klan resolutions adopted by labor unions. Ideal for union activists. Sponsored by United Steel Workers of America.

Suggested donation $4.00.

Blood in the Face
Village Voice political correspondent James Ridgeway is the first to expose the full range of racist far-right movements in America and Europe. Describes "rise of the new white culture." 208 pages, photographs, illustrations.
Suggested donation $16.95

The Monitor
The newsletter of the Center for Democratic Renewal keeps you informed on the activities and trends among Klansmen, neo-Nazis, and other white supremacists on the far right. Six issues of unique information and analysis. Suggested donation $25.00 for individuals. $40.00 for libraries and institutions. $45.00 US for overseas.

Bitter Harvest: Gordon Kahl and the Rise of the Posse Comitatus in the Heartland
James Corcoran's definitive action-packed account of the 1983 murder of Kahl in an Arkansas hideout. Describes the influence of the Posse in midwest farming communities. Over $250 pages in paperback.
Suggested donation $9.00.

AVAILABLE FROM THE
CENTER FOR DEMOCRATIC RENEWAL

From Political Research Associates

Right Woos Left: Populist Party, LaRouchian and Other Neo-Facist Overtures to Progressives and Why They Must Be Rejected

Released in April 1992, this 63-page booklet is a critical look at right-wing attempts to enlist progressive activists in a coalition to challenge the U.S. government. Exposes the right wing, and often anti-Semitic, agendas and traces their continuing influence. Originally released during the Gulf War as a three-page memo.By Chip Berlet.

Suggested donation $6.50.

For Educators and Young People

The Invisible Empire: The Ku Klux Klan Impact on History.

This 166-page paperback was written for school age young people. It is ideal for classroom use, book reports and general information about the Klan. By William Loren Katz

Suggested donation $10.00

From NCARRV*

*North Carolinians Against Racial and Religious Violence

Report on Bigoted Violence and Hate Group Activity in North Carolina.

This model annual report chronicles the crossburnings, arsons, vandalism and other acts which have made North Carolina in recent years one of the worst states for incidents of bigoted violence. Reports available for years 1991, 1990, and 1989 and 1988. Specify year(s) desired when ordering. Price stated is per year per report.

Suggested donation $5.00

From National Gay-Lesbian Task Force

Violence, Victimization & Defamation: Annual Report documents nationwide epidemic of homophobic violence. Important information about a subject shrouded in prejudice and fear. With statistics. Available for 1991, 1990, 1989 and 1988. Price is per report, per year.

Suggested donation $5.00

Violence, the Ku Klux Klan and the Struggle for Equality.

A curriculum guide issued in 1981 by the Connecticut Education Association, the Council on Interracial Books for Children and the National Education Association and prepared with the assistance of CDR. 72 pages includes pictures. (Limited copies available)

Suggested donation $8.00

From Searchlight Publishers

Searchlight Publishers produce the only English-language anti-fascist monthly magazine. They provide the most comprehensive current coverage of fascist activities across Eastern and Western Europe, North America and South Africa. Includes focus on Germany. For subscription information contact: Searchlight Magazine; 37B New Cavendish Street; London W1M8JR; United Kingdom.

From Ballots to Bombs: The Inside Story of the National Front's Political Soldiers.

This 40-page booklet is the most up-to-date expose of the National Front's link to terrorism. Included is never-before seen material on the link between U.S. racists and the Front. Suggested donation $6.00.

NEW RIGHT, NEW RACISM. This 70-page booklet exposes the hidden agenda of the British new right on race. It compares and contrasts the new right with the far right, looking at both the differences and links between them. By Paul Gordon and Francesca Klug. With a Preface by award winning playwright David Edgar.

Suggested donation $10.00

From Coalition for Human Dignity

ORGANIZED WHITE SUPREMACISTS IN OREGON. A 1991 report detailing neo-Nazi skinhead, Christian patriot and other white supremacist activity in Oregon. Useful for reporters, students, and activists. Illustrations and maps.

Suggested donation $5.00

ROLLING BACK CIVIL RIGHTS: THE OREGON CITIZENS ALLIANCE AT RELIGIOUS WAR. Detailed 1992 report on the program and personalities of an Oregon-based new right organization which is leading the attack on civil rights for lesbians and gay men.

Suggested donation $7.00

Important Collections

Mark of the Beast — Southern Exposure #8.

Special issue of journal published by the Institute of Southern Studies devoted to history and activities of the KKK. 72 pages with pictures.

Suggested donation $4.50

The Ku Klux Klan / A History of Racism and Violence.

A Special Report by the Southern Poverty Law Center. Fourth edition, 1991. 64 pages with pictures.

Suggested donation $3.75

New Era of Hate.

This 32-page booklet contains six essays on the rise in hate group activity. Published in June 1987 in Engage/Social Action journal of the General Board of Church and Society United Methodist Church.

Suggested donation $2.00

The Klan Unmasked.

Reissue by University of Florida of Stetson Kennedy's classic 1954 account of KKK activity in Georgia and Florida during the Forties and Fifties, based on the author's undercover investigation.

Suggested donation $16.50

Lyndon LaRouche and the New American Fascism.

New York-based investigative journalist Dennis King has spent 10 years digging into LaRouche's shadowy past and convoluted empire. The 400-plus pages of this book reflect those thousands of hours of interviews and scrutiny of mountains of documents.

Suggested donation $12.00

You Can Help Defeat the Politics of Fear!
Join the Center For Democratic Renewal!

If you want to help end hate group activity and bigoted violence, join the **Center for Democratic Renewal**. Founded in 1979 as the National Anti-Klan Network, the CDR is a multi-racial, multi-ethnic, interfaith, non-profit organization dedicated to promoting constructive non-violent responses to hate violence and the white supremacist movement. Your membership entitles you to a subscription to our bi-monthly newsletter, *The Monitor*, and notice of special publications and events. Please send in your dues today. Fill in the order form below.

ORDER FORM

PLEASE MAKE CHECKS PAYABLE AND SEND TO:
Center for Democratic Renewal and Education, Inc.
P.O. Box 50469, Atlanta GA 30302
(404) 221-0025 — Call for bulk order pricing and info.

TITLE	HOW MANY	PRICE	LESS DISC.	ITEM TOTAL	TITLE	HOW MANY	PRICE	LESS DISC.	ITEM TOTAL
MONOGRAPH SERIES (15% discount on 10 or more of one title)					**THE MONITOR**				
					For individuals		25.00		
					For libraries and institutions		40.00		
Quarantines and Death		5.00			For overseas		45.00		
The Thin Edge		8.00			The Klan Unmasked		16.50		
They Don't All Wear Sheets		5.00			Bitter Harvest		9.00		
"Christian Identity"		4.00			Right Woos Left		6.00		
RESOURCE MANUAL					Organized Oregon Supremacists		5.00		
When Hate Groups Come to Town		18.95			Rolling Back Civil Rights		7.00		
10 % Discount on order of 10 or more "Hate Group" manuals					New Right, New Racism		5.00		
BACKGROUND REPORTS					Inv. Emp.: KKK Impact on Hist.		12.00		
Ballot Box Bigotry		4.50			NEA Curriculum Guide		8.00		
Racist Organizing in the Northwest		4.00			NCARRV Bigoted Violence 19____		4.00		
Solidarity or Division		4.00			LaRouche & New American Fascism		12.00		
Profile of Tom Metzger		4.00			NGLTF Violence in 19_____		4.00		
Intervention in Farm Movement		2.00			New Era of Hate		1.00		
It's Not Populism		6.00			Blood in the Face		16.95		
IEKKK: A History of Violence		5.00			Mark of the Beast		4.00		
INFORMATION PACKETS					The KKK: SPLC Special Report		3.75		
A – Thom Robb and the KKK		5.00							
E– International Connections		7.50							
All Others (specify which)		5.00			Other (specify publication)				

Name _____

Address _____

City/State/Zip _____

Day Phone _____
(In case we have questions about your order)

Subtotal _____

POSTAGE AND HANDLING
Charged on Overseas Orders Only
Add 25% of total (U.S. funds, please!) _____

Ctr. for Dem. Renewal Membership ($30)
(includes *Monitor* subscription) _____

Additional donation _____

Total _____

Bibliography

The following titles are useful additions to the library of anyone interested in developing an in-depth understanding about far right organizations and movements as well as other manifestations of bigotry.

Bennett, David H. (1988). *The Party of Fear. From Nativist Movements to the New Right in American History.* Chapel Hill, N.C.: University of North Carolina Press.

An excellent history of the early Ku Klux Klan that also covers important 20th century historical developments related to anti-democratic organizations and religious movements.

Bennett, Jr., Lerone (1982). *Before the Mayflower: A History of Black America. The Classic Account of the Struggles and Triumphs of Black Americans.* New York: Penguin Books.

This definitive account of the enslavement of Africans and African Americans is required reading for any serious student of American history and the African American experience.

Berrill, Kevin T. and Gregory M. Herek (1992) *Hate Crimes: Confronting Violence Against Lesbians and Gay Men.* Newbury Park, California: Sage Publications.

This book is a straightforward analysis of gaybashing: the victims, the perpetrators and responses to it.

Blee, Kathleen M. (1991). *Women of the Klan. Racism and Gender in the 1920s.* University of California Press.

Through impeccable scholarship, Blee provides critical insight into how large numbers of otherwise "normal" people — in this case, women — can join a social movement dedicated to depriving others of their human rights. This book will stand as the definitive work on the role of women in the KKK for years to come.

Carlson, John Roy (1943). *Under Cover.* New York: E.P. Dutton & Co.

The first book ever published in the United States to document the activities of America's pro-Nazi organizations and movements, *Under Cover* recounts the first-hand experiences of John Roy Carlson who successfully infiltrated the fascist far right during World War II.

Chalmers, David M. (1989). *Hooded Americanism: The History of the Ku Klux Klan.* Durham, N.C.: Duke University Press.

A definitive history of America's most notable white supremacist organization.

Cohn, Norman (1966). *Warrant for Genocide. The Myth of the Jewish World-Conspiracy and the Protocols of the Elders of Zion.* New York: Harper & Row.

The best book available that comprehensively explains the lies and fabrications behind the myth of the "international Jewish conspiracy."

Corcoran, James (1990). *Bitter Harvest. Gordon Kahl and the Posse Comitatus: Murder in the Heartland.* New York: Viking.

An excellent and comprehensive account of the activity and ideology of America's rural radical right during the 1980s.

Flynn, Kevin and Gary Gerhardt (1989). *The Silent Brotherhood: Inside America's Racist Underground.* New York: The Free Press.

The best book yet about the far right, para-military underground known as The Order.

Horsman, Reginald (1981). *Race and Manifest Destiny. The Origins of American Racial Anglo-Saxonism.* Cambridge: Harvard University Press.

A comprehensive account of how the twin ideologies of white supremacy and Manifest Destiny have impacted American history, particularly during the early periods of settlement and westward expansion.

Jaynes, Gerald David and Robin M. Williams, Jr. Eds. (1989). *A Common Destiny. Blacks and American Society.* Washington, D.C.: National Academy Press.

Copiously documented, yet easy-to-read, this historic academic study is crammed with essential information about both the quantitative and qualitative impact of discrimination and segregation in American life.

Katz, William Loren (1986). *The Ku Klux Klan Impact on History.* Seattle, Wa.: Open Hand Publishing.

Excellent for college students, high school age youth and anyone else interested in a hard-hitting assessment of the Klan's impact on public policy and American life.

Kennedy, Stetson (1990). *The Klan Unmasked.* Gainesville, Fla.: University of Florida Press.

The classic "insider" story, Kennedy has written a riveting account of his singlehanded journey inside America's far right. According to historian Wyn Craig Wade, Kennedy accomplished more to stem the growth of the KKK in the post-World War II era than any other individual.

Kennedy, Stetson (1990). *Southern Exposure.* Gainesville, Fla.: University of Florida Press.

A back injury prevented the author from joining the war against fascism so he turned his energies to infiltrating an array of pro-Nazi groups in the U.S. Written in 1946, this book describes Kennedy's exploits. An excellent companion volume to *The Klan Unmasked.* Other books by Kennedy are available from University of Florida Press

Kevles, Daniel J. (1985). *In the Name of Eugenics. Genetics and the Uses of Human Heredity.* New York: Alfred A. Knopf.

An excellent, scholarly account of the relationship between eugenics, public policy and academia.

King, Dennis (1989). *Lyndon LaRouche and the New American Fascism.* New York: Doubleday.

The only definitive, critical biography of Lyndon LaRouche that also provides an analysis of the LaRouche organization.

Lutz, Chris and Leonard Zeskind (1987). *They Don't All Wear Sheets: A Chronology of Racist and Far Right Violence, 1980-1986.* Atlanta: Center for Democratic Renewal.

This 91-page book provides a state-by-state chronological listing of hate crimes and bigoted violence.

McLennan, Trisha and Paul (1985) *Solidarity or Division: The True Story of the Ku Klux Klan vs. Organized Labor.* Atlanta: Center for Democratic Renewal.

An excellent resource available from CDR which discusses the historical relationship between the Ku Klux Klan and the trade union movement.

McNickle, D'Arcy (1975). *They Came Here First. The Epic of the American Indian.* New York: Harper & Row.

Essential reading for any student of American history and the Indian experience.

Mintz, Frank P. (1985). *The Liberty Lobby & the American Right.* Westport, Conn.: Greenwood Press.

The only comprehensive book ever written about America's most professional and well-endowed anti-Semitic, racist organization.

Montagu, Ashley (1974). *Man's Most Dangerous Myth: The Fallacy of Race.* New York: Oxford University Press.

Montagu, an anthropologist, provides extensive documentation and brilliant analysis to explain how the entire concept of race and racial groups is scientifically and ethically flawed.

Myrdal, Gunner (1964). *An American Dilemma. The Negro in a White Nation.* Vol. 1. New York: McGraw Hill.

Myrdal, Gunner (1964). *An American Dilemma. The Negro Social Structure.* Vol. 2. New York: McGraw Hill.

Thorough, critical and filled with extensive documentation, Myrdal's work is the classic social scientist's study of segregation and Jim Crow in America.

Pharr, Suzanne (1988). *Homophobia: A Weapon of Sexism.* California: Inverness.

A feminist and human rights activist, Pharr links the hatred of gay men and lesbians to sexism and misogyny.

Poliakov, Leon (1971). *The Aryan Myth: A History of Racist and Nationalist Ideas in Europe.* New York: Basic Books. An excellent history and analysis of the ideology and false science that undergirded fascist movements in Europe and ultimately led to the Holocaust.

Ribuffo, Leo P. (1983). *The Old Christian Right: The Protestant Far Right from the Great Depression to the Cold War.* Philadelphia: Temple University Press.

One of the best historical accounts - accompanied by brilliant analysis - of the activities and impact of America's classic far right figures and their organizations: Henry Ford, Gerald B. Winrod, Gerald L. K. Smith, William Dudley Pelley and others.

Ridgeway, James (1990). *Blood in the Face. The Ku Klux Klan, Aryan Nations, Nazi Skinheads, and the Rise of the New White Culture.* New York: Thunder's Mouth Press.

The most recently published - as well as the most comprehensive and up-to-date - overview of America's white supremacist movement. Easily accessible and thorough, *Blood in the Face* incorporates into its text material (cartoons, essays, letters, etc) produced by the racist right.

Rose, Douglas. Ed. (1992) *The Emergence of David Duke and the Politics of Race.* Durham: University of North Carolina Press.

If you want to understand the sources of Duke's past electoral strength and the potential of those white supremacist candidates who will follow, this book, edited by Tulane University political scientist Douglas Rose, is indispensable.

Segrest, Mab and Leonard Zeskind (1989). *Quarantines and Death. The Far Right's Homophobic Agenda.* Atlanta: Center for Democratic Renewal.

This 39-page booklet explains how and why hatred of lesbians and gay men is an integral part of the philosophy and recruitment tactics of the far right.

Sims, Patsy (1978) *The Klan.* New York: Stein & Day.

Of all the historical accounts written about the

Klan, Sims' book ranks at the top of the charts.

Stanton, Bill (1991) *KLANWATCH: Bringing the Klan to Justice*. New York: Grove Weidenfeld.

Told from an inside point of view, *KLANWATCH* provides a blow-by-blow account of some of the Southern Poverty Law Center's most well-publicized legal cases.

Thornton, Russell (1987). *American Indian Holocaust and Survival: A Population History Since 1492*. Norman: University of Oklahoma Press.

This thoroughly researched text offers a chilling yet precisely academic treatment of the subject of Native American genocide and the destruction of indigenous peoples in the Western hemisphere.

Wade, Wyn Craig (1986). *The Fiery Cross: The Ku Klux Klan in America*. New York: Simon & Schuster.

Wade's historical account of the KKK is an invaluable resource for students and activists who need the facts about America's foremost hate group and a critical analysis about its role in shaping our history and society.

Zeskind, Leonard (1986). *The 'Christian Identity' Movement: Analyzing Its Theological Rationalization for Racist and Anti- Semitic Violence*. New York: Division of Church and Society, National Council of Churches.

Learn how and why 30,000 Americans believe that white, anglo-saxon Christians are the true descendants of the lost tribes of Israel, Jews are satanic and people of color are "pre-adamic mistakes" in this 47-page monograph written by the research director of the Center for Democratic Renewal.

Sample Intake Form

VIA: TEL_____
       MAIL_____
       OTHER_____

DATE __ / __ / __

NAME_____

ORG_____

ADDRESS_____

CITY_____ ST_____ ZIP_____

HOW THEY FOUND OUT ABOUT CDR_____

_____

REPORT/REQUEST_____

_____

_____

_____ (USE OTHER SIDE FOR ADD. INFO.)

KEY PERSONS/ORGS._____

_____

HARR_____ VAN_____ ASSAULT_____ ARSON_____ MURDER_____ WEAPONS_____ MTG_____

LIT DIST_____ MARCH/RALLY_____ OTHER_____

REPORTED TO POLICE? (Y / N) POLICE RESPONSE_____

_____

FOLLOW UP_____

ROUTE COPY TO_____ REFER TO OTHER AGENCY? (Y / N)

ACTION TAKEN:_____

_____

_____

SIGNATURE_____ DATE_____

Ten Points to Remember When Responding to Hate Groups

▼ 1. Document the problem and stay informed. Your first step should be to conduct thorough research about hate group activity and bigoted violence in your community. Develop a chronology of incidents drawing on newspaper accounts, victim reports and other sources. Stay informed about developments by clipping your local newspaper, subscribing to other publications and networking with other individuals and agencies.

▼ 2. Speak out and create a moral barrier to hate activity. Communities that ignore the problem of hate group activity and bigoted violence can sometimes create the impression that they don't care. This silence is often interpreted by hate groups as an invitation to step-up their activities. Through press conferences, rallies, community meetings and public hearings you can create a climate of public opinion that condemns racism and bigotry right from the start.

▼ 3. Match the solution to the problem. Whatever strategy you use to respond should be tailored to the specific situation you are dealing with; don't rely on rigid, formula-type solutions.

▼ 4. Build coalitions. Hate violence and bigotry against one targeted group helps to legitimize activities against other groups. If you involve a wide spectrum of people representing diverse constituencies you will have a better chance of achieving a unified, effective response.

▼ 5. Assist victims. Providing support and aid to hate violence victims is central to any response strategy. Don't get so busy organizing press conferences and issuing proclamations that you forget to make a housecall and express your personal support.

▼ 6. Work with constituencies targeted for recruitment. People who join hate groups usually do so out of frustration, fear and anger; they might even be your neighbors next door. By offering meaningful social, economic, spiritual and political alternatives you can discourage participation in hate groups by the very people most vulnerable to recruitment.

▼ 7. Target your own community as well as the hate group. Organizations like the Ku Klux Klan don't create social conflict out of thin air, they have to feed off existing community tensions in order to exist. The enemy of community harmony is not always the hate group itself, but the existing bigotry and division the group can exploit. For these and other reasons it is also essential to conduct anti-bigotry education programs on an ongoing basis, *after* the hate group has left your community.

▼ 8. Encourage peer-based responses among youth. Young people respond best to leadership that comes from within their peer group. While adults can provide valuable resources and insight, it is essential that youth groups develop and cultivate their own leaders and implement programs of their own design to combat bigotry.

▼ 9. Remember that hate groups are not a fringe phenomenon and their followers don't always wear sheets. Although the number of active white supremacists and neo-Nazis probably totals no more than 25,000 in the United States, as many as half-a-million Americans read their literature. This movement is complex and made up of numerous sometimes competing and sometimes cooperating organizations. Hate groups impact the mainstream of society in a variety of ways including: running candidates for public office; publishing sophisticated propaganda; buying radio time and media outlets; distributing cable television programs; manipulating the media; and building alliances with more respectable conservative groups, including some fundamentalist and evangelical Christian organizations.

▼ 10. Broaden your agenda. The problem is more than criminal. Hate activity is a political and social problem requiring a range of responses beyond those initiated by police. Citizen advocacy groups, religious agencies and others should develop a public policy agenda that addresses a wide range of issues including appropriate legislation, mandatory school curricula, expanded victim services, etc.

Center for Democratic Renewal • P.O. Box 50469, Atlanta, GA 30302-0469 • 404/221-0025

Welfare Myths and Facts

Politicians and others who use racial fears to promote their campaigns usually base their demagoguery on myths about poverty, welfare and race, leading their followers to conclude that African Americans or immigrants are responsible for the nation's woes and demands for "solutions" targeting specific ethnic groups. These myths must be countered with accurate, factual information to convince people to reject the "politics of fear."

MYTH #1: WELFARE RECIPIENTS HAVE LARGE FAMILIES

FACT #1: The majority of welfare recipients already voluntarily limit family size. The average AFDC family consists of only two children. The problem of poverty is not family size, but the fact that even small families find it nearly impossible to survive on minimum wage service sector jobs.

MYTH #2: WELFARE PAYS WOMEN TO HAVE MORE CHILDREN

FACT #2: In the state of Louisiana, for example, a welfare mother receives only $13 per week in additional AFDC benefits when she has a second child. For each additional child she bears, she receives a mere $11 extra and only $18 extra in food stamps per week. A mere $31 per week offers little incentive to women to bear more children. Children are far more expensive than that to raise. In addition, women receiving AFDC have one-fourth the number of babies as do those who do not receive AFDC.

MYTH #3: AFRICAN AMERICAN WOMEN HAVE LARGER FAMILIES

FACT #3: The family size of low-income African American women is actually decreasing, compared to whites. The fertility rate among single black women has decreased substantially over the past decade, while the fertility rate for single white females has risen.

MYTH #4: POVERTY IS THE RESULT OF INDIVIDUAL BEHAVIOR

FACT #4: Poverty is the result of unemployment, low wages, a poorly trained workforce, the loss of family farms, and the lack of daycare and other support services for poor families. The rise of the "underclass" corresponds to diminishing economic opportunities not irresponsible behavior by poor people. Eliminating poor people through government-sanctioned sterilization and criminal justice programs does not eliminate poverty. Poverty is built into our economic system as economists urge the government to maintain at least 5 percent unemployment to ensure a "healthy" economy. Such policies guarantee chronic unemployment and poverty.

MYTH #5: "RESPONSIBLE" BEHAVIOR WILL ELIMINATE POVERTY

FACT #5: African American women who engage in "responsible behavior," (i.e., avoiding out-of-wedlock pregnancies), suffered a 32 percent drop in real family income between 1972-1985, compared with only a 7 percent drop for "responsible" white women. And only a small percentage of black women avoiding out-of-wedlock pregnancies were able to end up in with a combined family income of $25,000 per year or more, compared with 60 percent of their white counterparts. This proves that race is a far more significant determinant of poverty than "behavior."

MYTH #6: WELFARE RECIPIENTS DO NOT WANT TO WORK

FACT #6: Between 1979-1984, the number of Americans working at jobs paying sub-poverty wages quadrupled. Only 8-12 percent of the poverty population can be defined as "persistently poor" (the so-called "underclass"). The bulk of the persistently poor do not live in large urban ghettos, but rather in rural areas where there are no jobs. The average welfare mother stays on AFDC for less than 24 months. For most recipients, welfare is a temporary stopgap between jobs. Fifty-five percent of the children on welfare have at least one working parent, according to the National Center for Children in Poverty, at Columbia University. Government statistics indicate that 90 percent of adult AFDC recipients are either disabled, already working at sub-poverty wages, or single mothers with small children and no access to child care. Among adults on welfare who are not disabled, retired, or taking care of small children; 70 percent of heads of poor households worked full or part-time in 1984 (the last year for which figures were available).

MYTH #7: ALL WELFARE RECIPIENTS ARE AFRICAN AMERICAN

FACT #7: The race of welfare recipients is: White (38.1%); African American (39.7%); Latino (16.6%); Native American (1.3%); and Asian (2.8%). Approximately the same number of white families are on welfare as African American families. While it is true that people of color are disproportionately represented in the welfare statistics, this is a function of socioeconomic status, not race or ethnicity. When whites and blacks of the same economic status and income level are compared, both groups are equally likely to be on welfare.

MYTH #8: REDUCING WELFARE CONTROLS STATE AND FEDERAL BUDGETS

FACT #8: Welfare accounts for only 2 percent of most state budgets. Totally eliminating welfare would still leave 98 percent of the budget unaffected. Motivations for cutting welfare are not just fiscal, but political.

While many parts of state budgets are protected by powerful special interests, programs for the poor make the easiest targets when states are confronted with deficits. Every hour, the federal government spends 33.7 million dollars on defense; 23.6 million on the national debt; 8.7 million on the savings and loan bailout. The government spends 2.9 million on all levels of education, 1.8 million on children's health. If we raised the income of all poor families to the poverty level of 1989, the cost would be $28 billion annually. The cost in 1991 of extra tax breaks to the richest 1 percent of the U.S. population was $55 billion. The 1993 federal budget will spend $589 billion on the military (despite the collapse of the Soviet Union), $120 billion on defending and assisting Europe, $101 billion on the savings and loan bailout, while spending only $11.3 billion on American children. The federal budget spends $.47 out of every tax dollar on the military and $.12 on health care. Our economy supports subsidies to the rich, while it is politically opportunistic to take aim at the poor as if they are the cause of the national deficit, as opposed to excessive military spending and tax breaks for the rich.

Compiled from information provided by the Louisiana Coalition Against Racism and Nazism, the Center on Budget and Policy Priorities, and Women Against Military Madness

WHAT TO DO IF YOU'RE A VICTIM OF HATE VIOLENCE

If you're a victim of a hate crime, it is sometimes difficult to know what to do first. These guidelines have been prepared in case a hate crime happens to you or someone you know. It is important to remember that these are just guidelines — not rules — that should be adapted to your particular situation.

1. Call the police. If you live in a city, report the crime or harassment to the city police. If you live in a rural area or outside of municipal jurisdiction, report the incident to the Sheriff's Department. When you call, be specific and insistent about the details you want to report. Write them down, if it will help you remember the facts. If the crime damaged your personal property, make certain that the police make an inspection. Take pictures of the damage if you can. During your contact with law enforcement, get the officer's name and badge number. It may help to write down your recollection of the conversation. If you are assisting a victim, always get the permission of the victim first, before calling the authorities.

2. Report the crime. It is important to report all hate crimes. One of the most persistent myths about hate crimes is that publicity leads to "copy cat" incidents. Hate violence is often cyclical; sometimes the same person gets attacked several times or one attacker chooses multiple targets. Not reporting crimes does not reduce the risk of further attacks. Instead the opposite may happen.

Perpetrators of hate violence perceive the lack of response as encouragement to commit additional acts. If this is happening to you, it may be happening to others in your community. You should not feel alone — hate violence is a community problem, not an individual one, although hate violence can lead to victim isolation. Many victims find themselves safer when they take action to show their attackers they are not easy targets. When victims come together and get community support, it also puts law enforcement on notice to provide protection.

After filing a report with local authorities, call the U.S. Department of Justice national hate crimes hotline at 1-800-347- HATE.

3. Stop telephone harassment. Using call tracing and the cooperation of your telephone company, you can stop telephone harassment. This service is available in most areas of the country. It is worthwhile investing a few dollars a month to have the perpetrator arrested, fined and possibly jailed, if you can afford it. If call tracing doesn't successfully identify the perpetrator, try call blocking which will simply prevent you from receiving calls from a specific number. These services usually require a one-time setup fee and a small monthly charge of less than $10. This may be more than you can afford, but for a period of several weeks or months it may be all you need to prevent your family from being harassed.

4. Alert your community. Members of your community cannot help you unless they know about the situation. Contact local religious organizations (churches, synagogues, mosques or community centers), community groups, and civic organizations. They may be a source of support and can add their voices to yours to help generate action by local authorities. They can also provide additional support and security, such as establishing a Neighborhood Watch or safety escorts for children. Community groups can also help investigate the attack by contacting neighbors, reporters, police, or taking photographs. Advocacy groups can provide follow-up by working with social service agencies or helping draw attention to the problem through press conferences and demonstrations.

5. Don't increase your danger. It is important not to take steps that increase the danger to you or your family. In particular, don't chase attackers; just try to get safely away. Don't brandish weapons unless you are trained to use them; weapons in the hands of the untrained can be taken away and used against you. Use common safety precautions, such as walking in groups or being continuously aware of your surroundings when out alone. Before moving into a neighborhood, investigate and ask questions. Will you be the first African American or Jewish family in the neighborhood? Have there been racial, religious, or anti-gay tensions or incidents in the community? Have there been racial incidents in local schools? Answers to these types of questions may inform you about what kind of welcome you may receive.

6. Contact an advocacy organization. There are several local and national organizations that monitor hate crimes and assist victims. For information or a referral to a group in your area, contact the Center for Democratic Renewal at (404) 221-0025. Victims of anti-gay and lesbian violence can also call the National Gay & Lesbian Task Force Anti-Violence project at (202) 667-5139. Similar advocacy groups exist to respond to acts of anti-Asian violence and to protect immigrant rights; contact CDR for more information.

Adapted in part from "What Can We Do About Bigoted Violence?" published by North Carolinians Against Racist and Religious Violence (NCARRV), P. O. Box 240, Durham, NC 27702.

STYLE AND USAGE GUIDE

Introduction

One of the purposes of this section is to bring clarity and common sense to the frequent difficulties encountered when writing about the many cultures and peoples represented in the United States. In general, the self-descriptions of the people being referred to are the preferred terms. Recognizing that the first goal of writing is to be read, the conventions of standard American usage have been taken into consideration.

African American. This is the preferred noun for referring to persons of African descent who are permanent residents of the United States. *John Lewis, an African American from Troy, Ala., serves in the U.S. House of Representatives.*

African-American. Adjective form. Always hyphenated.

Anti-Indian. Use this modifier when referring to hate activity. *Reports indicated that anti-Indian activity in the area was increasing.*

Anti-Semitism. Dislike, hatred, prejudice, discrimination or persecution directed against people of Jewish descent or of the Jewish faith. Note the S in Semitic is capitalized in common usage.

Arab. Refers to persons from Arab countries as defined as those nations in which Arabic is the principal language. Note that Iranians are not Arabs. Note that the term has nothing to do with belief in Islam. There are Christian Arabs as well as Muslim Arabs.

Asians. Recognize that Pacific Islanders are Asians from a different part of the world and that members of the groups note the distinction in self-descriptions. The two terms should be used together except when inaccurate or awkward. *The hearing was attended by a large number of Asians and Pacific Islanders from the Seattle area.* Use specific nationalities — Vietnamese, Cambodian, Laotian, Japanese, Chinese — whenever possible. Never use *oriental.*

Asian-American. Refers to Asian individuals or groups who are United States residents but of Asian or Pacific Island origins. *Pacific Islander-Americans* is awkward and should not be used. However, *Asian-Americans and Pacific Islanders* is a construction that can be used.

Black. Used today interchangeably with African-American as a modifier, and used in lower-case form. *The two black men were beaten by a gang of white youths, police said Thursday.*

Caucasian. Literally, a native of the Caucasus, a mountainous region forming part of the traditional border between Europe and Asia. Once but no longer commonly used as a descriptive term for white persons. See *White.*

Chicano, Chicana. The term references specific populations of Latinos, *i.e.,* those located in the U.S. west and southwest primarily of Mexican and Mexican-American descent, as well as persons of Mexican-American and Native-American ancestry. *All Chicanos are Latino but not all Latinos are Chicano.* See *Latino, Mestizo.*

Christian Identity. May be used interchangeably with **Identity** or **Kingdom Identity.** Denotes a specific white supremacist theological movement derived from British Israelism. Should not be confused with the Reconstructionist movement, the neo-Covenantors or other fundamentalist movements.

Christian Right. Often used (incorrectly) interchangeably with New Right. Denotes that sector of the right-wing political movement which came to prominence during the mid-70s and 1980s, with its ideological roots and constituency in fundamentalist and evangelical Christian movements. It is primarily conservative or ultra-conservative and authoritarian, rather than revolutionary, in outlook. May also be used to denote those sectors which are Reconstructionist or "theonomist." The Christian Right is a subset of the New Right.

Church. Lower case except when referring to a specific denominational body, entity or policy, usually on subsequent references, or as part of a name. *The church was burned.* But, *Members of the Mt. Hebron Church participated.* Or, *Catholic bishops issued a statement affirming Church policy against euthanasia.*

Cross, Crucifix. Protestants and other non-Catholics generally refer to the Cross, while Catholics refer to the Crucifix. In describing the religious symbol, use the appropriate term if the discussion involves one line or the other of Christianity; otherwise use the more widely accepted *Cross.* Note that either would be capitalized. However, if referring to the symbol often used by hate groups, cross is always used, and in lower case. *The protestors carried crosses.* Or, *Police arrested two in Friday's cross-burning incident.*

Extremist. This is an indeterminate term with a pejorative connotation designed to separate the

Center for Democratic Renewal • P.O. Box 50469, Atlanta, GA 30302-0469 • 404/221-0025

"mainstream" from the "margins." It is used in some quarters to describe the Left as well as the Right. Do not use interchangeably with white supremacist or far right. In those circumstances when a term to connote the political margins is appropriate it may be used advisedly.

Facist. Describes an organization, ideology or individual which resembles that of the historic fascist parties of World War II, *i.e.* Italian, Spanish, Bulgarian, Japanese. Avoid using this term as a generic pejorative. Use **neo-fascist** to describe some current re-development of that ideology. Use **quasi-fascist** to describe an ideology that is not quite fascist, but leading in that direction. Attempt to distinguish between fascist as an adjective and those measures associated with it. Use *Senate Bill One contained politically repressive measures as well as genuine anti-crime provisions* rather than *Senate Bill One was a fascist law.* Lyndon LaRouche's ideology could properly be described as either fascist or neo-fascist.

Far right. Used as an umbrella term which describes extremist or ultra-conservative elements further to the right than the New Right. These elements are dominated by various conspiracy theories mixed with anti-communism and anti-elite or right-wing populist agendas. Includes the white supremacist movement as well. *The John Birch Society is a far right political organization more radical than the Moral Majority but less dangerous than the Liberty Lobby.* Used without capitalization. As a noun, no hyphen is used: *The far right has embraced Christian Identity.* As a compound adjective, the hyphen is correct: *Several farmers in the area were recruited by the far-right Posse Comitatus.*

Hispanic. Adj. Used only in reference to a governmental category. The term was artificially created and in modern usage has no descriptive value. See Latino.

Homophobia. Fear, dislike or hatred of gay men and/or lesbians; **-ic,** having or demonstrating such fear, dislike or hatred.

Indian The term used most commonly within tribes to refer to a member of a tribe, many people from different tribes, and tribal societies which populated the Western hemisphere prior to colonization. Note that the most accurate way to describe a tribe or member of a tribe is with the commonly accepted name of the tribe, *i.e.*, Navajo, Haudenosaunee, Lillooet, Quechua, etc. The terms "Indian" or "American Indian" carry historical value and common meaning throughout Indian country. Used interchangeably with Native American. Usually, Indian is the preferred adjective or noun for referring to individuals, territories, artifacts, etc., or when only one or two references are

being made in a shorter item or article. When referring to peoplehood, either term can be used, and in a longer article or when writing from a broader perspective, the term Native American should be included. In general, tribal names should be used as often as possible. See Anti-Indian, Native American, Tribe, Tribal.

KKK. See *Ku Klux Klan.*

Klan, Klansman. See *Ku Klux Klan.*

Ku Klux Klan, **Klan**. The terms are used interchangeably and are always capitalized. Often abbreviated **KKK,** though *Klan* is the preferred term. The terms should refer specifically to a member of an organized faction of the Ku Klux Klan. Where appropriate, the specific Klan faction should be used, such as White Knights of the Ku Klux Klan or Confederate Knights of America. Use **Klan-type** when referring to a similar type of organization or activity, such as *The group of youths engaged in Klan-type activities such as burning crosses.*

Latino. Used generally to refer to Spanish-speaking U.S. residents (except, obviously, those whose origins are of the country of Spain, in which case the proper adjective is Spanish-American). However, Mexican-, Cuban-, Puerto Rican-, etc., should be used when an individual's or group's origin is known. Hispanic will be used only when referring to a governmental category. Note the gender specificity of the term when used as a modifier. *The Latina woman was attacked. All the men were Latinos.*

Melanesian. Refers to those populations which occupy islands in the west Pacific from Australia to Malaysia and the Philippines, the archipelago sometimes referred to as the "East Indies." The Phillipines, for instance, are often referred to as an Asian state, but in reality consists of the Melanesians.

Mestizo. Persons of mixed Indian and European (white and/or Hispanic) ancestry. Mestizo populations are found throughout the Americas, including the United States.

Native American. This term came into use, mostly outside Indian reservations, after 1970 when efforts began in U.S. colleges and universities to establish politically acceptable terms for specific minority studies programs. While "Native American" has won increasing acceptance among "academic and bureaucratic Indians" as an identifying term, the tribal name and the term Indian remain the preferred terms. The order of usage should be: Tribal name, the term Indian, the term Native American, depending on context. See *Indian.*

Nazi. Always capitalized. Used to refer to the organization, ideology and paraphernalia of the National Socialist German Workers Party circa 1923-1945;

to war criminals or others associated with that period in their current manifestation; and to political forces which collaborated with the NSDAP during that period. Use lower-case **nazi** when using the term as an adjective such as, *They were concerned about the growth of nazi-type activities in their community*. Do not use interchangeably with neo-Nazi to describe current manifestations.

Negro. Term used to refer to black Americans until the 1960s. See *Black*.

Neo-conservative. Describes a political movement of former liberals, primarily among intellectuals, who adopted and adapted conservative ideology in the 1970s and 1980s. Neo-conservatives differ from traditional conservatives in that they promote a strong role for state intervention in the economy, favor national authority over "states rights" structures, and are interventionist rather than isolationist on international issues.

Neo-Nazi. The *neo-* is lowercase, and the term is always hyphenated. *Five neo-Nazis were charged with the crime*. Describes post-War phenomenon such as *There was little neo-Nazi activity in the United States until George Lincoln Rockwell organized the American Nazi Party*. Do not use *Nazi Party* as a generic term. Use this term to describe organizations or individuals whose ideology directly resembles or attempts to resemble that of the historic German Nazi Party or one of its factions; i.e., *Third Way is a British neo-Nazi group with a Strasserite twist*. See *Nazi*.

New Right. Denotes the popularly-based right-wing political movement which came to prominence in the 1970s and 1980s. Includes secular forces (such as Richard Viguerie), Christian Right (as above) and other elements of the Religious Right . Sometimes used to include neo-Conservatives. Use term to distinguish from Old Right (pre-WW II) which was isolationist and contained patrician and anti-Semitic elements. While the New Right is implicitly politically, socially and economically racist, they are not dominated by an ideology of genetic superiority of the white race.

Race. Biological categorization of human beings by physical characteristics transmitted genetically. At one time, anthropologists generally described three groups: Cacucasoid, Mongoloid, and Negroid. However, all anthropologists today reject race as a meaningful biological concept, pointing instead to a basic heterogeneity of world population. The term is always inappropriate when referring to cultural, religious or national groupings.

Racist. Used to refer to an individual or group or action based on emotional or cultural dislike or hatred for those unlike oneself grounded in perceived or actual racial or ethnic differences. More powerful term than prejudice or discrimination. *All white supremacists are racists, but not all racists, or even white racists, are white supremacists*. See *White Supremacist*.

Tribal. A supplemental modifier which is frequently used as a mild substitute for "Indian," as in "tribal government" and "Indian government." See *Indian, Native American, Tribe*.

Tribe. Any one of the historical groupings of American Indians who are linked by governmental structure, common heritage, ancestry, custom, or faith. See *Indian, Native American, Tribal*.

White. Noun or adjective. Refers generally to those persons of European ancestry. Used in lower case. See *Black*.

White supremacy, -ist. Use to refer to an individual or group or action embodying the ideological notion of biological, intellectual, genetic or other inherent superiority of whites over all others. Avoid using terms such as *white resistance* or *white separatist* which have been developed by Klansmen and neo-Nazis as a term for media gloss. See *Racist*.

Center for Democratic Renewal • P.O. Box 50469, Atlanta, GA 30302-0469 • 404/221-0025